PENGUIN BOOKS

A-Z OF SOUTH AFRICAN POLITICS

Contributors:

Julia Beffon, Farouk Chothia, Jacklyn Cock, Carole Cooper, Lesley Cowling, Gaye Davis, Shaun de Waal, David Fig, Philippa Garson, Mark Gevisser, Ferial Haffajee, Mduduzi ka Harvey, Stephen Heyns, Bafana Khumalo, Eddie Koch, Stephen Laufer, Chris Louw, Jacques Magliolo, Nombuyiselo Maloyi, Vuyo Mvoko, Sibusiso Nxumalo, Justin Pearce, Ivor Powell, Estelle Randall, Carmel Rickard, Reg Rumney, Pat Sidley, Paul Stober, Jan Taljaard, and Steuart Wright.

WEEKLY
MAIL&GUARDIAN

A-Z of South African Politics

The Essential Handbook

1995

Edited by

Anton Harber and Barbara Ludman

PENGUIN BOOKS

PENGUIN BOOKS

Published by the Penguin Group
27 Wrights Lane, London W8 5TZ, England
Viking Penguin, a division of Penguin Books USA Inc, 375 Hudson Street,
New York, New York 10014, USA
Penguin Books Australia Ltd, Ringwood, Victoria, Australia
Penguin Books Canada Ltd, 10 Alcorn Avenue, Toronto, Ontario, Canada
M4V 3B2
Penguin Books (NZ) Ltd, 182-190 Wairau Road, Auckland 10, New Zealand
Penguin Books, Amethyst Street, Theta Ext 1, Johannesburg, South Africa

Penguin Books Ltd, Registered Offices: Harmondsworth, Middlesex,
England

First published by Penguin Books 1995

Copyright © The Weekly Mail & Guardian 1995

ISBN 0 140 25025 5

Typeset by Iskova Image Setting
Printed and bound by Creda Press
Cover design by Hadaway Illustration & Design

To

Jesse, Harriet and David —

the A-Z of supportive families

CONTENTS

INTRODUCTION

The only thing certain about South Africa in 1995 is change.

New policies, new institutions, new laws, new leaders — that's the agenda prescribed by the new constitution and the election of 1994, and that's why the 1995 *A-Z of South African Politics* is so different from last year's.

It's not just the faces and names that are different, but the styles and approaches which dictate a fundamentally different kind of politics.

Anyone spending even a few hours in Parliament will notice a most remarkable aspect: active, assertive, independent thinkers transforming the venerable Assembly and Senate into open, lively and vibrant chambers — a far cry from the rubber stamp houses of the previous regime.

This is true of all our national institutions — such as the nine provincial legislatures, the judiciary, the South African Broadcasting Corporation and the diplomatic corps.

It is not easy to find one's way around all these changes. This book is intended to provide an easy-to-read guide through the maze of power. It is a road map to the new South Africa.

What we have tried to capture in writing our book is the vibrancy and dynamism in our national politics.

Bald statistics would not capture the vitality and flux in our country, and so we have made full use of the personal knowledge possessed by our range of specialist writers about the individuals and the issues likely to dominate our country in the coming year.

We have had to make assessments: which rising stars will quickly fade, which are likely to shine rather more brightly in the coming year. We have tried to capture their personalities, rather than the details of their CVs. We have not limited ourselves to politicians, but added figures from, for example, business, the military, the police, the Bench, the church, and the trade unions where we felt they were likely to play a significant role.

We have favoured personal insight and entertaining writing over dry detail. And we have thrown in our assessment of these individuals' important characteristics, strengths, weaknesses and reputations, their notable foibles and quirks. That way we hope you will get a real under the skin sense of the individuals and issues we have dealt with, rather than a mere technical outline.

Our 32 contributors include *Weekly Mail & Guardian* journalists and other expert observers who have covered all aspects of South African politics thoroughly over the years. They are writing about people they know and issues they have engaged in, and it shows in the depth of their insight.

The individuals we profiled last year have changed — only a handful are in the same job — and so have the issues. We have tried to focus on those issues that will grow increasingly important, day by day — such as who will rule the airwaves, how the homeless will be accommodated, what the government's attitude will be to privatisation, how new priorities will change health care, how gender issues will be dealt with, and more.

We have also included an analysis of the election results, the way the provinces voted, and a run-down of each of the political parties in Parliament. We have written an easy to understand, step-by-step guide to the new constitution and the Bill of Rights. And added a chapter of the most up-to-date statistics on each of South Africa's new provinces. The *A-Z* is a reference book, but an unusual one, intended to be readable and continually useful.

Because change is such a byword in our politics, the *A-Z of South African Politics* is becoming an annual event, no doubt featuring new faces and new issues in every edition. Our hope is that our national politics remains as vibrant and exciting as it has been in the past year, making the writing of the *A-Z* as interesting and enjoyable as it was this year and last.

Anton Harber and Barbara Ludman
Johannesburg
January 1995

1

PROFILES

Ackermann, Lourens Wepener Hugo ('Laurie')   Born in Pretoria, Ackermann studied at Stellenbosch and Oxford where he was a Cape Rhodes scholar in 1954. He is one of four sitting judges appointed to the Constitutional Court in terms of a special provision of the constitution.

Ackermann took silk in 1975 and was appointed to the Transvaal Bench in 1980. He resigned his post in 1987 to take up the HF Oppenheimer Chair of Human Rights Law at Stellenbosch University, where he taught human rights and comparative constitutional law. At the time it was considered a radical move. Colleagues felt it showed that he thought more could be achieved by teaching human rights to aspirant lawyers than by trying to administer oppressive laws. However, he did not stay an academic for very long and was back on the Bench in 1993, this time in Cape Town.

He served on the Lesotho Court of Appeal from 1988 to 1992, and in 1991 and 1992 as an acting judge of appeal on the Namibian Supreme Court. He was a visiting scholar at the Columbia University Law School, New York, during 1988. Among other activities, he serves on the advisory board to the Equal Opportunities Research Project at the University of Cape Town. His long residence in the Cape has had a pleasant effect on the judge: among his interests are the collection of wine, wine books and memorabilia, and when he can find the time, trout fishing.

Born 14 January 1934. Family: wife Denise, three adult children.

Andrew, Ken   A flaccid public profile belies Andrew's abilities as a politician of competence and consistency. Colleagues use the words 'dedicated' and 'methodical' to describe the Democratic Party's spokesman on finance and economic affairs; it's clear the reason he has never been party leader is not lack of ability but, rather, flair.

Born in Cape Town, Andrew matriculated in the first class from Rondebosch Boys' High School, where he was head boy and represented Western Province in cricket. He followed up a BSc degree from the University of Cape Town (where he chaired the local committee of the National Union of South African Students, was secretary of the debating society and captained a rugby team) with a Master's degree in business administration and a career as a director of companies.

He joined the DP's progenitor, the Progressive Party, in 1961, becoming a federal council member of its successor, the Progressive Federal Party, in 1978, a position he held through the party's subsequent metamorphosis into the DP.

Andrew was the DP's federal chairman from 1991 to 1994, has chaired its national policy advisory committee and served as vice-chairman of the party's parliamentary caucus. Known for his commitment to following through whatever he does, he embodies the DP's reputation as the voice of the liberal business sector. Together with party stalwart Colin Eglin, he played a significant role in drafting the interim constitution.

It is as a dogged and determined financial expert that he has won the respect of all parties, and that has been reflected in his election to a key post as chairman of the parliamentary joint committee on Public Accounts. He also serves on other parliamentary committees, on which he plays an important and influential role, such as the joint Finance committee.

Born 30 May 1943. Family: wife Adrianne, two children.

Asmal, Kader   Asmal was one of the more notable victims of the horse-trading between the African National Congress and the National Party for cabinet posts in the government of national unity. Widely expected to become minister of Constitutional Development — an area in which he is regarded as an expert — the live-wire and amiable Asmal was given the relatively minor post of minister of Water Affairs and Forestry.

He immediately took up the challenge, however, of turning Water from a minor ministry to a keystone of the Reconstruction and Development Programme and transforming an old-style, high-tech department into one that serves the majority.

A lifelong commitment to human rights began with his meeting Chief Albert Luthuli while still a schoolboy in Stanger, Natal. He qualified as a teacher and taught while studying further through Unisa, realising a long-held dream when he enrolled at the London School of Economics in 1959.

In England he got the British Anti-Apartheid Movement off the ground before moving to Ireland where he joined Trinity College, Dublin, teaching for 27 years and specialising in human rights, labour and international law. He formed the Irish Anti-Apartheid Movement and served as vice-president of the International Defence and Aid Fund while qualifying as a barrister at both London and Dublin Bars and earning an LLM (LSE) and MA (Dublin). His involvement in Irish civil liberty campaigns led him to participate in a number of international inquiries into human rights violations, and in 1983 he was awarded the Prix Unesco.

From 1986 he served on the ANC's constitutional committee, and soon after returning to South Africa in 1990 was elected to the ANC's National Executive Committee. He was until recently professor of human rights at the University of the Western Cape. He is vice-president of the African Association of International Law and chairman of the Council of the University of the North.

Born 8 October 1934. Family: wife Louise Parkinson, two sons.

Bacher, Aaron ('Ali')   The managing director of the United Cricket Board of South Africa now plays as central a leadership role in South Africa's return to international sport as he did in the 'rebel' tours of the 1980s, and has become an adherent of the new South Africa as fervent as he was an opponent of the long boycott of apartheid. He is widely respected internationally as one of the best cricket administrators in the world.

Born Aaron Bacher of Lithuanian parents, Bacher was nicknamed 'Ali' (as in Ali Baba/Bacher) at the age of seven. He first represented Transvaal at cricket as a 17-year-old and played 12 tests for South Africa, four as captain. He led what was probably the greatest South African side ever, which included Graeme and Peter Pollock and Barry Richards, to a whitewash of Bill Lawry's 1970 Australian side before the beginnings of the sporting boycott meant the cancellation of that year's tour to England.

He studied medicine at the University of the Witwatersrand and worked as a GP until 1979, when he switched to marketing. That year, as chairman of the Transvaal Cricket Council, he began the move to run the game along professional lines. In 1981, after heart bypass surgery, he devoted even more of his time to cricket.

He was instrumental in organising the first of the 'rebel' cricket tours, in 1983. As, first, professional consultant to the South African Cricket Union (Sacu) and, later, managing director, he established grassroots cricketing coaching in the townships, with the assistance of then Sacu president Joe Pamensky and businessman Mervyn King.

This programme came under threat in January 1990, when unprecedented opposition to Mike Gatting's English rebels led to a clash between the cricketing authorities and local anti-apartheid organisations. Bacher was almost ousted from his Sacu post when he stuck by an agreement forged with the National Sports Congress and cancelled the second leg of the Gatting tour.

But once the African National Congress had been unbanned, cricket was one of the first sports to get its house in order. Cricket bodies came together as the United Cricket Board of South Africa (UCB), with Krish Mackerdhuj as president and Bacher as managing director, in June 1991, and South Africa returned to the international fold during an emotional tour of India in November 1991.

Bacher's efforts to develop the sport among black South Africans and his frank admission that the sporting boycott was justified have consolidated his position at the top of South African cricket. His insistence on the removal of the springbok emblem — replaced first by the UCB's emblem and then by a protea — was evidence of the cricketing authorities' reconciliation efforts. This acceptance is signalled by the frequency with which Sports minister Steve Tshwete is seen at his side.

Born 24 May 1942. Family: wife Shira Teeger, two daughters, one son.

Baskin, Jeremy   Too young to be called a veteran, Baskin is certainly a figure of long standing in South Africa's relatively young labour movement. He has been associated with trade unionism since the birth of militant black unions in the 1970s, was general secretary of Cosatu's Paper, Printing, Wood and

Allied Workers' Union and in 1991 wrote *Striking Back*, the semi-official history of the Congress of South African Trade Unions.

Baskin is set to remain a key thinker and architect of Cosatu's direction: he recently took on the mantle of director of the federation's think-tank, the influential National Labour and Economic Development Institute (Naledi), based in Cosatu headquarters in Braamfontein, Johannesburg. Naledi is increasingly filling the policy vacuum left in Cosatu by the exodus of some of the movement's best brains to the new government. Already the institute has put out policy papers on centralised bargaining and immigration policy which, with other policy papers, are likely to inform Cosatu's direction in negotiations with employers and the new government. Labour watchers would do well to keep an eye open for Naledi's work on industrial restructuring and the role of trade unions under a new government.

Born 1 September 1956. Single.

Bengu, Sibusiso   The minister of Education is a quiet, learned man with strong diplomatic skills. Having travelled widely and lived abroad for many years he is equipped with a sound knowledge of education systems around the world. But despite his lifelong involvement in education he has remained outside the process of policy formation here. As a man who shies away from publicity and confrontation, he is considered by many to lack the political authority and dynamism required to preside over a fairly volatile constituency and steer the nightmarish process of dismantling apartheid education structures.

There are strong doubts about his ability to withstand the pressures of the job since he suffered a mild stroke shortly after taking office. However, he is regarded as a man of integrity and President Nelson Mandela is said to hold him in high regard.

Vice-chancellor of Fort Hare University before taking up his ministerial post, he has an honours degree in history from Unisa and a PhD in political science from the University of Geneva.

He is a staunch Lutheran and a former secretary-general of Inkatha. His years of teaching experience from the 1950s to the 1970s culminated in the founding of the reputable Dlangezwa High School in Natal in 1969, of which he was principal until 1976. His belief that Inkatha should develop into a democratic, mass-based organisation led to clashes with Inkatha chief Mangosuthu Buthelezi and persecution by Inkatha members.

Bengu left the country in 1978 and returned only in 1991. While serving as secretary for research and social action for the Lutheran World Foundation, he became close to the African National Congress and developed a strong working friendship with Oliver Tambo. Bengu has authored several publications and served on numerous boards.

He regards Chief Albert Luthuli, his uncle, as his mentor and hero: the man who encouraged him 'to study until he died'.

Born 8 May 1934. Family: wife Fundeka, four adult daughters, one son.

Botha, Roelof ('Pik')   Once known as the world's longest-serving minister of Foreign Affairs, Pik Botha did justice to his reputation as 'the ultimate political survivor' when he was appointed to the cabinet of President Nelson Mandela, albeit in the far more junior position of minister of Mineral and Energy Affairs. His lower profile did not deter the rotund and flamboyant Botha from controversy: he hit the headlines —

and strong opposition — when he announced a dramatic increase in the petrol price shortly after assuming office.

He grew used to controversy during the apartheid years, and even developed a penchant for it during decades of defending white minority rule against a hostile outside world. He survived the scandal of being caught lying about South Africa's involvement in the Mozambican war when he was found to have personally visited Renamo bases. And he survived being publicly slapped down by then president PW Botha for suggesting that South Africa might one day have a black president.

Not surprisingly, the gravel-voiced minister was one of FW de Klerk's strongest supporters in the 1989 power struggle that saw PW Botha ousted as state president.

Pik Botha became minister of Foreign Affairs in 1977, after serving as a high-profile South African ambassador to the United Nations in 1974, followed by a stint as ambassador to the United States. An advocate by training, he had previously been a member of South Africa's legal team in the 'South West Africa case' at the International Court of Justice in The Hague, Netherlands, from 1963 to 1966, and again in the early 1970s.

In spite of his public image as a verligte, even in the days when this was not a popular asset, Botha has always been a great crowd-drawer for the National Party. An excellent public performer with an actor's sense for the dramatic, he was always the most popular speaker on the campaign circuit in white elections and could swing marginal constituencies the NP's way. His skill at preparing potjiekos is legendary, although he claims a preference for eating rosebuds. He delights in being a raconteur and even occasionally playing the jovial buffoon: during negotiations, he once donned a uniform and acted the role of a visiting French general with a special message for the negotiators.

He has, however, never been the typical party hack jostling for position. This aloofness has cost him heavily: he has almost always been the first candidate to fall out in leadership elections. It is also one of the reasons why he was voted the NP's Transvaal leader only in 1992. Early in 1994, however, he convincingly beat off a challenge by his colleague Roelf Meyer for the leadership of the party in the powerful Gauteng province.

Botha was born at Rustenburg, matriculated at the Hoër Volkskool Potchefstroom, and received his BA and LLB degrees from the University of Pretoria.

Born 27 April 1932. Family: wife Helena, four adult children.

Botha, Thozamile   The new chairman of the important Commission on Provincial Government proved his capacity for leadership in the 1970s, spearheading the formation of the country's early civic and trade union structures under the banners of the Port Elizabeth Black Civic Organisation and the Motor Assemblies and Component Workers' Union of South Africa.

Following long detention and banning orders, Botha fled into exile in 1980 and continued his focus on strengthening the union movement as a national executive member of the South African Congress of Trade Unions. He worked with the late Chris Hani in Lesotho before moving to Lusaka and then to Essex where he completed a Master's degree in political science and public administration.

On his return to South Africa in 1990 he was elected head of the African National Congress's Department of Local and Regional Government and was a founding member of the

National Housing Forum. He also played a key role in the Local Government Negotiating Forum and was elected to the executive of the South African National Civic Organisation.

Elected to Parliament, he relinquished his seat to assume his current position, where his task is to oversee the charting of provincial constitutions and the transition to non-racial municipalities, in tandem with the drafting of a final constitution in the Constitutional Assembly. Within his first year in office he intends forming the nucleus of new regional governments from what remains of the provincial and Bantustan administrations and, in the longer term, rearranging the civil service.

Hard-working and friendly, with interests that range from chess to soccer and rugby, Botha is popular in the Eastern Cape where he has won the respect of colleagues, who describe him as flexible, accommodating and sensitive.

Born 16 June 1948. Family: two children.

Brink, David   The non-executive chairman of Absa, the country's biggest banking conglomerate, Brink has been voted one of South Africa's top five businessmen on several occasions.

He is proud of his history, which is steeped in mining. His father was one of Anglo American's most successful mine managers, ending up on the Zambian copper belt. Brink followed in his father's footsteps, working for Anglo between 1962 and 1970 and completing a Master's degree in mining engineering from the University of the Witwatersrand.

He has a 23-year association with RUC, Murray & Roberts's mining arm. In 1986 he was appointed chief executive of M&R and followed a logical progression, considering the links between the two, into Absa.

Local businessmen respect Brink, referring to him as 'a businessman of unusual breadth and vision'. In addition to being chairman of the Business Forum, he holds memberships in a number of important political and business bodies, including the President's Economic Advisory Council, and has a keen interest in sport and conservation.

Born 9 August 1939. Family: wife Marilyn Driver, two daughters, one son.

Buthelezi, Mangosuthu   The minister of Home Affairs, Chief Mangosuthu Buthelezi, is likely to prove the hardest to please element of the government of national unity. If there is a major fault-line in the cabinet, it is represented by the unpredictable Buthelezi, who is capable of switching between unbridled charm and ruthless bellicosity, and between ardent Zulu nationalism and friendly liberalism.

Buthelezi had a traditional upbringing, working as a herdboy in his youth. At the University of Fort Hare in the late 1940s, he joined the African National Congress Youth League and came into contact with ZK Matthews, Robert Mugabe and Robert Sobukwe. He was expelled after student boycotts and completed his degree at the University of Natal.

In 1953, he took up his position as chief, though not without controversy — his brother Mceleli would have taken the post if he had not run foul of the police. In 1970, he was appointed head of the kwaZulu Territorial Authority and became chief minister of the homeland in 1976.

Buthelezi used kwaZulu to build up a political power base in the 1970s and 1980s, based on homeland patronage, the exploitation of ethnic nationalism, policies on sanctions and violence that were much appreciated by the white establishment, and a combination of political guile and ruthlessness. The emerging Black Consciousness Movement of the 1970s branded him a homeland collaborator, though he consistently declined to accept homeland independence or enter into political deals with the government until Nelson Mandela was released from prison and the ANC unbanned.

He revived Inkatha in 1975 with the blessing of the ANC, but broke with the movement in 1980; his relationship with the ANC deteriorated sharply and, over the next few years, consistently. He built a minor personality cult within the IFP, establishing himself as an unchallenged leader, dealing toughly with any challenges to his policies or position, and often running the organisation as his personal fiefdom.

Since 1990, severely damaged by revelations of covert and extensive Security Police and Military Intelligence support in the 1980s, Buthelezi backed off from his claim to national leadership and turned to secure his regional base with a combination of ethnic nationalism aimed at a traditional constituency and liberalism aimed at white supporters.

At one point secure in his partnership and likely election alliance with the National Party, Buthelezi was deeply affronted by the 1992 Record of Understanding between Nelson Mandela and FW de Klerk, which restarted negotiations but also isolated Buthelezi and doused his dreams of being a third and equal talks partner. He also lost much moderate and white support by his refusal to rejoin the negotiations process and his disruption of the election process. He surrounded himself with some dubious hardliners. His political weakness and isolation led him into a negotiating alliance with the white right, originally in the Concerned South Africans Group and then in the Freedom Alliance.

Buthelezi chose to enter the April 1994 elections at the very last minute, disrupting the process severely, but emerging with a narrow victory in kwaZulu/Natal. His precarious hold on the province was not matched by any significant strength in the rest of the country. For the peace and reconciliation process, it was an ideal response — enough power to satisfy him and to shelve his threats of violence and disruption, but not sufficient to pose a national threat. The three pillars of his political base — homeland patronage, control of the kwaZulu security machinery, and his link to the king — are either gone, or under threat.

As minister of Home Affairs, Buthelezi has been vocal in his threats to illegal immigrants, whom he views as a major threat to the Reconstruction and Development Programme and against whom he has been threatening firm action. He is also responsible for censorship and has pledged that no longer will anyone decide what adults can see or hear, in line with the new constitution.

There are signs that he is approaching the 1995 local government elections in much the same way as he did the 1994 national elections, threatening to boycott unless they are conducted on his terms. Having proved himself a master of the political cliff-hanger, he is likely to follow the same tactics to maximum effect in this crucial poll and in the government of national unity.

Hanging over his head is an investigation into kwaZulu Police hit squads, for which he would have to assume responsibility as former minister of Police in the homeland.

Buthelezi holds the Guinness Book of Records entry for the longest-ever speech, a 400-page, five-day performance in the kwaZulu Legislative Assembly. He has also had a brief film career playing Cetswayo in the movie Zulu. He is known as a dedicated workaholic, an enthusiastic amateur historian and one of the least charismatic and most awkward speechmakers in national politics. He is supremely sensitive to criticism, which has been manifest in a difficult relation-ship with the media. This reached a head in 1994, when he stormed into an SABC studio while one of his rivals was on the air and provoked an ugly confrontation. He later apologised publicly for the incident.

Born 27 August 1928. Family: wife Irene, seven adult children.

Calitz, Estian   Directors-general's jobs were advertised after the April 1994 election, and incumbents invited to apply. Calitz's October 1993 appointment as director-general in the Department of Finance was quickly confirmed, an indication of his reputation in the field.

Calitz was born in George, where he spent most of his early years. He completed his undergraduate studies at the University of Stellenbosch before moving to Pretoria to complete his postgraduate education in economics and econometrics. However, he soon returned to the Cape where he obtained a doctorate in economics from Stellenbosch, specialising in public finance.

These qualifications opened a wide choice of career path. He opted to start in the Economics Department of the South African Reserve Bank in 1972, but left the Bank to lecture in economics at the University of Pretoria and Rand Afrikaans University.

Less than five years after obtaining his doctorate he had achieved recognition in the economics world; enough to be appointed deputy director in the then office of the economics adviser to the prime minister.

He has since held several positions in the civil service related to economic policy analysis and advice. In December 1989 he was appointed deputy director-general: financial planning in the Department of Finance, responsible for macro-aspects of fiscal and budgetary policy and policy analysis. In this capacity he served on various policy committees and has led a number of research and policy formulation projects.

He is a keen hiker, getting back to the George area as often as time allows him to.

Born 23 May 1949. Family: wife Karin, four children.

Carolus, Cheryl   Carolus is unusual among prominent African National Congress activists in having turned down the chance of parliamentary fame and fortune, preferring to remain an extra-parliamentary activist. She is currently secretary of the ANC's Policy Department, the ANC's secretary in charge of matters relating to the Reconstruction and Development Programme and, in December 1994, was elected ANC deputy secretary-general − a key post in plans to rehabilitate ANC structures and lead the 1995 local election campaign. A teacher by training, Carolus is a trustee of the Joint Education Trust in addition to her ANC posts.

She has been involved in politics since her schooldays, but first became prominent as an activist after the formation of the United Democratic Front in 1983. She served on the Western Cape regional and the national executive committee of the UDF, remaining politically active in the Western Cape despite personal banning orders and the 1988 restriction order which all but immobilised the UDF.

In May 1990, Carolus was appointed to the ANC delegation which held talks with the government. Later the same year, she became part of the South African Communist Party's interim leadership group which was formed to rebuild the party as a legally operating structure. In July 1991, she was elected to the ANC's National Executive Committee and assumed responsibility for the health, education, human resource development and arts and culture portfolios. This role entailed moving to Johannesburg − so she runs for an hour every morning, now that she is no longer able to hike on Table Mountain.

Born 27 May 1958. Family: husband Graham Bloch.

Chandler, Jeff   As president of the South African Associa-tion of Arts (SAAA), Chandler wields a fair amount of official power. He oversees the prestigious Volkskas Atelier art competition, is an ex-officio member of the Department of National Education's Art Advisory Committee, the National Gallery's Board of Trustees and the committee of the Durban Arts Corporation, and co-ordinates the 14 branches of the SAAA, organising South African participa-tion in almost every international exposition to which the country is invited.

It is the kind of post which in the past has been associated with retired judges, senior Broederbond membership and political favours, but nothing could be more remote from Chandler. Born into an Afrikaans farming family in the Queenstown district, he is an ex-parabat with one-time aspirations of becoming a mercenary, changing direction to become instead a Rhodes University student anarchist of the generation influenced by the 1968 student uprisings in Paris. Employed, after earning his BA, as a retail manager in the Oude Meester liquor group (though he himself is a diehard Tassenberg drinker), he returned to university for postgrad-uate studies.

He earned a Master's degree in fine arts, has taught ever since at the Durban Technikon and is a painter of some note, mainly of nudes and erotic works. As president of the Natal Society of Arts, he changed a late-colonialist association of whites into the most vibrant and community-involved of the SAAA's regions, with a strong outreach programme, much of its funding and revenue rerouted into township art projects, community teacher training and work with such groupings as terminally ill and handicapped children.

In 1993, the SAAA's credibility was at an all-time low after an abortively managed South African re-entry into the international art scene via the Venice Biennale. Elected SAAA president in 1993, Chandler has systematically worked to realign the organisation and transform its identity. His vision of the SAAA is summed up in his often-repeated assertion that he takes the name literally. To this end he has introduced a significant democratisation in the organisation's formerly highly centralised and barely accountable operation, and opened up the selection processes for which he is responsible. He has worked towards establishing links with cultural organisations of a grassroots nature and with the National Arts Coalition. His vision is one in which the SAAA will operate as an umbrella body with a diverse affiliated organisational membership.

Born 5 October 1947. Family: wife Pasquale Jacobs, one son.

Chaskalson, Arthur   In what many see as a reward for a life of brilliant service to the cause of human rights, Chaskalson has been appointed president of the new Constitutional Court. Together the 11 members of the court must certify whether the new constitution, still to be drafted, conforms with the principles laid down during the pre-election negotiations. They must also act as guardians of the interim constitution and weigh competing rights when cases involving the Bill of Rights come to them for adjudication.

In his capacity as president of the new court, Chaskalson also serves on the Judicial Service Commission, and thus will help select judges for all the country's higher courts.

Chaskalson recently retired as director of the Legal Resources Centre, an organisation he helped to found and headed for 15 years, successfully arguing some of the most important legal challenges to apartheid legislation.

He graduated from the University of the Witwatersrand with a BCom LLB, was admitted to the Johannesburg Bar in 1956 and took silk in 1971. Human rights and legal organisations, both international and local, awarded him many honours. Among the most important was his election in 1985 as an honorary member of the Bar Association of New York, an honour shared by very few and only one other South African — Jan Smuts in 1930. He was also consultant to the Namibian constituent assembly and helped draft the Namibian constitution.

However, he was never given a judicial appointment in South Africa during the apartheid years, partly because he apparently let it be known he would not be prepared to administer the unjust laws then on the statute books, partly because the government was, in any case, not willing to honour him in this way.

He has continued his association with Wits University as a board member of the law faculty for the past 15 years, and as honorary professor of law since 1981.

During pre-election negotiations Chaskalson was a member of the African National Congress's constitutional committee and served on the technical committee which drafted the interim constitution. This has led to some concern whether it was proper for him to lead the judges who will interpret the constitution. However, experts point out that he did not serve on the committee which drafted the Bill of Rights — the chapter of the constitution which will feature most in the Constitutional Court.

Born 24 November 1931. Family: wife Lorraine, two adult sons.

Chikane, Frank   At the annual conference in July 1994 of the South African Council of Churches (SACC), general secretary Frank Chikane announced his intention to resign, but said he would stay on until a successor was found.

Young, bright and extremely able, he is likely to remain influential politically whatever role he chooses to fill. He is one of the few commissioners of the Independent Electoral Commission who emerged unscathed by a stint with that organisation. He was charged with the responsibility of getting the elections belatedly off the ground in what was Bophuthatswana, which proved to be one of the few relatively trouble-free rural areas for balloting and counting.

Chikane was a child of the Black Consciousness Movement of the 1970s. His education both at school and university was repeatedly interrupted by spells of detention. He trained as a pastor in the black section of the Apostolic Faith Mission (AFM) between 1975 and 1979 but was defrocked by the church for his political activity. He was only recently reinstated and now heads the black section of the AFM, which is moving slowly towards uniting as one non-racial church.

Under his stewardship, the SACC was a formidable foe of apartheid, but suffered from the tag of being 'the African National Congress at prayer'. Now, however, the SACC has welcomed back into its fold several of its more conservative brethren in the church and is well placed, though perhaps not very well funded, to provide for the needs of millions of Christians.

He has left his mark as an activist priest, a leading light at the Institute for Contextual Theology and one of the coauthors of the seminal Kairos Document which espoused a liberation theology answer to apartheid and successive States of Emergency during the second half of the 1980s.

Born 3 January 1951. Family: wife Kagiso, three sons.

Cobbett, William John ('Billy')   Well before lunchtime on the day Housing minister Joe Slovo moved into his new offices he had fired the incumbent director-general and installed Cobbett in the post. Slovo's speed said much about the working relationship between the minister and his director-general. Normally, the ministry sets policy and the department carries it out; but in Housing, Cobbett and Slovo worked together. This has put Cobbett in a position to supply valuable continuity − after the death of the minister in January 1995 and the appointment of his replacement, deputy Welfare minister Sankie Nkondo − in an attempt to solve the housing crisis.

Cobbett arrived at African National Congress head-quarters at the end of 1991 and was pointed in the direction of the National Housing Forum (NHF), then just a glint in the eye of development non-governmental organisations determined to tackle the hostel crisis.

Charming, direct, plain-speaking, he characterises himself as a fast learner and his career as 'chequered'. Ten years ago he was lecturing in sociology at the University of the Witwatersrand, armed only with a Middlesex Polytechnic honours degree in modern European history. When invited to join the developmental agency Planact as co-ordinator in 1988, his background in the area was scanty and theoretical, centred on research for his uncompleted PhD: a critique of apartheid development focused on Botshabelo in the Free State.

He left South Africa for England in the mid-1970s and returned seven years later to research his PhD; but the project didn't survive the 1986 State of Emergency. Cobbett returned to England, coming back to South Africa two years later when Planact offered a post.

It was at Planact, he says, that he picked up on development issues generally. He says he learned to negotiate by watching Cyril Ramaphosa run talks with Planact client, the Soweto People's Delegation which led to the Greater Soweto Accord in 1990. Cobbett became an expert on local government, worked on the design of the Central Witwatersrand Metropolitan Chamber, advised civics throughout the Transvaal, and at the end of 1991 was co-opted briefly as site manager for Codesa I before moving on to a headquarters job at the ANC, an organisation he didn't join until it was unbanned, on the theory that one didn't have to belong to the ANC to work for it.

His crash course in housing concentrated on hostels, which put him close to the centre of talks leading to the September 1992 Record of Understanding which restored multiparty negotiations that had been diverted three months earlier by the Boipatong massacre.

At one point, he was the NHF vice-chairman, the ANC representative on the National Electricity Forum, the ANC representative on the Transitional Executive Council's local and regional government sub-council, a member of the TEC's local government sub-council and co-chair of its traditional authorities sub-council.

In a combination of Cobbett's personal, transparent manner and Planact-style consultation, he has said all housing policy proposals will be put out for public discussion.

Born 27 December 1957. Family: wife Mary Clulverd, three children.

Coetsee, Hendrik Jacobus ('Kobie')   When he was named president of the Senate, Coetsee was being rewarded for his central role in opening negotiations between the National Party government, in which he was minister of Justice, and Nelson Mandela, when the latter was still in prison. For that, he has won the praise and admiration of Mandela, who would like to have appointed Coetsee to his cabinet. However, the National Party's poor showing in the polls did not permit a large enough number of NP cabinet positions to extend as far as Coetsee.

An enigmatic person, Coetsee has earned both respect and criticism from political opponents — most notably during the negotiations when he almost allowed the African National Congress to appoint the members of the Constitutional Court. His *faux pas* was exposed by the Democratic Party's Tony Leon, and he withdrew what was perceived by the ANC as a generous gesture.

An advocate, Coetsee became MP for Bloemfontein West in 1968 and, after 1985, leader of the NP in the Free State. From 1978, he served in the cabinet as deputy minister of Defence responsible for the Directorate of National Security; in 1980 he became minister of Justice and in 1990 Correctional Services was added to his portfolio. In 1992 he took over National Intelligence.

Coetsee was responsible for a number of reforms in the judicial and legal system, including improvements in the position of women and children. He also introduced the small claims courts.

Born 19 April 1931. Family: wife Ena, five children.

Corbett, Michael McGregor   Judge Corbett is making legal history by serving a second term as acting chief justice. Originally he was asked to stay on beyond his normal retirement age and caretake the Appeal Court during the pre-election transition period. However, the new government asked him to extend his stay in office yet again. Public reaction to his additional two terms has been very positive, unlike the uproar when his predecessor, Mr Justice Pierre Rabie, architect of controversial security legislation under the *ancien régime*, was asked to serve a period as acting chief justice. Judge Corbett's acceptance of a second term in this capacity reveals his strong sense of duty — friends say he had many plans for his retirement, all of which have had to be put on hold.

With his appointment to lead the Appellate Division, its character and standing changed significantly. Judge Corbett's scrupulous fairness has provided an enabling environment for pro-human rights judgments from the courts. This, coupled with his successful handling of the inauguration of Nelson Mandela, clearly impressed the government and largely explains the request that he stay on.

Under the new constitution he has the additional task of co-ordinating and serving as a member of the Judicial Service Commission (JSC) — the body which must help choose all future supreme court judges and justices of the Appeal Court. His role on the JSC will be important to watch: the constitution commits the JSC to choosing a Bench which reflects the country's race and gender composition. However, he is no radical on this question and has spoken strongly in the past about the need to preserve standards on the Bench, even if this means that in the immediate future the judiciary continues to be dominated by white males.

He is a graduate of the Universities of Cape Town and Cambridge, and has honorary doctorates from UCT, Rhodes, University of the Witwatersrand and the University

of the Orange Free State. He was appointed to the Cape
Supreme Court in 1963 and to the Appellate Division in 1974.

Born 14 September 1923. Family: wife Margaret, four
adult children.

Crump, Alan   In the 1980s Crump, professor of fine arts at
the University of the Witwatersrand, used to be referred to as
the godfather of the 'fine arts mafia'. He sat on and
powerfully influenced practically every fine arts competition, museum, educational and policy committee of note in
the country. While his real power base has, if anything,
grown with his appointment in 1990 as chairperson of the
Standard Bank's National Arts Festival in Grahamstown, the
persona has mellowed somewhat in recent years. Ever one to
confound expectation, he has also, over the past few years,
been quietly building a reputation as a producer of finely
wrought watercolours.

Attaining his professorship in 1980 at the age of 31 on the
back of a Fulbright scholarship, a senior lectureship at Unisa
and a fairly promising career at the cutting edge of
conceptual art, Crump was an *enfant terrible* with the
institutional muscle of an *éminence grise*. It was not long
before he made his presence felt, building the Wits Fine Arts
School to a point of uncontested pre-eminence in South
African art by the mid-1980s, and promoting a new
professionalism in South African art through sponsorships
and the creation and/or expansion of a number of lucrative
and usually controversial national art competitions, the most
notable of which was the now defunct Cape Town Triennial.

Since that time, however, Crump's involvement in the fine
arts has moved increasingly in the direction of cultural
development, and has overseen the transformation of the
massive Grahamstown Festival from a late-colonial celebra-

tion of English heritage to the more democratic and representative showcase it is today. Crump's plans for the future of the festival revolve particularly around a greater directedness towards the African continent.

Born in Durban, Crump gained BA(FA) and MA(FA) degrees at the University of Cape Town, and, in 1973, as a Fulbright scholar, an MFA from the University of California in Los Angeles. He is honorary director of University Art Galleries at Wits, as well as chairperson of its Museum User Committee and of the University Art Galleries' Selection and Acquisitions Committee. He is a long-standing trustee of the Johannesburg Art Gallery, a trustee of the African Institute of Art at Funda, art adviser to the Standard Bank Corporation, serves as external examiner in fine arts for nearly every tertiary educational institution of note, and is adviser to nearly every public art museum in the country.

Born 28 April 1949. Family: wife zoologist Caroline Robinson.

De Klerk, Frederik Willem ('FW')   From the last white state president to second deputy president in the country's first non-racial government: FW de Klerk says he prepared himself psychologically for the inevitable lowering in status that democracy would bring. However, there is little doubt that he would have preferred more clout than he has. His National Party's election results reflected the 'worst scenario' projections of party strategists.

His new status does not mean that De Klerk does not wield strong influence on government decisions. The contrary is true: most (white) senior civil servants, defence force personnel and the strong farming industry form his constituency; few decisions can be taken by the government without considering the opinions of these sectors.

De Klerk shared the Nobel Peace Prize with President Nelson Mandela in 1993.

His insistence that he will play a constructive role in the government of national unity is borne out by the gracious way in which he conceded election defeat to the African National Congress and accepted the third-in-command post. His role in the transition to democracy can only now — after the elections — really be seen in context.

It is an ironic twist of history that the role of overseeing the transformation fell on a member of one of the staunchest families of Nationalists in South Africa. De Klerk's father was a member of HF Verwoerd's cabinet and former prime minister JG Strijdom was his uncle.

The most outstanding characteristic of De Klerk's political career after he joined Parliament in 1972 was probably his elusiveness. He was thought to be closer to the verkrampte section of the National Party. Nothing prepared South Africa for his dramatic announcements on 2 February 1990, releasing Nelson Mandela and unbanning, among others, the ANC and the South African Communist Party.

Although it belongs to the politics of the past, the calm and determined way in which he ousted his redoubtable predecessor, PW Botha, earned him respect, as did the sophistication he brought to the party. He was the first television president in the country, developing a friendlier, more open and accessible relationship with the media than any of his predecessors and turning it to his advantage. He also showed a steely determination in keeping the country on the negotiations path and a remarkable calm and self-confidence in the difficult period of the last few years.

He is credited with the abolition of apartheid, but his refusal to admit that apartheid was immoral still counts against him in many quarters. He has also been criticised for failing to take adequate steps when irregularities in his security forces were revealed in the early 1990s. As could be expected, he voiced strong opposition to Justice minister Dullah Omar's proposed truth commission to investigate political crimes of the apartheid era which could lead all the way to the top, including De Klerk.

De Klerk was born in Johannesburg, grew up in Krugersdorp and completed his BA LLB at the University of Potchefstroom. In January 1973 he was offered the chair of administrative law at Potchefstroom, but instead decided on a political career.

Apart from National Education, he served mostly in low-profile portfolios in the previous white-dominated Parliament, including Posts and Telecommunications, Sports and Recreation, Mineral and Energy Affairs, and Internal Affairs.

He was elected leader of the NP in the Transvaal in 1982 following the breakaway of the Conservative Party. In February 1989 he became leader of the NP and in August the same year state president. He claims credit as the one who took the initiative for change, but the politics he represents are expected to become increasingly less relevant as the new black elite governs itself into effective power.

Born 18 March 1936. Family: wife Marike, three adult children.

De Klerk, Peter   De Klerk has moved from the advertising and marketing industry to the most powerful position in broadcasting today: he is, along with Sebeletso Mokone-Matabane, the co-chair of the seven-member Independent Broadcasting Authority (IBA), which is empowered with restructuring and re-regulating the broadcasting industry. It is a five-year appointment, and De Klerk did not immediately resign his post as chief executive officer of the Association of

Advertising Agencies, causing many in the broadcasting sector to worry about a conflict of interests: one of the most important tasks of the IBA will be to look at the restructuring of the South African Broadcasting Corporation, and at how it is to be financed. However, by September he had relinquished the AAA post.

De Klerk was elected to the chairmanship of the IBA by a panel of political leaders, including current Broadcasting minister Pallo Jordan and former Home Affairs minister Danie Schutte. Even though he is not known to have any political affiliation, his appointment was a political compromise, wrought to assuage Schutte, who saw the IBA as being too heavily weighted with members of the African National Congress.

De Klerk started his advertising career at Adverto (later D'Arcy Masius Benton and Bowles, then Sonnenburg Murphy Leo Burnett). He was chairman and managing director of D'Arcy, and has also been managing director of another agency, J Walter Thompson. He has also been general marketing consultant to Mercedes-Benz in South Africa.

Born 5 May 1939. Family: wife Elizabeth Elaine, three adult children.

De Lille, Patricia   The hard-nosed and forthright De Lille is certain to have impact as chairperson of the National Assembly's select committee on Transport. A behind-the-scenes operator, she was thrust into the limelight when she took over from Benny Alexander (now known as !Khoisan X) as Pan Africanist Congress chief negotiator at the World Trade Centre and won respect for her firmness and clarity.

De Lille's organisational and negotiating skills were honed in the trade union movement. After a brief involvement in the Western Cape uprising in 1976, she worked for a paint company where she and other workers, frustrated with trying to represent workers on an internal liaison committee, joined the South African Chemical Workers' Union. She became Western Cape regional secretary in 1983 and a member of the national executive in 1985. In 1987, she was the first woman to sit on the executive of the National Council of Trade Unions (Nactu) and was elected vice-president the following year.

De Lille was involved in Africanist organisation in the Western Cape in the late 1980s. She left her job to work for the PAC in 1989 and declined renomination to the Nactu leadership to concentrate on this. After the 1990 unbannings, she was elected PAC foreign affairs secretary, and in 1992 moved to the PAC's relief and aid portfolio.

The PAC's poor election showing relegated her to a back seat in Parliament, but she was given a committee chairman-ship in the spirit of national unity and can be expected to make a strong mark there.

Born 17 February 1951. Family: husband Edwin de Lille, one son.

De Villiers, Dawie   The minister of Environment Affairs and Tourism was one of the driving forces behind the reforms of the FW de Klerk government. His reconciliatory speech during the first session of the new Parliament in Cape Town was described by President Nelson Mandela as the best of the sitting.

A qualified dominee in the Nederduits Gereformeerde Kerk, the mild-mannered former Springbok rugby captain has over a period of time distinguished himself as the National Party's moral philosopher. De Villiers led the NP team at the last round of negotiations, where he made his mark as one of the more capable chairmen.

After the national poll, he was re-elected leader of the NP in the Western Cape ahead of controversial premier Hernus Kriel. This gives him a powerful hold on the only province where the NP showed overwhelming strength.

The former philosophy lecturer and ambassador to the United Kingdom has been in Parliament as long as FW de Klerk. He was first elected to the all-white Parliament of prime minister John Vorster in 1972, and was appointed to the cabinet in 1980 when PW Botha was in power.

In spite of his philosophy background (he holds a PhD from the University of Stellenbosch) his cabinet positions were mostly of a technical nature: minister of Industrial Affairs, Trade and Tourism, Mineral and Energy Affairs, minister of Economic Co-ordination, and minister of Public Enterprises.

A staunch supporter of the NP since his student days at Stellenbosch — where he served on the management committee of the NP — De Villiers is now an equally staunch defender of human rights and a severe critic of the Conservative Party.

Born 10 July 1940. Family: wife Suzaan, four children.

Dexter, Phillip David   Tough and clear-minded — he impressed colleagues who sat with him on the National Economic Forum and on the Transitional Executive Council's task force on the public sector — Dexter is one of the fastest-rising stars in South African politics.

He was elected to Parliament as one of the Congress of South African Trade Unions officials on the African National Congress list, then appointed to an ANC post involving the co-ordination of the party's legislative pro-grammes at national and provincial levels.

In 1982 he went into exile halfway through a politics and philosophy degree course at the University of Natal. He spent almost a decade doing work for Umkhonto weSizwe and the ANC abroad, apparently in the intelligence area. On returning to South Africa in 1990 he completed his degree at the University of Cape Town, and immediately joined the National Education, Health and Allied Workers' Union (Nehawu).

In 1992 he was elected Nehawu general secretary, with responsibility for invigorating and reorganising a rudderless union with neither coherent structures nor finances. The union is now on its feet and is an influential force within Cosatu and the public sector. It has a tough relationship with the government and Dexter, a key figure on the parliamentary committee on the public service, will have an important role to play here.

The private life of this ardent communist, who insiders say reluctantly accepted a position on the ANC election list, has suffered since his return from exile; his Brazilian wife first followed him back, then left.

Born 1 December 1962. Family: one son.

Dipico, Manne Emsley   In his mid-30s, Dipico could well have found himself contemplating the end of his career as a semi-professional soccer player. But politics intervened, steering him away from sport and towards government. Hanging up his boots prematurely, he chased — and narrowly gained — a majority for the African National Congress in the Northern Cape, where he is now premier.

Dipico is the youngest of the nine regional premiers. But his former colleagues in the National Union of Mineworkers (NUM) warn against underestimating him — he is an independent thinker, a hard worker and a popular figure in the region. And, they might have added, an example of how the unions nurtured a generation of political leaders through the 1980s.

Dipico was born in Kimberley's Greenpoint township and brought up by his mother, a domestic worker at the town's hospital. He started working life as a diamond miner, but was fired from De Beers' Finsch Mine for participating in a wages strike and later enrolled at the University of Fort Hare. An Azanian Students' Organisation activist while at university, he also joined the ANC's underground structures, and was detained for anti-Ciskei activities. He was denied readmission to Fort Hare on his release and became a full-time regional organiser for the NUM in Kimberley. He spent almost three years in jail for furthering the aims of the ANC and was released in 1990.

Displaying the kind of flexibility which will be needed to put his remote and underprivileged region on the map, Dipico named a Freedom Front member to his cabinet and the Democratic Party's only regional MP to the position of speaker. His task will be to turn an agricultural and raw materials-based economy into one which creates jobs in tourism and in adding value to those primary resources.

Born 21 April 1959. Single.

Duarte, Yasmin Jessie   It is perhaps symbolic of the person in charge of the portfolio that Safety and Security in Gauteng is way ahead of any of the other regions in developing a new way of policing South Africa.

Despite being frustrated at the start of her tenure by a lack of clearly defined powers and a budget, Gauteng Safety and Security MEC Duarte has forged ahead, starting vigorous policy debates and issuing a number of groundbreaking directives. Most notable is the boost she has given community policing — getting communities involved in deciding how their townships will be policed — by personally pushing for community police forums to get off the ground.

Key to the progress in the region is Duarte's hands-on style of operating which has made it clear to the traditional police hierarchy that a new woman with new ideas is in charge, and there's not much point in fighting her.

She has been active in the PWV area, specifically in the coloured township of Riverlea, for the past 25 years. She is deeply committed to women's rights and it was as an official of the Federation of Transvaal Women that she served on the Southern Transvaal executive of the now defunct United Democratic Front, between 1985 and 1990. She was repeatedly banned and restricted during this time.

After the unbanning of the African National Congress, she was elected to the regional executive committee (REC) of the organisation and also served on the REC of the ANC's Women's League.

In May 1990, she was appointed as a special assistant to ANC president Nelson Mandela. This position and strong backing from the ANC's women's lobby made her one of the most influential people in the organisation and a certainty for a national position. But Duarte wanted a position in the Gauteng regional government and left Mandela's office to accept the portfolio in the province.

Born 19 September 1953. Family: husband John Duarte, two teenaged children.

Eglin, Colin   The leading theorist in the Democratic Party and its longest-serving parliamentarian, Eglin is serving under the fourth consecutive national constitution. His parliamentary career started in 1958 when he was elected to the all-white Parliament of the Union of South Africa. In

1974 he was re-elected to the Republican Parliament; in 1983 he survived the transition to the tricameral constitution allowing limited coloured and Indian representation in Parliament; and during the last three years he has helped negotiate the country's first democratic constitution, under which he was elected to Parliament in April 1994, one of only seven surviving DP MPs. Previously MP for Sea Point in Cape Town, he acted as the DP's chief negotiator at the multiparty negotiating forum leading up to the elections.

He has won respect for many years for his dogged commitment to principle, detailed knowledge of foreign affairs and dedicated liberalism. The dry and pedantic manner that served him well in Parliament and the negotiating council — he was a member of the 10-person planning committee — was not as helpful during his two short-lived and unsuccessful terms as party leader.

Born in Cape Town, Eglin graduated with a BSc degree in quantity surveying at the University of Cape Town in 1946, having interrupted his studies for war service with the South African forces in Egypt and Italy in 1944/45.

In 1959 he was one of the founders of the Progressive Party, which he served as leader from 1971 to 1979 and again from 1986 to 1988, by that time leading the Progressive Federal Party.

Born 14 April 1925. Family: wife Joyce, three adult children.

Erwin, Alexander ('Alec')   As deputy Finance minister, academic economist Alec Erwin has emerged as a central figure in the economic policy formulation of the government of national unity, and in the corporatist stance of that government.

Among the few cabinet recruitments from the labour movement, Erwin has the credibility to reconcile the economic blueprint of the African National Congress, the Reconstruction and Development Programme, with the restraints of the broader economic environment.

Erwin's credibility is hard won, as a typical diehard, overworked and underpaid white unionist who battled state adversity through the 1970s and 1980s to shape the unions into a political force to be reckoned with.

He was general secretary in the Federation of South African Trade Unions, a forerunner of the Congress of South African Trade Unions, from 1979 to 1981, but afterwards was content to work quietly in the background for some years as national secretary for education in the National Union of Metalworkers of South Africa.

An economic thinker, he helped shape and give content to the economic analysis of the union movement, as Cosatu's co-ordinator of the Economic Trends Group, and to the labour movement's economic solution to South Africa's problems, the Industrial Strategy Project. He also played a role in the ANC-constructed Macro-Economic Research Group, now the National Institute of Economic Policy.

Rejecting 'a war of slogans', Erwin was in the forefront of the drive to cut through conflict on economic issues through the consensus politics of the National Economic Forum.

Erwin, once a doctrinaire socialist, is now brimful of phrases that suggest conservative economic rectitude; he was supportive of former Finance minister Derek Keys's emphasis on macro-economic discipline on a number of counts, not least the point that inflation erodes the wage gains of workers. He remains, formally at least, a member of the South African Communist Party.

Born 17 January 1948. Family: wife Annie Pretorius, two daughters.

Fanaroff, Bernard ('Bernie')   Fanaroff was recently elevated to the position of deputy director-general in the office of Jay Naidoo, minister without portfolio charged with implementation of the Reconstruction and Development Programme (RDP). Adviser to the minister, he is charged with the implementation and co-ordination of the RDP at provincial and regional levels.

Fanaroff was one of the longest-serving officials of the modern South African trade union movement, and one of the very few white unionists to have stayed the course, leaving his job as national organiser for the National Union of Metalworkers of South Africa (Numsa) only in 1994.

He cut short a promising academic career in the early 1970s after obtaining a doctorate in astronomy at Cambridge University because 'all I had was an interest in the working class'.

His union career spans the growth of the labour movement from the tiny splinter organisations that emerged from the 1973 Durban strike wave, through the formation of the Federation of South African Trade Unions, to the birth of the 1,3-million-strong Congress of South African Trade Unions.

Renowned in union circles for his understanding of the labour field, creative thinking and strategic subtlety, he belonged to Cosatu's inner circle, led the federation's anti-VAT campaign in 1991, was one of three union delegates on the Electricity Council in 1993, and spearheaded the formation of the Telecommunications Forum which grappled with controversies surrounding the launch of the cellular phone industry. He also played a central role in the pre-election campaign, calling for transparency in the arms industry.

Born 11 September 1947. Family: wife Wendy Vogel.

Felgate, Walter   A 1993 curriculum vitae of Felgate grossly underplayed the influence he wields within the Inkatha Freedom Party: it listed his membership of the party's central committee as an 'extra-curricular activity'.

Born in Pretoria, the bearded Felgate forged a friendship with IFP leader Mangosuthu Buthelezi over 20 years ago when he was African affairs adviser to the London-based Rio Tinto Zinc Corporation. Also a former personnel manager at the Phalaborwa mining company, he found a common bond with Buthelezi's strong desire to defeat the African National Congress's campaign to isolate South Africa internationally through sanctions and disinvestment.

As Buthelezi's closest confidant, Felgate played a behind-the-scenes role until the 1990s, acting as the IFP leader's researcher and speech writer. But as the political temperature rose — and after 1990, when Buthelezi lost his secretary-general, Oscar Dhlomo — Felgate shot into the public limelight. He was co-opted to the IFP central committee and became a key figure in IFP-ANC peace talks and, later, a delegate to the multiparty negotiation process. He was strongly in favour of the IFP's walking out of the negotiations forum and became chief IFP negotiator in bilateral talks with the ANC and National Party, which blamed him for Buthelezi's refusal to accept compromises and participate in the elections.

With his abrasive personality, Felgate is also deeply resented by his own colleagues who have desperately tried to curb his influence in the party. But he still has Buthelezi's confidence, having been placed third on the party's list for the National Assembly.

However, Felgate appears to have adopted a low profile since the election — perhaps to devote more time to such non-political interests as sailing and fishing. IFP moderates will breathe a sigh of relief.

Born 19 November 1930. Family: two children.

Fismer, Chris   The deputy minister of Justice was named to the newly created post of minister of General Services in December 1994 to top up the number of cabinet posts allotted to the National Party.

One of the rising young stars in the NP, Fismer served as parliamentary and political assistant to the previous state president in his last year in power. His job was to 'communicate the president's views to the public at large'.

Now Fismer, one of the more verligte members of the NP, finds himself in the difficult position of representing mainly white interests in the government of national unity.

As one of the post-1976 graduates in the NP caucus, shaped by the demands of black politics rather than the fierce nationalism of an earlier generation of Afrikaners, the slightly hesitant and bespectacled Fismer has always shown more sensitivity for the new politics than most of his older colleagues in the NP. This, combined with a growing awareness of the importance of public perceptions, was the reason why he was appointed as FW de Klerk's assistant.

In spite of his verligte tendencies, Fismer followed the typical Afrikaner road to NP office. Born and schooled in Pretoria at the prestigious Afrikaans Seuns Hoërskool, he obtained his BComm (Econ Science), BLC and LLB degrees from the University of Pretoria. As a student he served as chairman of the students' representative council and central rag committee and as president of the Afrikaanse Studentebond.

Fismer was first elected to the tricameral Parliament in 1987 when he unseated the Conservative Party's Daan van der Merwe in the Rissik constituency. In 1989 he was re-elected with a majority of 3 533 votes.

In Parliament he quickly made his mark as an outspoken — if not very dynamic — member of the reform-minded left wing of the NP.

Born 30 September 1956. Family: wife Linda, twin daughters.

Gerwel, Gert Johannes ('Jakes')   Gerwel felt it would have been arrogant to turn down an invitation to assume the post of director-general in the Office of the President — and so he stepped down from the heights of academe and accepted it. As the man in charge of administering President Nelson Mandela's public life, his duties include accompanying the president on state visits and advising him on the writing of his speeches.

His appointment has brought to an end a long association with the University of the Western Cape, the institution which saw the start of his brilliant academic career. The son of a poor family who put a high value on education, he was born near Somerset East in the rural Eastern Cape, educated at a farm school and later at boarding school before enrolling at UWC. He returned to UWC — from which he graduated cum laude — to lecture during the 1970s. At that time the university was an ethnically based training college for coloured students, staffed largely by conservative white academics. Gerwel, inspired by the black consciousness thinking which was then dominant in South Africa, was an important figure in protest politics at the university. Later he studied at the Free University of Brussels, graduating magna cum laude in 1979 with a doctorate in literature and philosophy.

Gerwel was appointed vice-chancellor of UWC in 1987 and declared his intention of turning the university into an intellectual home for the left. Under the leadership of this prominent activist, who was publicly involved in the United Democratic Front, the former apartheid college became a prominent centre of opposition to apartheid — and, after the unbanning of the African National Congress, Gerwel served on the ANC's regional executive committee.

Gerwel's reputation as an intellectual with his political feet on the ground has made him a respected adviser and decision-maker. While working in the President's Office he has retained his positions as chair of the Equal Opportunities Foundation, as a trustee of the Institute for Democracy in South Africa (Idasa) and of *Die Suid Afrikaan* magazine. He has also retained his abiding interest in cricket.

Born 18 January 1946. Family: wife Phoebe, one son.

Ginwala, Frene   The transition to democracy which changed the complexion of Parliament has also, in Ginwala, given the country its first woman speaker of the House. The redoubtable Ginwala immediately made her impact felt when she ruled that suits and ties were no longer obligatory for male MPs; within days after her appointment the traditionally staid Parliament was noticeably more relaxed. She has made it her aim to bring Parliament closer to the people, and the strict rules governing access to the National Assembly have been relaxed. Under her guidance the traditional Christian prayer has been replaced with a moment's silence for either prayer or meditation, and she has also sought to modernise and Africanise the symbols of Parliament.

Although she has little knowledge of parliamentary procedure, Ginwala has wide international experience. Usually sari-clad, she is an articulate and popular keynote speaker at any number of conferences. She has a reputation as a principled politician, is known for her incisive interventions in public debates, and has been extremely influential in getting the African National Congress and the negotiating council to put women's issues high up on the agenda. Of stern gait and even sterner countenance, she does not suffer fools gladly.

Ginwala left the country in the 1960s as a student to arrange the escape of the late Oliver Tambo, then ANC president, after the apartheid government started rounding up political opponents. As an ANC official, she worked in Tanzania, Zambia, Mozambique and the United Kingdom, where she was head of the political research unit in Tambo's office. She also served as ANC spokesperson in London, where she completed her LLB degree. She is a barrister at law (Inner Temple) and has a doctorate from Oxford.

She has wide experience as a journalist, having worked as a stringer in East Africa for British newspapers (including *The Guardian*) and the BBC. She was editor of the monthly political journal *Spearhead* and, from 1969 to 1972, managing editor of the Tanzanian national papers *The Standard* and *Sunday News*.

Ginwala has lectured at universities in a number of countries and participated at various United Nations, Unesco and other international conferences on South Africa, conflict research, women, and development and technology transfer. She was one of 14 experts invited in

1987 to advise the director-general on the Unesco programme on peace and conflict research.

She returned to South Africa in 1991 as part of the ANC task force to establish the Women's League and later became a member of Nelson Mandela's secretariat. She was a member of the ANC negotiating team at Codesa and the Multiparty Negotiating Process technical committee that drew up the procedure for the 1994 elections. She headed the ANC's Research Department in Johannesburg, was deputy head of the ANC Commission for the Emancipation of Women and convener of the Women's National Coalition.

Born: 25 April 1932. Single.

Godongwana, Enoch   The outspoken general secretary of the National Union of Metalworkers of South Africa (Numsa) commands enormous respect among his colleagues in the top echelons of the Congress of South African Trade Unions. Renowned for his strategic thinking skills and love of debate, this leader of Cosatu's second-largest affiliate was nominated for the position of general secretary in 1993 when it was apparent that Jay Naidoo was destined for Parliament. However, he stepped down to concentrate on his union whose leadership had been weakened by the departure of people like Moses Mayekiso and Bernie Fanaroff.

A former Border regional secretary of the South African Communist Party, he has now become one of the party's ideologues. 'I'm red from head to toe,' he says.

Godongwana started his working life as a dispatch clerk at Barlows Heavy Engineering where he joined the Metal and Allied Workers' Union, later becoming a shop steward and organiser. Following the merger of metal and engineering unions to form Numsa in 1987, he enjoyed a rapid rise within the union, becoming national organiser, regional secretary, acting general secretary, and now general secretary.

Although his Unisa law degree is an unfinished story, his mental stamina has been tested in many areas: as founder member and chairperson of the Border-Kei Regional Development Forum, former chairperson of Cosatu's Economic Development Task Force, and as labour representative on the Job Creation Technical Committee of the National Economic Forum.

Godongwana has no intention of leaving the trade union movement: 'I do not have any other skills except organising workers,' he says.

Born: 9 June 1956. Single.

Godsell, Robert ('Bobby')   Executive director of the giant Anglo American Corporation, Godsell is a rare example of a business leader who has a sophisticated understanding of society as well as influence in business circles. He has established a firm role as a liberal thinker while steadily building his clout in the business world.

Since joining Anglo American's Industrial Relations Department in 1974 he has risen rapidly through the ranks, and is now in charge of industrial relations and public affairs.

One of the visionary businessmen who has helped negotiation forums like the National Economic Forum succeed and helped enhance the perception of business as a willing partner in change, Godsell is active in leading business institutions such as the South African Employers' Consultative Committee on Labour Affairs (Saccola), and has been a president of the Chamber of Mines.

A keen squash player who relaxes by reading detective stories, he holds a Master's degree in liberal ethics from the University of Cape Town.

Born 14 September 1952. Family: wife Gillian, three children.

Golding, Marcel   Golding has taken to his new job as MP like a bulldog to a fresh bone. He will need such gusto for the task of helping restructure Mineral and Energy Affairs, as chairman of the National Assembly select committee dealing with this department.

He is well equipped for it: Golding's quick grasp of concepts and cocky style helped build the National Union of Mineworkers (NUM) into the country's biggest trade union. Although he left the NUM in 1993 to hit the campaign trail as a parliamentary candidate, there can be little doubt that the unionist in Golding will come out to play in the department. He's started by taking civil servants down mines. And he is also taking many NUM campaigns to government.

Golding's plans for his first term in office include establishing a commission of inquiry into marginal mines, changing the system of deferred pay of migrant workers, winning citizenship for migrant workers and working on social legislation for miners retrenched in the downscaling of mining operations. The Department of Mineral and Energy Affairs must serve all stakeholders in the industry and cease to be a lackey of the mining magnates, says Golding.

But it is not only to mining that he will turn his attention. Golding is also part of the ANC's informal left caucus in Parliament and has pushed for the assignment of constituencies to ANC MPs. And if there is any time left in the day, he will pursue a spread of interests, from growing herbs and listening to classical music to running.

Born 29 June 1960. Single.

Goldstone, Richard   In a real-life version of the frying pan and the fire, Judge Goldstone has gone straight from the Standing Commission of Inquiry into Violence and Intimidation — better known as the Goldstone Commission — to The Hague as chief prosecutor in the United Nations-sponsored Yugoslavia war crime trials. He takes with him the experience gained in four years of heading the Goldstone Commission. During those investigations, however, his brief was to expose the truth rather than to bring individuals to trial, and his new position could pose completely different challenges. The current joke that Judge Goldstone has his eyes on the UN secretary-general's job has led to the nickname 'Richard Richard'.

During the years the commission has operated, Judge Goldstone has continued his work as a judge of the Appellate Division and his involvement in a number of legal and other issues, including business law reform.

He gained his early reputation as a specialist in commercial cases and became a judge at the early age of 41. During his career on the Bench, however, he developed a reputation for precedent-setting judgments on human rights issues. In one of his best-known cases he delivered a judgment which prevented evictions under the Group Areas Act unless alternative accommodation was provided. In effect, this made a key apartheid law unworkable. While on the Appellate Division he has written most of the important labour law judgments.

During the Emergency years of the 1980s he developed a reputation for visiting and helping detainees. The respect this earned him among political radicals was shared by other parties too, and there was widespread approval of the decision to appoint him to head the commission into violence.

Even so, there have been critics of his work on the commission: some say it is inappropriate for a judge to be involved in such overtly political work; others criticise the commission for its failure to stop political violence or even find the causes of it. His report on the police shooting of nine people in Sebokeng in 1990 found all parties must share the blame; it was a precursor of his commission's findings, where more often than not all parties to a conflict were criticised.

Although his new UN post seemed to exclude him from eligibility for the Constitutional Court, as it would engage him full time for two years, he accepted a seat on the court, countering widespread criticism by pointing out that he intended to return after his UN post had expired and the Constitutional Court appointment was a seven-year posting. In the event, one or more acting Constitutional Court justices will stand in for him until he has completed his overseas assignments. A special amendment to the new constitution was needed to facilitate this.

At the time of his UN appointment he was president of the National Institute for Crime Prevention and Rehabilitation of Offenders.

Born 26 October 1938. Family: wife Noleen, two adult daughters.

Gomomo, John   The president of the Congress of South African Trade Unions is said to have removed his name from the list of Cosatu officials selected to stand for Parliament because he was concerned about a leadership drain on the trade union federation. A hard worker with a reputation for organisational and procedural skills, he is known as a tough disciplinarian, expecting from others the high standards he has set for himself.

His rise to prominence started in 1963 when Gomomo, born into a family of Eastern Cape farmworkers, began work at Volkswagen, making silencers on its Uitenhage production line. A decade later he became involved in union activity through United Automobile Workers, which became part of the National Automobile and Allied Workers' Union (Naawu) in 1980. A full-time shop steward from 1984, he was made vice-president of Naawu in 1987 and elected Cosatu second vice-president in 1989. After the February 1990 unbannings of political organisations, Gomomo became part of the internal leadership corps of both the African National Congress and the South African Communist Party. He is a devout Roman Catholic who fasts on Fridays. A widower, he is devoted to his children.

Born 25 October 1946. Family: eight children.

Gordhan, Ketan ('Ketso')   Long a powerful behind-the-scenes organiser, Gordhan was a natural choice for a director-generalship, and it was minister of Transport Mac Maharaj who plucked him from Parliament for his department. Gordhan was a key figure in the African National Congress's election campaign, as one of the triumvirate — with Popo Molefe and Patrick 'Terror' Lekota, both now premiers — who led the strategic thinking and organisational work behind the ANC's success.

Gordhan comes from a politicised family (MP Pravin Gordhan is his uncle) and was involved in resistance politics at school, cutting his teeth on civic and youth work in Phoenix and Newlands, Durban. In 1984, he was appointed full-time organiser for the United Democratic Front in Natal, joined the Natal Indian Congress executive and co-ordinated the UDF's Million Signature Campaign.

He was detained in the 1987 Emergency and left to study in England, where he earned an MPhil in development economics at the University of Sussex. He returned in 1990 to work for the Labour Economic Research Project in Durban and joined the ANC's Department of Economic Policy in July 1990 for two years. In September 1992, he became assistant co-ordinator of the ANC elections commission. He won a seat in Parliament, but was named director-general shortly thereafter.

Born 12 July 1961. Family: wife Roshene.

Gordhan, Pravin   Political pundits expect this highly talented politician to keep popping up in positions of prominence. Elected to the National Assembly on the African National Congress list, he spent only a few weeks out of public gaze before being appointed chairman of the National Assembly's select committee on Constitutional Affairs.

Long an influential figure in the Natal 'struggle', Gordhan was thrown on to the national stage with a vengeance when he was elected co-chairman of the multiparty negotiations forum at the World Trade Centre in 1993. He won widespread acclaim for his skilful and firm — and sometimes openly manipulative — handling of the talks, but also made enemies for what was seen by some as unprovoked jabs and sarcasm from the chair, aimed at those not in agreement with the ANC. Gordhan was in the chair at two crucial points (and some maintain intentionally put there to drive matters to a head): when 27 April 1994 was adopted as the election date, and when delegates met for a tense, last-minute agreement in November 1993. He was later one of four joint chairpersons of the Transitional Executive Council.

Sidelined after the ANC's unbanning because of allegations that he was part of a Natal 'cabal', Gordhan overcame this hitch with strategic thinking and good organisational skills.

He is a leading member of the South African Communist Party, having actively built the underground structures of the party in the period of illegality.

Gordhan pursued his political career through the ranks of the Natal Indian Congress and the Durban Housing Action Committee but was also in the ANC underground network and played a role in Operation Vula, an ANC plan to revitalise and rebuild internal structures. He was arrested in 1990 for alleged treason and possession of weapons, but was granted indemnity in March 1991. In the post-election period he served as one of the advisers to the ANC kwaZulu/Natal regional representatives negotiating with the Inkatha Freedom Party. His new tasks will probably leave even less time than ever for his other, non-political interests, including cinema and hiking along country trails.

Born 12 April 1949. Family: wife Vanitha, two children.

Govender, Pregaluxmi ('Pregs')   Govender is a worker bee who could be queen bee if she chose to. But instead this young gender activist and trade unionist recently turned parliamentarian often shuns the limelight, preferring to get on with the job, even if it means that others take the credit.

Govender has extraordinary organising and managerial skills and the word 'founder' and 'first' must appear often on her curriculum vitae. She was a founder member of the Natal Organisation of Women, and a member of the National Women's Committee of the Congress of South African Trade Unions. The national education officer of Garment and Allied Workers' Union, now the South African Clothing and Textile Workers' Union, she was also the first director of the successful Cape Town based Workers' College and the first project manager for the Women's National Coalition.

In 1993 Govender engineered the most authoritative research report ever released on South African women. It reached a record two million women and has become the basis of the new Women's Charter. It is no wonder that the minister without portfolio, Jay Naidoo, has chosen Govender as part of the team responsible for the implementation of the Reconstruction and Development Programme (RDP). Govender is a member of the RDP and Finance standing committees; she edited the government's report on the status of women that will be presented this year at the United Nations conference in Beijing, and in 1994 edited the gender sections of the RDP book, booklet and White Paper.

She was formerly married to Cosatu assistant general secretary Jayendra Naidoo.

Born 15 February 1960. Family: two children.

Groenewald, Tienie   The grand strategist of the Afrikaner Volksfront (AVF) has maintained an unusually low profile since his appointment as a Freedom Front senator, but his continuing influence in right-wing policy-making should not be underestimated.

Groenewald has arguably wielded more back-room influence than any other person in the far-right sphere. It was largely Groenewald who engineered the formation of the AVF, who played an instrumental role in the formation of the Concerned South Africans Group, later the Freedom Alliance, and whose volkstaat ideals eventually became part of broad right-wing policy.

Although articulate and an ambitious power-player during his tenure as a career officer, once out of the military and into right-wing politics he elected to work largely out of the spotlight. It was a wise decision, for he succeeded in exerting considerable influence on right-wing strategy without having to perform the function of a public flak-catcher. He will in all probability continue to serve in this behind-the-scenes role as strategist for General Constand Viljoen's Freedom Front.

A former fighter pilot and military attaché, Groenewald was born on a farm outside Koster in the Western Transvaal. He joined the Air Force in 1955 and obtained an honours degree in military science. After rising to the rank of major-general he was appointed as security adviser to the State Security Council by then president PW Botha in 1982.

From 1985 to 1986 he held the post of chief director of Military Intelligence. After a four-year spell as deputy head and chief director of planning of the Bureau of Information he requested early retirement in June 1990. Although he prefers to spend his time in such pursuits as hunting and woodwork, since his retirement he has involved himself full time in right-wing activities.

Born 7 July 1937. Family: wife JudiMaria, two children.

Gwala, Harry Renowned for his fiery rhetoric — 'When our enemies come to attack us, we do not meet them with Bibles. We kill them' — Gwala has been the longest-serving African National Congress and South African Communist Party leader in kwaZulu/Natal. Born in the Natal Midlands in 1920, Gwala joined the SACP in 1942, before becoming an ANC member two years later.

He believes he has been badly treated by the SACP, which took a decision in July 1994 to suspend him from the party for alleged 'ill-discipline' in the midst of allegations that he operated hit-squads that had targeted three senior ANC and SACP leaders for assassination. Vehemently denying the charges, Gwala accused the SACP of engaging in an act of

Stalinism by attempting to purge 'honest comrades' from the party, as had happened in the Soviet Union in the 1930s. (Gwala also defends Stalin — 'Let me remind you that he defeated Hitler,' he notes — and backed the 1992 Moscow coup attempt by hardliners.)

One of the few ANC/SACP leaders who opted to remain in a black township rather than move to a leafy suburb, Gwala is the ANC's chief whip in the kwaZulu/Natal provincial legislature. He has built support for himself around his militant stance — 'How can you negotiate with a man who has a sword when you have no sword yourself?' he asked in 1990 — and by remaining active at grassroots level. Let there be a massacre of ANC supporters and Gwala will be among the first to arrive on the scene to console the bereaved. His reputation as one of the ANC's best orators was under-used in the election campaign as the party's upper echelons tried to marginalise him. President Nelson Mandela made two failed attempts to oust Gwala as ANC Natal Midlands chairman.

Ironically, Gwala has been the political tutor of several moderate ANC leaders, including Jacob Zuma, who successfully challenged him for the ANC's premiership candidacy in kwaZulu/Natal.

Having never opted for exile, Gwala remained active in Umkhonto weSizwe after his release from an eight-year jail term in 1972. He was re-arrested in 1975 and given a life sentence. But he was released before the ANC's unbanning in 1990 on 'humanitarian grounds' because he suffers from a degenerative motor neuron disease that has paralysed both his arms. Widowed while in prison, Gwala had planned to remarry in 1993 but the wedding was called off.

Born 30 July 1920. Family: four adult children.

Hanekom, Derek   One of Hanekom's first acts as minister of Land Affairs was to acquire a bakkie instead of the official Mercedes sedan. Admittedly, it was a R180 000 luxury four-wheel drive, but it signalled his determination to spend much of his time on the poor roads of the country's far corners.

It was in Hanekom's ministry that the first real controversy hit the new government of national unity, when it was revealed that large portions of kwaZulu/Natal land had been quietly transferred to Zulu King Goodwill Zwelithini by former state president FW de Klerk the day before he was voted out of office. Hanekom initially reacted angrily, but then maintained a diplomatic silence while leading a cabinet committee of investigation into the issue.

Hanekom will need all the diplomatic skills he can muster to balance the demands of the country's dispossessed black landowners with white farmers' right to property. Land redistribution is one of the most sensitive issues facing the new government, but Hanekom is well placed as an Afrikaner who won respect among land-rights activists in his previous role as African National Congress spokesperson on agricultural matters. He has a firm grasp of the political and economic complexities of land redistribution in South Africa and played a key role in developing the ANC's land policy. He got off to a fast start in the first session of Parliament by tabling a White Paper and legislation to get land reform and restitution moving early in 1995.

Hanekom is one of many government members who graduated from jail to Parliament; he served three years in prison in the 1980s for leaking information to the ANC about South African Defence Force support for Renamo. After his release he lived in exile in Zimbabwe and worked for development projects, co-ordinating the Popular History Trust.

Born 13 January 1953. Family: wife Patricia Murray.

Hartzenberg, Ferdinand ('Ferdi')   The author of a highly acclaimed doctoral thesis on cattle breeding, Hartzenberg is the leader of the Conservative Party as well as chairman of the Afrikaner Volksfront's executive council.

His personal relationship with Freedom Front founder General Constand Viljoen is amiable, but the two are engaged in a battle for the right-wing constituency. Viljoen's Volkstaat Council has been sanctioned by the government to pursue Afrikaner aspirations; no less a personage than Deputy President Thabo Mbeki spoke at its founding meeting. Meanwhile, Hartzenberg is desperately trying to further the CP cause on at least an equal footing. But he is hindered in this attempt by, among other problems, a certain lack of the charisma that characterises his rival right-wing leaders. Although he is well liked and respected within the upper echelons of both the CP and the AVF, grassroots supporters tend to see him as bland.

He was active in National Party politics from his days as a student and was elected MP for Lichtenburg in 1970. Six years later he was appointed deputy minister of Development Aid and in 1979 promoted to the post of minister of Education and Training. In 1982 he left the NP to become one of the founding members of the CP.

Born 8 January 1937. Family: wife Judy, four adult children.

Haysom, Nicholas ('Fink')   Haysom was given a choice of jobs in the new government: the next commissioner of police, or legal adviser to the president. It was some surprise to observers who know his appetite for tough challenges and his preference for action over legal practice that he chose the latter posting. Now this affable and energetic lawyer, known as much for his political and strategic thinking as his legal skills, will play an important role as adviser to Nelson Mandela.

Haysom cut his teeth in student politics, serving on the students' representative council of the University of Cape Town and as president of the National Union of South African Students. He went on to law and the formation of one of the country's foremost human and labour rights firms: Cheadle, Thompson and Haysom. He was also deputy director of the Centre for Applied Legal Studies at the University of the Witwatersrand, an associate professor of law and a member of the African National Congress's Constitutional Committee. He has written on a number of subjects, including human rights, labour law and policing.

In 1992, he was appointed to the new Police Board where he played a role in reshaping the South African Police and won sufficient respect to be considered as the next commissioner by his good friend, minister of Safety and Security Sydney Mufamadi.

Instead, posted in the president's office, he is the political lawyer who advises the country's foremost lawyer-politician.

Born 21 April 1952. Family: wife Murie Ann, three children.

Holomisa, Bantubonke ('Bantu')   As head of the former Transkei's military council, Major-General Holomisa was engaged in a string of diplomatic battles with the former South African government in its final days of apartheid rule. The ushering in of a new dispensation saw the demise of the homeland and Holomisa's conversion to civilian life with his appointment as African National Congress deputy minister of Environmental Affairs in the new government. He has now

declared war on the plastic packet and coined the rallying cry
'*Phantsi ngeplastic, phantsi!*' (Down with the plastic bag,
down).

Although some have questioned Holomisa's appointment
and commitment to the environment, considering his strong
military background, nature conservation has always been
high on his agenda.

Holomisa was released from detention in the homeland in
April 1987 at the demand of Transkei troops and seized
power from Stella Sigcau's government in a bloodless coup
eight months later, vowing to fight corruption.

However, his efforts at eradicating corruption were largely
unsuccessful — it was under Holomisa that more than 1 600
Transkei soldiers received rapid promotion shortly before
their incorporation into the South African National Defence
Force. The shrewd and popular leader used his position
instead to establish himself as a key critic of the South
African government and a voice for its opponents. He was
the first South African leader to release political prisoners
and allow banned organisations to operate freely.

Holomisa easily survived a coup attempt, allegedly
orchestrated by Pretoria, in November 1990 and went on to
embarrass the South African government with his well-timed
release of a Military Intelligence signal authorising the 1985
murder of Eastern Cape activist Matthew Goniwe, which led
to the reopening of the inquest, and later the release of the
Katzen Document detailing plans to destabilise the region.

A friend of Nelson Mandela and the late Chris Hani,
Holomisa is well known for his 'open door' policy and
practice of broad consultation. He enjoys widespread support
among the youth and former Umkhonto weSizwe cadres,
who called for his intervention in their bumbling integration
into the SANDF.

He has made a name for himself with his sometimes outrageous claims. Before the April election, for example, he accused the National Party of stirring invisible ink into the puthu served at NP rallies in ANC strongholds, which would bar ANC supporters from voting. He was often used by the ANC to launch its more vigorous attacks on its rivals, partly because he was prepared to issue more startling statements than most politicians, partly because of his spirited independence.

But Holomisa's general outspokenness, together with his concern for the environment, should win him the support of conservationists as he shifts his focus from liberation politics to the affairs of his department.

Born 25 July 1955. Family: wife Tunyelwa, two sons and a daughter.

Jiyane, Ziba   A graduate of American Ivy League universities, Jiyane has catapulted high within the ranks of the Inkatha Freedom Party in a short space of time: having joined the party in the post-1990 era, he was elected to the key post of secretary-general at the IFP's annual general conference in July 1994.

His rapid rise comes as something of a surprise: he quit as national secretary of the Inkatha Youth Brigade in 1978 to join the exiled Pan Africanist Congress and head its Radio Freedom. Disillusioned with the PAC's socialist policies, Jiyane later withdrew from politics to concentrate on academic studies in the United States where he obtained, amongst others, a DJuris from Yale University Law School with an emphasis on constitutional and international law.

On Jiyane's return to South Africa, he was lecturer and consultant to the Institute for Multi-Party Democracy's Political Leadership Programme and a senior political science lecturer at the University of Zululand. Chief Mangosuthu Buthelezi persuaded Jiyane to rejoin the IFP in 1993 as its media spokesman and national political director. Also an adviser to the party at the multiparty negotiation process, Jiyane soon found himself at odds with Buthelezi over his hardline stance and refusal to participate in the April 1994 election. Some IFP insiders have suggested that Jiyane's confrontations with Buthelezi cost him a cabinet post, though his current post of secretary-general places him in an ideal position to bid for the IFP presidency if Buthelezi ever retires.

Born 22 September 1958. Family: wife Zodwa, one child.

Jordan, Pallo   The most prominent and respected left-wing thinker in the African National Congress but outside the South African Communist Party, Jordan was a natural choice for the post of minister of Telecommunications and Broadcasting. As head of the ANC's Department of Information and Publicity, he led many of the negotiations and the policy planning in this field. He made a major contribution to the talks and planning that led to the change of guard at the South African Broadcasting Corporation and the creation of an Independent Broadcasting Authority.

However, not much has been heard from him since he took this cabinet post. This is partly because he does not yet have much of a ministry, and partly because he sees his job as a passive, non-interfering one, letting independent bodies get on with their work.

Jordan has impeccable left-wing credentials, but has always been strongly critical of SACP policy. His fiercely independent thinking has not always been well received, and he was detained for six weeks by ANC security in the early 1980s. However, his intellectual leadership and strategic input ensure that his voice carries weight within the ANC.

He comes from an intensely political Kroonstad, Orange Free State family, with both parents prominent in the Non-European Unity Movement. He received history degrees, including a doctorate, from the University of Wisconsin and the London School of Economics, and then worked for the ANC in various capacities: as head of Radio Freedom and head of Research before moving to Information and Publicity.

During World Trade Centre negotiations, Jordan led the argument against Joe Slovo's proposal for 'sunset clauses' in the new constitution, then fell back into line when his position was defeated. But his prominence and popularity were reflected in a strong showing on the ANC election candidates list.

Born 22 May 1942. Single.

Kasrils, Ronnie   When he returned illegally to South Africa in 1989 as a member of the African National Congress's Operation Vula network, Kasrils took a long walk through his old home of Yeoville, changing direction, checking in shop windows, stopping to tie his shoelaces. The object was to check whether he was being followed. Named deputy minister of Defence in June 1994, he is likely to need all his counter-surveillance skills. Watching his — and Defence Minister Joe Modise's — back as the battle for the hearts and minds of the military unfolds could be among his more important functions.

Kasrils, an almost lifelong member of the Communist Party, has a long history in guerrilla strategy and tactics, and was the founder and head of Umkhonto weSizwe's Military Intelligence. He learned a great deal about conventional military forces in the 18 months of talks between MK and the

South African Defence Force on the integration of standing armies and non-statutory forces.

Sceptics believe that while Kasrils and his minister appear to have done a good job of drawing the military establishment towards the government's policy of reconciliation, they have become too much a part of that establishment in the process. There have been few, if any, critical words from either on the military hawks' demands for expenditure. And minister and deputy minister appear to have bought wholesale into the military's contention that there is a need to plan and equip for an ongoing though diffuse threat.

Having spent his early years in the advertising industry, Kasrils has a natural flair for self-presentation which, to the casual observer, can obscure the political savvy he couples with a tenacious and essentially romantic commitment to a set of increasingly unfashionable socialist ideals.

Kasrils's own version of the years when he became the 'scarlet pimpernel' are contained in his entertaining autobiography *Armed and Dangerous*, the wording on a police poster when he was being sought while underground. He has also co-written two books on English philosopher Bertrand Russell.

The 'Yeoville boykie', as he likes to refer to himself, seems largely to have overcome the criticism he took for his leadership of a march on Bisho, Ciskei, in September 1992 against the administration of Brigadier Oupa Gqozo; the march ended in a massacre when Ciskei troops opened fire on the African National Congress demonstrators.

Born 15 November 1938. Family: wife Eleanore, three adult children.

Kgositsile, Baleka   An African National Congress MP who serves on two important committees — constitutional affairs and land affairs — Kgositsile is one of the few people who can make her voice heard, not only in committees but on the floor of Parliament as well. One cannot really miss the outspoken Kgositsile. Before the elections the former secretary-general of the ANC Women's League and National Executive Committee member was the ANC's national spokesperson.

She was one of a group of exiles who spread the ideology of feminism among South African women. She had fought strongly for gender equality within the ANC and was a member of the gender emancipation commission which was chaired by Frene Ginwala. A member of the ANC negotiating delegation during the multiparty talks at the World Trade Centre, she fought hard and ultimately successfully for a quota of positions to be filled by women in the future government.

Born in Durban, she was influenced during her childhood by the political atmosphere at the University of Fort Hare, where her father lost his job as a librarian in the 1950s for being a member of the Communist Party. She obtained a teacher's diploma, then fled South Africa in 1976 because police were looking for her in connection with illegal political activities. In exile she worked as a journalist on the ANC's Radio Freedom and was active in both cultural and women's politics. She returned in 1990 as a member of the interim leadership corps.

Born 24 September 1949. Family: five children.

Khanyile, Vusumuzi   Charming, intelligent and highly ambitious, Khanyile has seen it all. His long walk from treason trialist and African National Congress activist to his present position as managing director of the Thebe Investment Corporation has not been a country stroll. Nor is his present position an easy one. Thebe is seen as the ANC's investment arm despite the corporation's claims to independence. Khanyile and his company have been under close local and international media and business scrutiny since the inception of Thebe in August 1992 and the ostentatious investment and acquisition spree it promptly undertook in the name of black empowerment.

The company was started by Nelson Mandela and Walter Sisulu, who acted as trustees to the Batho-Batho Trust, reputedly Thebe's income source. Despite its embryonic status the company has already ventured into a multitude of controversial areas of business, achieving this through a number of business partnerships. The most pertinent ventures include those with Macmillan Boleswa publishers (the school textbook market), HNR Computers (Apple Computer products) and SA Express (an air charter company). Thebe most recently and most optimistically announced it was planning to start up its own merchant bank.

The company also inherited a number of projects from the ANC, including Movement Marketing Enterprises, which was originally set up to promote ANC products and memorabilia and now sells upmarket clothing in the town-ships. Other sectors Thebe is involved in include printing, property, car rental, catering and haulage.

Despite the directors' insistence that they are independent of the ANC, rumours persist that they use their political connections to gain entry into these sectors. In essence, the suggestion is that giving a shareholding to Thebe will facilitate quick and easy access to the new government. When the company was formed, the board consisted of now-Gauteng premier Tokyo Sexwale and former KaNgwane chief minister Enos Mabuza. Both have since resigned. Khanyile comes armed with a BComm Hons from the University of Birmingham.

Born 5 November 1950. Family: wife Nombulelo, three children.

Khoza, Themba The leader of the Inkatha Freedom Party Youth Brigade in the PWV region, Khoza revels in his role as the IFP's strong-arm man and repeated allegations of his involvement in 'third force' killings seem only to have served to cement his position in the party. Despite his strong position, Khoza was not elected to the regional parliament, but this means he is now free to behave like a party boss without the constraints of a government of national unity. When the IFP wanted to block a television drama in July 1994 which hinted at the involvement of party members in pre-election train violence, Khoza was sent to browbeat the SABC into suspending the broadcast. (The decision was later reversed.)

Khoza first joined the IFP Youth Brigade in 1975. He gained national prominence in January 1990, when he opened the first IFP office in the Transvaal. During the violence which flared on the Reef shortly afterwards, Khoza played a key role in projecting the IFP as a strong national party, not the Natal-based ethnic grouping it was perceived to be.

During the 1990/91 violence, Khoza was accused of supplying weapons to hostel dwellers and charged with illegal possession of weapons, but in January 1992 he was acquitted.

In March 1994, the Goldstone Commission of Inquiry named him as a recipient of arms manufactured by renegade policemen, while a Transitional Executive Council investigation alleged he planned the massacre of the family of an African National Congress-aligned chief in Natal. More recently, he has played the role of peacemaker, serving on the

National Peace Committee and the local dispute resolution committee in Soweto.

Khoza was born in Eshowe in Northern Natal.

Born: 17 May 1959. Single.

Kriel, Hernus As the only National Party provincial premier, Kriel has the difficult task of steering the Western Cape without upsetting a central government dominated by African National Congress rivals who know that Kriel's failure in the NP's last remaining power base would harm his party's fortunes. If Kriel intends to show the world that the NP can do better at regional politics than the ANC, he will find his manoeuvrability considerably constrained by national politics.

He is watched with an eagle eye by ANC supporters who still suspect him of racial motives, but he has already stated his support for the ANC's Reconstruction and Development Programme. Otherwise he is deliberately keeping a low public profile, refraining from addressing meetings. This has not deterred the Western Cape ANC from appointing shadow ministers to scrutinise every move the NP regional government makes.

Kriel's personal history is not likely to endear him to the ANC. As minister of Law and Order in ex-president FW de Klerk's cabinet, he had the task of steering the South African Police through the difficult waters of transition and chose to do so with a combination of bluster, threats and kragdadige posturing. This was seen as a deliberate strategy to muster conservative white and coloured support and secure his leadership position in the Western Cape. Kriel's most infamous moment came during 1993 when Pan Africanist Congress members, including PAC chief negotiator Benny Alexander (now !Khoisan X), were arrested in a night-time raid later termed a 'fishing expedition'; nearly everyone arrested was later released. Kriel was summoned by the multiparty negotiating council to explain the actions of his police, the first time a South African cabinet minister had ever been forced to account for himself in public.

In spite of his image as the NP's 'Mister Tough', he is known to be 'one of the boys', is a keen golfer and has never been averse to having a drink with political opponents in the parliamentary bar. A lawyer, he became an MP in the tricameral Parliament in 1984, representing Parow.

Born 14 December 1941. Family: three adult children.

Kriel, James   The Air Force chief's passion for the skies may have cost him the top job of the South African National Defence Force. Regarded as a top military intellect and a man of integrity, Lieutenant-General Kriel was among the front-runners for the position of SANDF chief when Kat Liebenberg stepped down. But the job went to Army General Georg Meiring because of the overriding importance of land troops to maintaining internal stability in South Africa through the transition period. Military politicians were unsure whether Kriel would be sufficiently able to command the loyalties of the Army.

A chain-smoker, Kriel was born in Cape Town and joined the Air Force after matriculating at Tygerberg High. He commanded several Air Force units before becoming a staff officer in 1985, since when he has spent most of his time flying a desk and racing pigeons whenever he has the time.

Born 8 March 1942. Family: wife Nellie, three adult children.

Langa, Pius Nkonzo   His appointment to the Constitutional Court came as no surprise to Langa's colleagues; he has a breadth of working experience probably unmatched in the legal profession. After completing a junior certificate at Adams College in 1955, he had to go out to work. He studied matric part time, and his first job, in 1957, was as a factory worker. In 1960, the Department of Justice hired him as an interpreter and messenger. Over the next decade he studied with Unisa, obtaining a BJuris and an LLB. By 1971 he was transferred to Ndwendwe as a prosecutor and later as a magistrate.

Once he completed his LLB he resigned from the department and joined the Durban Bar in 1977 where he has practised ever since. At the same time, he had a full political life and was a founder member of the Release Mandela Committee in Natal. He was also an early member of the Democratic Lawyers' Association, later to become the National Association of Democratic Lawyers (Nadel), which he served as president, a post which he has resigned. He was awarded senior counsel status in 1994.

Langa comes from a deeply religious family. He is the second of seven children; one of his brothers was killed in political conflict during 1984. Two others went into exile in the late 1970s.

Born 25 March 1939. Family: wife Beauty Thandekile, six children.

Lekota, Mosiuoa Patrick ('Terror')   Ask any observers which province has enjoyed the most successful transition and they will tell you the Free State, under the premiership of the popular and charismatic Lekota. Admittedly, his was one of the few provinces to inherit a single and coherent bureaucracy and a region with little history of violence. But the Free State was notoriously the most conservative of provinces, the heart of National Party rule, and it is no small credit to Lekota and his personal charm and political skills that he has swung so much support behind his leadership. The African National Congress had overwhelming support among the black voters in the province, but Lekota has gone out of his way also to win over the white farmers so crucial to the regional economy, which may have contributed in November 1994 to his narrow defeat as regional leader during the ANC regional conference.

Lekota was born in the Free State and rose to prominence in the Black Consciousness Movement while a student at Turfloop. He served six years on Robben Island for his part in organising pro-Frelimo rallies in the early 1970s, and joined the ANC while in prison.

In 1983, not long after his release, he was appointed publicity secretary of the newly formed United Democratic Front and played a key role in mobilising against the tricameral Parliament. He was imprisoned again after the Delmas Treason Trial and only released when his appeal against conviction was upheld.

Since the ANC's unbanning, he has served the organisation in Natal, the Free State and at head office, first in the unlikely role of deputy head of the Intelligence Department and later as deputy head of the Elections Commission, where he brought his organising and mobilising experience to play in the 1994 election campaign.

He is known for his courage, his dedication and his popular touch. The nickname 'Terror' was earned on the soccer field.

Born 13 August 1948. Family: wife Cynthia, four children.

Leon, Tony The leader of the Democratic Party has the arduous task of putting his party back on the map as a liberal voice following the party's catastrophic performance in the

April 1994 elections. As the party's routing was announced, Dr Zach de Beer relinquished the leadership and Leon — who led the party in the powerful PWV province — was elected acting leader, pending a full party congress.

Leon will need all his skills to keep the DP together: the party has recently suffered a string of defections to the African National Congress. Shortly after his election he announced major structural changes to make the party more representative of the population. However, the DP has suffered badly in public perceptions for preferring to send mostly white members of the 'old boys' club' to Parliament instead of black candidates. It has also been outmanoeuvred by the National Party with its newfound liberal image.

The tenacity and audacity of this ambitious young man, previously MP for Houghton, have won him almost as many supporters as critics in his short parliamentary career. A lawyer, and the son of well-known Natal Judge Ramon Leon, he first made his name in politics as a talented and eloquent Johannesburg city councillor but chose to leave local politics when Helen Suzman retired from her safe Houghton seat in 1989. Amid controversy, he took on Suzman's hand-picked successor — and won, demonstrating his ruthless determination and campaigning skills.

He has been clearly identified with the old-style DP liberals, having no time for those who have flirted with the ANC and aiming some of his most potent eloquence at the left. At one stage, shortly after the unbanning of the ANC and the NP's shift to the left, he was urging his party to support ex-president FW de Klerk.

He was severely criticised in July 1994 for defending the Johannesburg City Council's forced removal, in the midst of a winter cold snap, of illegal squatters from shacks pitched on a site in Johannesburg marked for a low-cost housing development.

At the multiparty negotiations, Leon made his mark as an uncompromising defender of free market guarantees in a Bill of Rights, taking the technical committee to task for emphasising equality in its draft documents and not, as he would prefer, freedom. He also led the attack, eventually successful, on a proposal to allow the cabinet to choose Constitutional Court judges.

Under his leadership, and with his forceful oratory and knack for the pithy sound-bite, the DP will attempt to reassert its position by playing the role of outspoken parliamentary watchdog.

Born 15 December 1956. Single.

Liebenberg, Chris   Very much the professional banker, Liebenberg was a surprising choice to replace Derek Keys as minister of Finance from October 1994. The ex-chief executive of the Nedcor group attracts the descriptions 'grey', 'solid', 'likeable' and 'professional' as well as the epithet 'colourless'.

No one doubts his integrity or capability, however. And he does exude a calmness and confidence that will help assuage doubts about the fiscal prudence of the new government. Perhaps it is unfortunate he has stepped into the shoes of as formidable a personality as Keys, who would always have been a hard act to follow.

A consensus man, Liebenberg is certainly as popular as his predecessor and enjoys a measure of political credibility. As head of Nedcor he was one of the first business leaders to involve himself in the Consultative Business Movement. Like Keys, Liebenberg is a strong advocate of market-orientated policies linked to fiscal and monetary discipline. He is also said to be a 'Stals man', a supporter of Reserve Bank governor Chris Stals.

Doubts about his appointment centre on his lack of political power base: he has refused to embrace any party. Keys had built up a political profile and was, at least, a National Party candidate in the election. Liebenberg accepted the job on the basis that he would not join any political party, thus forcing a constitutional change to allow a non-MP to join the cabinet.

The worry is that his lack of a power base makes him dependent on the president for cabinet clout and may make it harder for him than for his predecessor to resist pressures to abandon monetary and fiscal discipline. Liebenberg summed up his philosophy in an interview once as 'You will reap whatever you sow', and described his management style as that of 'delegation and control'. The same interview showed the glimmer of a sense of humour, if not gender sensitivity, when Liebenberg described his 'likes' as 'quality, expertise, professionalism ... and pretty girls'.

Born 2 October 1934. Family: wife Elly, two children.

Louw, Mike   His confident and humorous performance in front of an open session of the parliamentary Security Committee showed how secure the present head of the National Intelligence Service (NIS) is of his status in South Africa's new National Intelligence Agency (NIA). It was Louw's handling of the NIS — and some quiet undermining of rival state security agencies, according to critics — which enabled him to secure the top place among South Africa's intelligence organisations for the civilian-controlled NIA.

As the only intelligence agency allied to former state president FW de Klerk, and the one that played a key role in establishing covert talks with the ANC and Nelson Mandela in 1988/89, the NIS was at its zenith during Louw's tenure. Louw was on the secret government committee that met Mandela in prison, setting the scene for the ANC leader's release. But, although the National Party has put up a strong fight for control of National Intelligence, Louw has made it clear he is equally able to work with both his new and old masters. As a result he is assured of one of the top three positions in the new system. African National Congress intelligence operatives see Louw as a man they can work with, and he will be retained to instil confidence in, and keep in check, old NIS agents.

Born 1939. Personal details not available.

Luyt, Louis   One of the most controversial but enigmatic of sporting administrators and power-brokers, the president of the South African Rugby Football Union (Sarfu) has an ego to match his formidable bulk. Luyt, a former Free State and Northern Transvaal lock who rose from railway clerk to self-made millionaire, holds a doctorate in law and has seldom been far from the spotlight.

He made his fortune from the Triomf Fertiliser company and became a beer baron with a brew — Luyt Lager — named after him. In 1973 he sold Luyt Breweries to Anton Rupert's Oude Meester, and in 1975 launched into the media business with a government-inspired attempt to take over the liberal South African Associated Newspapers. When this failed, Luyt, with his Triomf empire crumbling, took a secret and illegal R12-million loan from the Department of Information to front the establishment of *The Citizen*. The exposure of the operation led to the Info Scandal which eventually toppled prime minister John Vorster. Luyt has maintained his innocence in the matter, and has complained bitterly of being 'used'.

By 1985 Luyt had begun looking politically leftward. His presence on rugby missions to speak to the African National Congress in exile in Europe in 1988 provoked then Education and Sport minister FW de Klerk to threaten the end of government support for rugby. Meanwhile, in 1988 Luyt hosted a meeting which led to the merger of the Independent Party, National Democratic Movement and Progressive Federal Party into the Democratic Party.

He had already stepped into rugby administration, leading the palace coup which led to the fall of Jannie le Roux's regime in the Transvaal. Luyt brought modern business practices to the running of rugby, and turned around the financial fortunes of the Transvaal Rugby Football Union. It was another decade before the administrative turnaround was mirrored on the field and the province won the Currie Cup.

He was almost ousted from the Transvaal executive in 1990 after allegations about financial discrepancies and complaints about his dictatorial style of management. He stayed on, and purged the administration of dissenting voices. Other provinces complained about Transvaal's lenient attitude towards payments to players in what is still, allegedly, an amateur game.

Luyt's determination to do things his way as Sarfu president has led to a string of major confrontations with powerful colleagues, from the management of the rugby side that performed poorly in New Zealand in July 1994 to ANC Sports minister Steve Tshwete. Tshwete called for Luyt's resignation when Luyt led the Ellis Park throng in a rendition of Die Stem during the first official test match against the New Zealand All Blacks in 1992; but two years later, when Luyt resigned after losing a bid to oust South African rugby manager Jannie Engelbrecht, Tshwete talked him into staying on.

He has strayed only briefly from the rugby field: late in the 1980s he bought 26 per cent of the Moroka Swallows football club, ensuring that the team used Ellis Park for its home games, and in 1990 was banned from the National Soccer League under suspicion that he was trying to form a rival league. He sold the stake in Swallows in 1993.

Born 18 June 1932. Family: wife Adri, four children.

Madala, Tholakele Hope   A contentious appointment to the new Constitutional Court, Judge Madala was relatively unknown outside the Eastern Cape and Transkei. He was the surprise choice on the list of four sitting judges given seats on the Constitutional Court under a special provision of the constitution. One reason for the surprise at his elevation to the court is his brief experience as a judge — he was appointed to the Transkei Bench in January 1994 — and the fact that he did not fight a long list of human rights cases while he was still an advocate or attorney.

Judge Madala was born in Kokstad, and holds a BA from Rhodes, a teacher's diploma from Unisa and an LLB from Natal University. He taught at Lovedale High School and at St Michael's in Swaziland before starting his law degree. He served articles at Venn, Nemeth and Hart in Pietermaritzburg before being admitted as an attorney (of both the South African and Transkei Supreme Courts) in 1977. Almost immediately he began lecturing at the University of Transkei in the Department of Private Law. In 1978 he joined a firm of attorneys in Umtata although he continued lecturing part time until 1980, when he was admitted to the Transkei Bar, making him one of the few judges with experience as both an advocate and attorney. He served as chairman of the Society of Advocates of Transkei between 1991 and 1993. In 1992 he was admitted as an advocate in the Supreme Court,

Pietermaritzburg, and he took silk — from then Transkei ruler, Major-General Bantu Holomisa — in 1993.

Judge Madala has a strong record with regional lawyers' organisations — he formerly served as chairman of the Black Lawyers' Association, Umtata and districts branch, and sat on the BLA's extended national executive committee. However, he retains his links with the organisation, and is still on the board of trustees of the BLA's Legal Education Centre.

Until his appointment to the Transkei Bench he was vice-chairman of the board of directors of the Transkei National Building Society and served on the management board of Thembisa School for the Handicapped.

Despite his judicial commitments, he has continued to serve on a number of community and educational institutions, including the Transkeian Medical Council, the Council of the University of Transkei and as director of the Thembelitsha Centre for the Rehabilitation of Alcohol Dependants.

He is deeply involved with the Anglican Church, holding the position of deputy chancellor of the diocese of St John's. He also sits on the diocesan finance board, the executive committee of the diocese and the board of trustees.

The South African Law Reports indicate he has been involved in six reported cases since he joined the Bar. Two of these concerned security detainees, and in one of them he was led by Ismail Mahomed, then senior counsel, now his colleague on the Constitutional Court.

Born 13 July 1937. Family: wife Patricia Alice Ndileka, three children.

Maduna, Penuell Mpapa   Known not long ago as an 'angry young man' and a fierce debater with a short fuse, the deputy minister of Home Affairs has settled into the new establishment quite comfortably. The stocky Maduna still has the aura of a hurried man with a mission, but the responsibilities of his office have led to a more reflective attitude.

A legal man by training, Maduna has a reputation for clinically and effectively cutting through issues despite an apparently emotional presentation. His fiery looks — he was an amateur boxer in his younger days — can easily intimidate opponents. But he is regarded as highly intelligent and is held in high esteem by his colleagues in the African National Congress's Department of Legal and Constitutional Affairs.

Maduna — a Zulu-speaker like his minister Mangosuthu Buthelezi — was born and bred in the struggle against apartheid. During his student years at the University of Zululand in the 1970s he organised the underground structures of the ANC in Natal, while publicly acting as chairman of the interim committee that was established in 1973 to revive the South African Students' Organisation (Saso) branch at the university. He was incarcerated and prosecuted twice under Section 6 of the Terrorism Act of 1967.

He went into exile in 1980, first working in the office of the treasurer-general of the ANC in Tanzania before moving to ANC headquarters in Lusaka, Zambia, where he helped establish the movement's Department of Legal and Constitutional Affairs. He played an active role in the formulation and adoption of the ANC's constitutional guidelines and participated in virtually all the meetings the organisation had with white South Africans, including the highly publicised encounter with prominent Afrikaners in 1987 in Dakar.

Maduna was closely involved in constitutional negotiations, having had a direct hand in the adoption of the Harare Declaration which ushered in the era of negotiations. In 1990 he was one of the first ANC officials sent to South Africa to 'talk about talks' with the government; he was also a member of the ANC team at the Groote Schuur and Pretoria talks in May and August of that year, as well as the DF Malan Airport talks in February 1991 which reaffirmed the ANC's decision to suspend armed activities unilaterally.

Maduna participated in the process that established Codesa, was part of the ANC team that revived negotiations after they were broken off in June 1992, and was among those who met with then president FW de Klerk in September 1992 to adopt the Record of Understanding.

He played an active role at the World Trade Centre in the development of the chapter on fundamental human rights in the interim constitution.

Maduna obtained a BJuris degree from Unisa, an LLB from the University of Zimbabwe and an LLM from the University of the Witwatersrand. He is a member of the board of the Faculty of Law of the University of the Witwatersrand and co-author of the book *Fundamental Rights in the New Constitution*, and is studying for a higher diploma in tax law at Wits.

Born 29 December 1952. Family: wife Nompumelelo Cheryl, two children.

Maharaj, Satjandranath Ragunanan ('Mac')   The minister of Transport has been described by one commentator as 'one of the best brains in the African National Congress'. Ironically, he received his most appropriate training for his new job while serving a prison sentence.

Maharaj's law studies at the University of Natal were interrupted by his political activities. He served 12 years in prison for sabotage, where he completed a BAdmin, an MBA and part of a BSc degree. On his release, he left the country and worked for the ANC in Lusaka.

He developed a formidable reputation as a wily and influential military and strategic thinker. When Operation Vula was launched in 1987, to re-establish an ANC underground network inside the country, Maharaj was one of two men hand-picked by then ANC president Oliver Tambo to return to the country in disguise. He left in 1990 in order to return legally, but was detained later that year when Operation Vula was uncovered by the police. After his release, he resigned his ANC and South African Communist Party posts and quit politics. He cited personal reasons, and has never been explicit about these, but it was suspected that he was also disgruntled at the lack of support he received from the political leadership. It is also known that he was under family pressure as the result of many years of hardship.

However, in 1991 he was re-elected to the ANC leadership and joined the negotiations team, where he played a key role. Although he had acted as an SACP representative after its unbanning, he never rejoined that organisation. Maharaj was the ANC alternate member of the Transitional Executive Council and was always a certainty for the new cabinet. He is married to Zarina Maharaj, a gender researcher at the Centre for Applied Legal Studies at the University of the Witwatersrand.

Born 22 April 1935. Family: wife Zarina, two children.

Mahomed, Ismail   Judge Mahomed must be one of the most distinctive legal characters in the country today. In his public life he is flamboyantly eloquent. In private, his passionate love affair with the law demands that he sustain the workaholic habits he developed as a young lawyer having to battle discrimination.

His career has been marked by a string of firsts, many of them relating to breaking racial restrictions which, under the old regime, hampered so many would-be lawyers who were not white. He was the first supreme court judge to break the all-white mould, and the first judge of colour on the Appeal Court. He is the first South African to be chief justice of Namibia, and in that capacity has been responsible for a number of precedent-setting human rights decisions based on that country's Bill of Rights. Despite being appointed to the South African Bench comparatively recently, he has wider judicial experience in other jurisdictions than any of his local colleagues, having served on the Bench in Botswana, Swaziland and Lesotho as well as Namibia.

He has personal experience of apartheid-related humiliation — being barred from Free State hotels when appearing in the Bloemfontein Appeal Court, for example — and was overlooked for appointment to the Bench until it became politically expedient for Pretoria to offer him a post.

During successive States of Emergency in the 1980s, Judge Mahomed led many of the most important legal challenges to the inroads on civil liberties created by Emergency legislation and scored some important human rights victories, such as the dismissal of all charges during the massive treason trial in Pietermaritzburg during the 1980s.

Soon after his appointment to the Transvaal Supreme Court, he was appointed co-chair of the constitutional negotiations then getting underway. This high-profile role was followed by his appointment to share the job of chairing the committee which selected the new board for the South African Broadcasting Corporation. During the public hearings of candidates for the board, television viewers were enthralled by his questioning. Ironically, while he made a name as a tough interviewer, he was criticised for not being tough enough, after the interviews, against then president FW de Klerk, whose subsequent interference in the selection process almost destroyed the new board before it could even begin its work.

Mahomed suffered a heart attack and underwent heart surgery shortly before the announcement of the Constitutional Court presidency, a post for which he was strongly tipped. In the event, the job went to long-time colleague Arthur Chaskalson. Several weeks later, Mahomed was named a member of that court.

Born 25 July 1931. Family: wife Hawa.

Makwetu, Clarence Mlamli   Despite the disastrous showing of the Pan Africanist Congress in the April 1994 election, the PAC leader narrowly overcame a leadership challenge at the party conference in December 1994.

Billed as the 'African hope', he failed to convince the electorate that his organisation could deliver 'real freedom for occupied Azania'. Even when he tried to put the 'we will win against all odds' spin on his party's campaign, he was unconvincing. He has also been accused by the party faithful of putting forward a dour impression in interviews and for making excuses for poor organisation after his claim that the election was rigged.

Sources in the PAC say Makwetu, now an MP, has failed to assert his presence in Parliament.

His position at the top of his party was threatened by New York-based political consultant Motsoko Pheko, who won the deputy presidency. Another contender was the movement's deputy president and former commander of the Azanian People's Liberation Army, Johnson Mlambo — a man popular with the youth, who refer to Makwetu as 'Imva' (the lamb), in contrast to the name they called his fiery predecessor, Zeph Mothopeng: 'Ibhubesi' (the lion).

A Transkei farmer, Makwetu was a founder member of the PAC and a former president of the Pan Africanist Movement, which acted for the PAC when the organisation was still banned. He was elected PAC president in 1991 at a time when it was wracked by internal conflict over whether to negotiate. In the face of fierce opposition from the youth wing — including the ultra-militant 'revolutionary watch-dogs' — he convinced Apla's commanders to lay down their arms and return to the negotiating table after an eight-month walk-out. But despite his lacklustre performance since the election, he is credited with having successfully negotiated the integration of Apla soldiers into the new defence force.

Born 6 December 1928. Family: wife Mandisa, two adult children.

Mandela, Nelson Rolihlahla   At a time when most men of his age would be ready for retirement, Mandela has shown an energy and leadership skill that have won him international admiration and, even more surprising, unanimous respect among the most diverse groups within the country. He has made the almost impossible task of uniting a deeply divided nation and facing up to formidable political, economic and social tasks seem easy. Problems that would have split most governments in the most stable countries — such as the kwaZulu/Natal land scandal that emerged days after the April 1994 election, and Chief Mangosuthu Buthelezi's disruption of a national television programme later in the year — have been quickly laid to rest because of Mandela's personal political skills.

It is difficult to imagine that his stature could have risen after his inauguration as the country's first democratically elected president, but it undoubtedly has, so much so that one of his biggest problems is preventing himself being drawn into the international political arena when he has so many demanding tasks at home. He is the only international leader who has the credibility and skills to mediate in the Middle East, Angola, or in the United States-Cuban conflict, but has had to resist because of the demands of his own constituency.

The negative side of all this is that extraordinary demands are being put on a man of his age, and there is evidence it is affecting his health. While he remains remarkably fit and able, he has shown signs of exhaustion and is plagued by an eye problem inherited from his days on Robben Island. He has also had a prostate operation. There is a growing demand for his load to be lightened by his two deputy presidents and for less direct and personal involvement in day-to-day political crises.

Nevertheless, he can take personal credit for the spirit of reconciliation and national unity that followed the April 1994 election. He quickly swung the country behind his call for political and racial reconciliation and his acclamation of a multicultural, ecumenical, 'rainbow' nation.

He managed to do this without relinquishing the African National Congress's commitment to radical social and economic reform. He has still shown firm leadership when called upon to do so, such as when dealing with rent and service payment boycotts, crime and violence and the troubled integration of restive former guerrillas into the South African National Defence Force.

Mandela was groomed to lead from his birth to chieftain-ship stock in Transkei in 1918. He attended Fort Hare, whence he was expelled, and later the University of the Witwatersrand, where he received an LLB and, with Oliver Tambo, opened the first black law practice.

He was a leading figure in the young guard that took control of, and radicalised, the ANC Youth League and, in the 1950s, the ANC itself. He was 'volunteer-in-chief' in the Defiance Campaign of the early 1950s and the M-Plan, drawn up to deal with the possibility of going underground, was named after him. He was one of the 156 accused in the 1956 Treason Trial and, although acquitted, was detained during the 1960 Emergency.

As chairman of the All-In National Action Council, he was central to the underground organisation of a three-day stayaway in 1961, and its failure in the face of severe repression led him down the path of armed struggle.

When the formation of the ANC's armed wing, Umkhonto weSizwe, was officially proclaimed on 16 December 1961, Mandela was named commander-in-chief and sent to Algeria for military training. He was captured near Howick in 1962 and was serving a sentence for incitement and leaving the country illegally when his fellow commanders were arrested in Rivonia and he was put on trial with them. His speech from the dock ('I am prepared to die for what I believe') received international attention and he was sentenced to life imprisonment.

During his 27 years in prison, he was recognised as the leader of the political prisoners and a massive international campaign for his release made him by far the best-known prisoner in the world. In the early years, he and his colleagues on Robben Island were subjected to extremely hard and degrading conditions and punishing hard labour, but this eventually eased off. He began contacts with the government from his prison cell in 1986, leading to his release in 1990 and the beginning of formal negotiations.

He separated from his second wife Winnie in 1992, which left him a solitary, even lonely, figure with one of his daughters standing in as his partner at his inauguration and similar formal events.

He brings to bear an old-worldly dignity and courtesy, combined with a firm and sometimes imperious leadership. His leadership of the ANC and the country as a whole is unchallenged.

Born 18 July 1918. Family: four children, 18 grand-children.

Mandela, Winnie   The great survivor of South Africa's relentlessly tough politics, Mandela's selection as deputy minister of Arts and Culture, Science and Technology was the surest sign of her rehabilitation from disgrace. What is less clear is whether, as an insider in the new power structures, she will continue to carve out a role for herself as a voice of populist radicalism.

She has done so in recent years with remarkable effect, off-setting her unpopularity in many central African National Congress circles with hard mobilising work in the squatter camps, where she voiced ultra-left criticism of the compro-mises that were driving forward the negotiations process. Since she has as many bitter enemies as ardent supporters, she is likely to remain a divisive figure in the government of national unity. She has already clashed with her minister, IFP's Ben Ngubane, when they each appointed their own arts policy task forces.

Her hard rhetoric pushed her to the national leadership of the South African National Civic Organisation and the ANC Women's League presidency within two years of being suspended from the league's PWV region and resigning from all her positions in the ANC, including membership of the National Executive Committee. Her 1992 withdrawal followed accusations of abuse of ANC funds and staging demonstrations against the leadership, making her swift comeback quite remarkable.

A social worker, she was young, strikingly beautiful and not particularly politically aware when she married Nelson Mandela in 1958 after his divorce from his first wife. But during his imprisonment, she won local and international admiration for her defiance of the government in the face of severe harassment: she was repeatedly banned and in the late 1970s banished to Brandfort in the Orange Free State. She was detained for many months and stood trial in 1969 for ANC activities. Her bravery, as the only person within the country who publicly mouthed ANC positions, drew international acclaim.

Her problems with the ANC began before her husband's release from prison. Her controversial group of bodyguards, the Mandela United football team, was wreaking havoc in Soweto when four young activists were kidnapped and one of them, Stompie Seipei, killed. She was later convicted of kidnapping and accessory to assault, and sentenced to four years' imprisonment; on appeal, the conviction was upheld but a fine imposed instead of the sentence.

In April 1992, Nelson Mandela announced his separation from his wife for 'personal reasons'.

Mandela has shown remarkable resilience and political cunning, and can be expected to be a vocal internal critic of the ANC if she feels it is failing its popular mandate or compromising unduly on its liberation tradition.

Born 26 September 1936. Family: two daughters.

Manganyi, Noel Chabani   As a former vice-chancellor of the often troubled University of the North, Professor Manganyi can be said to have leapt from the frying pan into the fire. Appointed director-general of Education in August 1994, he now occupies one of the hottest seats in the post-election administration, responsible for helping oversee the mammoth task of making whole the country's fractured education system.

His training as a clinical psychologist will no doubt stand him in good stead as he grapples with keeping calm a volatile sector already impatient at the pace of change. Described as an able administrator who enjoyed the respect of a range of stakeholders as executive director of the Joint Education Trust, Manganyi's competency and ability to operate under pressure have yet to be tested.

He has undoubted intellectual ability. Born in Louis Trichardt, Manganyi matriculated from the Douglas Laing Smit Secondary School at nearby Elim in 1959 before earning, in quick succession, his BA, BA (Hons), MA and DLitt et Phil degrees through Unisa. He served his internship as a clinical psychologist at Baragwanath Hospital.

In 1976, after returning from a post-doctoral fellowship at Yale University, he became professor and chairman of the University of Transkei's Psychology Department, becoming dean of arts the following year.

He spent the years between 1981 and 1990 as visiting professor and senior research fellow at Wits University's African Studies Institute and was also visiting fellow at Yale during the same period.

He was vice-chancellor of the University of the North from 1991, when he was also a member of the Joint Working Group on Education, a forum which brought together government and stakeholders, until his appointment in 1993 as executive director of the Joint Education Trust.

The recipient of numerous awards and study grants, Manganyi co-edited *Political Violence and the Struggle in South Africa* with political analyst André du Toit, one of eight books he has so far published. His biography of the late South African painter Gerard Sekoto is due to appear at the end of the year.

Born 13 March 1940. Family: wife Dr Peggy Sekele.

Manuel, Trevor   As Trade and Industry minister, Manuel has already shown to good effect the capacity to consult and to learn quickly that distinguished his tenure as head of the African National Congress's Department of Economic Policy.

Although the former Cape Town activist and founding member of the United Democratic Front has a political pedigree that includes several spells in jail in the 1980s, he is no ideologue, and has earned the grudging respect of business. That pragmatism, and his affable personality, will stand him in good stead as he oversees South Africa's reintegration into world trade.

However, he will have to deal with competing claims from business, labour and ordinary consumers as well as pressure from South Africa's trading partners, as tariffs are reduced in terms of the General Agreement on Tariffs and Trade.

Born 31 January 1956. Family: wife Lynnette Matthews, three children.

Marais, Jaap   The grand, obstinate old man of far-right politics clings desperately to the Verwoerdian concept of white supremacy in a white South Africa. As leader of the marginalised Herstigte Nasionale Party (HNP), Marais continues to tilt at windmills after more than 25 years in the political desert. However, he is still regarded as the voice of the civilised ultra-conservatives and may be speaking on behalf of more people than just those inside the HNP. A certain quaintness, bad timing, the formation of the

Conservative Party, a pedantic political style and, of course, obstinacy have prevented Marais and the HNP from ever capitalising on these feelings.

While ultra-conservatives are not always associated with the esoteric, Marais is a lover of poetry, with TS Eliot and John Keats among his favourites. A prolific author himself, he has also translated Shakespeare's *Julius Caesar* into Afrikaans. He is a breeder of budgies and a connoisseur of fine wines and cuisine.

Born 2 November 1922. Family: wife Maria Dorothea, three adult children.

Marcus, Gill   Often gruff and curt, Marcus has quickly established a much firmer reputation as chairperson of the parliamentary joint Finance committee than she did as a senior African National Congress spokesperson. In fact, members of all parties have been quick to praise her efficient and effective use of this sensitive position, as well as her even-handedness and fairness. Because of the 1994 Budget, she had to get her committee up and running before most others, and she set up an educational programme for committee members new to the intricacies of parliamentary budgets.

There is no doubting her passionate commitment to politics and to the ANC, demonstrated through many years of dedicated service in exile, mostly clipping South African newspapers for the ANC. On her return to South Africa, she took up a post in the organisation's Department of Information and Publicity and became one of its most frequently heard voices. She was also very influential in setting its media policies in the run-up to the 1994 elections.

She can be expected to play an extremely important role in her current parliamentary position and may be headed for more senior postings.

Born April 1950. Single.

Martin, Marilyn   The director of the South African National Gallery (SANG), a onetime prominent apologist for attempts by the PW Botha government to break the cultural boycott in Chile and elsewhere, has emerged as the most 'new South African' of institutional democrats.

In a few short years, the SANG in Cape Town has moved from the stodgiest neo-colonialist and most Eurocentric conservatism to somewhere near the cutting edge of community orientation and cultural representivity.

Attempts in the early 1990s to involve community-based organisations in policy- and decision-making have run aground. But Martin's vision for the SANG continues to be aimed towards greater participation by the gallery in the cultural life of the broader community. An educational division has been established with substantial outreach programmes in surrounding townships, and such projects undertaken as an exhibition celebrating 300 years of Malay presence in this country.

Despite a hopelessly inadequate acquisitions budget of around R200 000 per year, a buying policy has been pursued to supplement the gaps in the gallery's collection — notably in respect of black artists of the 1940s to the 1970s. Current collecting priorities, now that a core collection of Southern African beadwork has been put in place, include the work of early black painters George Pemba, John Koenakeefe Mohl and Gerard Bhengu.

Born in McGregor in the Cape, Martin matriculated from the Heidelberg Hoërskool before obtaining a BA Honours degree from Unisa and a Master's degree in architecture from the University of the Witwatersrand. In the 1980s she worked as an art critic for various publications including *Beeld, De*

Kat and *The Weekly Mail*, and lectured in the Architecture Department at Wits. During this period she was prominent in the South African Association of Arts, serving as national vice-president between 1984 and 1987, and being accorded an honorary life vice-presidency in 1990. Martin continues to serve on numerous official committees, including the board of directors of the Foundation for the Creative Arts; the Urban Foundation; the Military Art Advisory Board; the Committee of Heads of Cultural Institutions; the council of Southern African Museums Associations; and she serves as a patron of Cape Town's bid for the Olympic Games.

Born 16 August 1943. Family: two adult children.

Matsepe-Casaburri, Ivy Admirers and detractors alike call the chairperson of the first independent board of the giant, state-owned South African Broadcasting Corporation 'Dr Ivy' — the former with respect and the latter with derision. The PhD from Rutgers University in the United States, with a background in education, assumed the mantle of chairperson of the SABC board in August 1993 under difficult circumstances: she was only third choice for the job, after a political fracas involving then president FW de Klerk's veto of academic and author Njabulo Ndebele for the post and Frederik van Zyl Slabbert's refusal to accept the job. She walked into a largely male, largely Afrikaner *ancien régime* that was initially extremely hostile to her.

Her stewardship of the behemoth SABC has received mixed reports. She is slowly gaining the respect of the SABC staff (her 'brown bag' lunches are particularly popular), and, as someone with no prior knowledge of broadcasting, she has painstakingly assimilated a vast amount of knowledge about the field in her first year of tenure. But she presides over a flawed board: intended to give the SABC credibility by being 'representative', it is large, unwieldy, made up largely of people who do not have the requisite experience to govern the SABC, and caught up in its own internal politics.

Matsepe-Casaburri is to be credited with holding together a board of 21 governors with wildly disparate backgrounds and political affiliations, but the board's size and diversity, coupled with its chairperson's inherent caution, have meant that little, if anything, changed at the SABC in the first year of her tenure. The board has compiled lengthy reports on matters ranging from a rather controversial language policy to news programming, but none of these has been implemented. Most alarming, the board has done little actual restructuring of either personnel or programming, which means that the SABC is currently a minefield of insecurity, inefficiency and even sabotage.

There is little the SABC can do in terms of major restructuring until the Independent Broadcasting Authority (IBA) rules on its future. Matsepe-Casaburri played a major role in wresting the process of compiling a submission to the IBA from the hands of a defensive old management, and presenting a submission which is clearly in favour of a less commercial service that is more public broadcasting-orientated. She also approved an initiative by SABC supremo Zwelakhe Sisulu to put into place a 'transition team' to take control of the SABC. Given that her particular obsessions are affirmative action and public broadcasting, it is possible that the second year of her tenure will see more wide-reaching changes in the SABC.

Personal details not available.

Matthews, Joe   The deputy minister of Safety and Security owes much to the spirit of the government of national unity. How else would a lawyer wanted for embezzlement in a neighbouring country survive as second-in-command of the all-important campaign to restore law and order in a country beset by crime? Matthews fled Botswana in 1985 after being charged with the theft of some R130 000 in clients' funds. A warrant is still out for his arrest, but the African National Congress has allowed the matter to stand because Matthews is a notably moderate choice among the Inkatha Freedom Party hardliners who were possible candidates for top positions. And Matthews, who has earned a reputation as being both pragmatic and obstinate, has avoided ruffling feathers in the new government, staying out of the limelight in favour of his minister, Sydney Mufamadi.

Matthews has had a varied career. The son of the legendary Cape leader of the ANC in the 1950s, ZK Matthews, he started out as a communist, twice convicted under the Suppression of Communism Act, and national secretary of the ANC Youth League. He and his father were among the accused in the marathon treason trial that started in 1956. He went into exile in 1960 and represented the ANC in England, Holland, Botswana (where he was deputy attorney-general) and Canada and held top positions, including at one stage the chair of the ANC Revolutionary Council.

His friendship with IFP leader Mangosuthu Buthelezi dates back to 1948 and their years at Fort Hare University, and it was disagreement over the ANC's relations with the then chief minister of kwaZulu that led to his break with the exiled organisation. He returned home in 1991 and joined the IFP two years later as chief executive officer, a position phased out in the IFP's new constitution.

Matthews quickly became one of the IFP's top negotiators in the multiparty constitutional talks and earned a reputation and respect for his argumentative debating and lack of diplomacy. After the IFP pulled out of the talks, a move that Matthews was known to be uncomfortable with, he was sidelined in favour of the more hardline Walter Felgate, but returned to the fore with the participation of the IFP in the government of national unity.

Born 17 June 1929. Family: wife Regina, seven adult children.

Mbeki, Thabo   In exile, Mbeki was famed for his diplomatic skill and charm, playing a major role in defusing the fears of white South Africans through personal contact and careful moderation. Now, as vice-president, what is fast emerging is the shrewd and tough, even ruthless, politician behind the charm and diplomacy. It is this formidable combination that has made him the leading candidate to replace Nelson Mandela as president.

Mbeki grew up as a child of the 'struggle'. As the son of African National Congress stalwart Govan Mbeki, renowned for his organisational skills and leadership in the Eastern Cape in the 1950s, he went into exile when his father was imprisoned alongside Mandela. He received an MA in economics from Sussex University and, as was routine for all ANC recruits, military training in the Soviet Union in 1970. He then represented the ANC in Botswana, London, Swaziland, Nigeria and Zambia. He became best known as ANC president Oliver Tambo's right-hand man and was frequently the organisation's most visible diplomatic face, playing a key role in the international campaign against apartheid in the 1980s.

He returned in 1990 to be part of the Groote Schuur talks team, but afterwards his public profile seemed to recede into the background. He bounced back to be elected ANC national chairman in 1993 and was hand-picked by Mandela to be first deputy president after the 1994 election.

Mbeki's great strength is his political acumen, eloquence and diplomatic experience; his weakness is his penchant for jet-setting, and his identification with businessmen like hotel-and-casino magnate Sol Kerzner rather than with any sizeable grassroots constituency.

Born 18 June 1942. Family: wife Zanele, two children.

Mboweni, Tito   At first glance Mboweni's background and training ill-suit him to the post of Labour minister — he is a development economist. But he openly admits to a dislike for the legalistic way the labour market operates, and would like to bring more economic sense to it.

His desire to cut through the conflict and adversarial nature of South African labour relations was severely tested only two months after he assumed office, with a wave of strikes by restless elements of the union movement, suspicious that they were going to be sold out by a new government and eager to feel the benefits of political change. However, his general phlegmatic and unflappable nature may equip him for the tense times ahead.

Mboweni gained the public eye through statements that terrorised middle-class whites and business. During his term as number two in the African National Congress's Department of Economic Policy, he progressed from a position of moderation and even conciliation to the creation of anxiety with suggestions of a wealth tax along the lines of the German levy after World War II to rebuild the country, and by his backing for anti-trust legislation.

His wilder statements conceal a responsible approach to economics: he has tried to rein in the more irresponsible tendencies in the movement and has always been careful to

make economic sense. Since his appointment, he has
spearheaded the drafting of a new Labour Relations Act
that will fundamentally shift the country's industrial relations
towards a more co-operative system.

Born 16 March 1959. Family: married, two children.

Mdlalose, Frank   This moderate, gentlemanly doctor, with a
goatee beard and a generous paunch, was a surprise choice as
premier in the one province controlled by the Inkatha
Freedom Party, kwaZulu/Natal. He seemed to be at odds
with the hardliners of the IFP in the build-up to the 1994
election, but was probably chosen because he owes his entire
political career to IFP president Mangosuthu Buthelezi
personally.

Mdlalose was an African National Congress Youth
League member in the 1950s, but disappeared into the
political wilderness until Buthelezi asked him to help relaunch
Inkatha in 1975. He has been party chairman since 1977 and
has served in the kwaZulu government since 1978. Meanwhile, he obtained a BSc and BEd from the University of
Fort Hare and an MB ChB from the University of Natal.

He emerged as head of the IFP negotiations team at the
World Trade Centre talks, but disappeared from centre stage
when it seemed that the IFP would boycott the elections. But,
in the dramatic week when the IFP reversed its decision and
contested the poll, Mdlalose returned to the limelight to
spearhead the IFP victory in kwaZulu/Natal.

His reputation as a moderate, and the close relationship he
has forged with ANC provincial leader Jacob Zuma, sparked
hope that he would lead the strife-torn province to peace and
stability. But in his first few months in office, he surprised
everyone with an uncharacteristic belligerence, and even
arrogance. When asked to explain a reshuffle of his executive,

he replied: 'There is no reason I need to give anybody for choosing anybody to the cabinet.'

He also stood firm on insisting that Ulundi be the provincial capital, a move that was certain to bring disagreement and conflict. As a result, there was a three-month delay before the first meeting of the provincial legislature while parties sought a compromise.

A critical question will be whether he will rule the province, or merely serve as a conduit for Buthelezi to run it from afar. However, he does not have an independent political base and has not previously managed to stand up to Buthelezi when they have had political disagreements. It has been strongly rumoured − though never confirmed − that he tried to resign from office in early 1992, disillusioned with the level of conflict in kwaZulu/Natal, but was blocked by Buthelezi.

He has a keen interest in boxing and tennis.

Born 29 November 1931. Family: wife Eunice Nokuthula Sikhosana, five adult children.

Meiring, Georg The chief of the South African National Defence Force (SANDF) was rewarded for his willingness to work with new minister of Defence Joe Modise (it is said that he lobbied for Modise's appointment) with an immediate five-year appointment. It may seem ironic that these two former foes are now thrown together in the SANDF, but it quickly became apparent that as hawks who share a love for matters military, they have a great deal in common.

General Meiring has a history as a no-holds-barred opponent of the African National Congress and its military wing, but now he will be responsible for the integration of up to 30 000 Umkhonto weSizwe cadres and about 1 500

Azanian People's Liberation Army soldiers into the SANDF during his period in office.

Although he seems to have built a close rapport with Modise, his advice to the novice Defence minister to apply for an interdict against the *Weekly Mail & Guardian* just weeks after the new government had taken office gave rise to speculation as to his real agenda within the force.

Modise, who built a good relationship with his former adversary during integration negotiations, was initially happy to see Meiring in the top job because he commands the loyalty of the Army, the largest and hitherto politically most engaged section of the military. But Modise may well be questioning the wisdom of his decision. Meiring sees himself as a defender of the status quo, and he has fought hard to set the entry hurdles for MK cadres into the officers' corps as high as possible. He would clearly also like to retain a strong hold over Modise so that he can steer integration and change in a manner that is least unsettling to the Defence Force.

A tall and generally austere man known as a good strategist with a formidable intellect, Meiring's professionalism and loyalty to the government of the day are believed intact. He is expected to keep the military within the fold during the transition years, loyal and ready for action if called.

With a background in signals and logistics, Meiring saw action as commander of South African forces in Namibia and the far-northern command, responsible for counter-insurgency on the Zimbabwe border. His interests run to hunting and other outdoor activities.

Born 18 October 1939. Family: wife Anna Maria Gertruide ('Annchen'), five children.

Meyer, Anthon Tobias ('Tobie')   Roelf Meyer's elder, lesser-known brother, now deputy minister of Land Affairs, has farmed in the districts of Ficksburg and Humansdorp since 1956, and in 1983 was judged South African Farmer of the Year. At present he is a dairy and beef farmer in the Tsitsikamma area near George.

He has served in various posts in local organised agriculture, ranging from secretary of a farmers' association to president of the Eastern Cape Agricultural Union. He served on the National Regional Development Advisory Council, where he developed a reputation for improving relationships between agricultural role-players in the Eastern Cape, Transkei and Ciskei. He has also been a member of the South African Broadcasting Corporation board.

This background should equip him well to help minister Derek Hanekom in the tough balancing act between demands for land redistribution and the restitution of rights alienated under apartheid, and the needs of nervous white farmers.

Meyer started his political career as a National Party branch secretary and later chairman of his constituency. He was elected MP for Cradock in 1987.

He is one of very few ministers in the government of national unity keeping a position related to his portfolio in FW de Klerk's cabinet. He was elected deputy minister of Agriculture and Agricultural Development in 1991, and Land Affairs was joined to his portfolio in 1993.

Born 14 March 1939. Family: wife Marie.

Meyer, Roelf   The minister of Constitutional Development, Provincial Affairs and Local Government finds himself in the unenviable position of representing a minority party in the government of national unity while being in charge of highly sensitive portfolios. Meyer's chief task is to oversee the technical aspects of the transition period, which will come to an end in April 1999.

This task is not made easier by the fact that his deputy, Mohammed Valli Moosa, is one of the top strategists of the African National Congress, who earned his spurs during the constitutional negotiations in Kempton Park. Meyer has no access to the powerful ANC caucus, which has very definite ideas about the constitutional road ahead; it is doubtful that the minister will be able to take any substantial decisions without the agreement of his deputy.

However, Meyer's job continues the close relationship that developed during the negotiations with Cyril Ramaphosa, present chairman of the Constitutional Assembly. The two have built up a rapport — something that was often held against Meyer by his previous cabinet colleagues — and they should be able to ride the political storms.

Unassuming and quiet, Meyer came into the public limelight in 1993 as the government's chief negotiator, taking over from his cabinet colleague Tertius Delport after the failure of Codesa II. Always a proponent of the behind-closed-doors, coming-to-terms approach, Meyer lost support within his party for what was seen as an approach too accommodating to the ANC. Recently, he was convincingly beaten by Mineral and Energy Affairs minister Pik Botha in the National Party's Gauteng leadership stakes.

The fact that Meyer is a member of the country's first democratically elected government is proof of how far he has come since the days when, as deputy minister of Law and Order in PW Botha's cabinet, he openly supported the detention of youths during the State of Emergency.

His previous conservatism dates from his student days at the University of the Orange Free State, where he completed his BComm and LLB degrees and served as national president of the conservative Afrikaanse Studentebond. Later he became national chairman of the Junior Rapportryers, closely linked to the secretive Afrikaner Broederbond.

Meyer was elected to Parliament in 1979. His nine-month stint as minister of Defence ended in May 1992 amid allegations that he was not accepted by the Defence Force's tough guys. However, he survived most of his critics and is expected to be a force in politics for some time to come. He shares an interest with many of his NP colleagues in hunting — he is a passionate game farmer — and his pragmatism and quiet determination are probably his strongest assets.

Born 16 July 1947. Family: wife Carene, four teenaged children.

Mhlaba, Raymond Mpakamisi   The election of political veteran Mhlaba as premier of the Eastern Cape is the crowning of his early successes in mobilising support and laying the foundation of the liberation struggle in the Eastern Cape in the 1950s.

Born in Fort Beaufort, 'Oom Ray' became involved in the trade union movement in the 1940s and, using organisational skills learned from the Communist Party, rapidly garnered support for the African National Congress in Port Elizabeth as New Brighton township chairman. Under Mhlaba, ANC officials consolidated structures in surrounding towns as far afield as East London.

From his first banning under the Suppression of Communism Act in 1950, his activities mirrored events in the ANC's campaign against the apartheid government, from the 1952 Defiance Campaign to the adoption of the armed struggle, culminating in a life sentence in the Rivonia treason trial.

Mhlaba emerged from 25 years' imprisonment on Robben Island in 1989 and now serves on the executive committees of the ANC and the South African Communist Party, of which he is currently deputy chairman. He also co-chairs the Eastern Cape Regional Economic Development Forum. But his life is not entirely tied up in politics: he is also a keen cricket fan.

Though feisty at times, Mhlaba has adopted a tone of reconciliation in the provincial government, welcoming the opportunity to work with the National Party. His leadership will be put to the test as the Eastern Cape government faces the daunting task of unifying what remains of the Cape Provincial Administration, Transkei and Ciskei. His first days in office were characterised by crises in the former Transkei which, together with Ciskei, includes some of the poorest areas in the country. But he showed his mettle by being the first premier to fire an executive member.

Born 12 February 1920. Family: wife Dideka Makazi Letitia, many grandchildren.

Modise, Joe   Umkhonto weSizwe's commander since 1965, Modise is South Africa's first black Defence minister. He is generally regarded as a hawk, and although the African National Congress is hoping to find resources for its Reconstruction and Development Programme within the Defence budget, the responsible ministers will find in Modise a tough opponent of military spending cuts.

Modise got off to a shaky start when, on the advice of South African National Defence Force (SANDF) chief General Georg Meiring, he attempted to interdict publication of a list of Military Intelligence operatives by the *Weekly Mail & Guardian* within weeks of taking office. Massively criticised by the ANC, the South African Communist Party and the Congress of South African Trade Unions, he withdrew the interdict application, exposing his dependence on the generals.

Unlike some of his cabinet colleagues, Modise — who had become chums with the Defence establishment through 18 months of integration negotiations — seemed unable to impress his stamp of authority on the vast military-industrial complex made up of Armscor, the arms sales and procurements organisation, and the SANDF. The appointment of the first MK cadres to positions as generals took him seven weeks, in marked contrast to rapid appointments made in some other departments.

Many have been the suggestions that Modise has been seduced by the trappings of office — large ministerial limousines, readily available helicopters and private jets, and hunting trips to SANDF game reserves.

With the appointment of Ronnie Kasrils to the position of deputy Defence minister, Modise should be able to build the envisaged civilian defence ministry which will allow him to reduce his dependency on the old-guard military establishment. Besides impressing on the Defence Force the primacy of democratically elected politicians, the new ministry will have to develop spending and deployment doctrines more responsive to the country's reconstruction priorities than at present.

Born in Doornfontein, Johannesburg, Modise's has been a life of militancy which took him from resistance to the Sophiatown removals to participation in MK's first acts of sabotage.

He received military training in Czechoslovakia and the USSR, and was involved in the planning and execution of MK operations, including the Wankie campaign and the strategy of 'armed propaganda' after 1976. He was criticised by the Motsuenyane Commission into human rights abuses at ANC camps during the 1980s because he failed to exercise sufficient control, but this looks unlikely to affect his future role.

Born 23 May 1929. Family: wife Brigadier Jackie Sedibe, five children.

Mofokeng, Mpu Daniel ('Dan') As a long-time general secretary of the Southern Transvaal region of the South African National Civic Organisation (Sanco), Mofokeng supported such tactics as rent and bond boycotts. He points with pride at the effect the Transvaal Civic Organisation had on black local authorities: two or three months after its launch in 1991, almost half the black local councillors had resigned.

Now that he's the Gauteng MEC for local government and housing, his emphasis has shifted somewhat. 'The new challenge,' he says, 'is how to rebuild those structures that you once destroyed. In the same way that people once preached ungovernability, we must now talk about governability.'

Mofokeng, elected on an African National Congress ticket and also a member of the South African Communist Party, still sees a role for the civics, although his view clearly reflects his new vantage point from the heights of provincial government. Civics, he says, can make it easier for the government to implement the Reconstruction and Development Programme. They can involve the masses, educate them about the constitution and their civic rights and duties. Then he becomes briefly the man who came to prominence in the civic movement: 'If South Africa wants democracy, we must allow organs of civil society to be established. We can't allow a situation where issues will only be debated by political parties.'

In early 1993, Mofokeng hit the headlines when he said Sanco did not believe 'white' political parties should be permitted to campaign in the townships. He still defends that view — despite accusations at the time of 'authoritarian fascism' — but says he only wanted the playing fields levelled, and once the Transitional Executive Council was established and other parties' 'bad behaviour' had been corrected, he had no problem with making the townships accessible.

Born in Katlehong, he started a B Admin at Turfloop, was detained in 1986 and when released spent time as an organiser for the Unemployed Workers' Co-ordinating Committee of the Congress of South African Trade Unions (Cosatu) before being seconded to other Cosatu unions. In 1989, back in Katlehong, he held office in the new civic movement while organising for the Transport and General Workers' Union, finding time, simultaneously, to finish his B Admin degree.

Soon after he assumed Gauteng office, his housing portfolios were surrounded in controversy, not all of his making. First his premier, Tokyo Sexwale, announced his own housing programme for the province; the national minister of Housing was not pleased, and negotiations ensued, leading to a compromise that left little of the provincial plan intact.

Once that was sorted out, Mofokeng hit the headlines by promising residents of coloured townships that their rent arrears would be written off and their houses handed over. The national minister of Housing was even less pleased — the ministry estimated it would cost R9-billion in government revenue nationally — and Mofokeng had to backtrack.

Mofokeng has been left with the reputation of being an 'unguided missile'. Even his local government portfolio became embroiled in battles over whether the region would be cut into several cities or only three. In the end, negotiators compromised on seven, but the new scheme had given extra emphasis to his view that ratepayers' associations should combine with civics for more clout.

Born 27 January 1960. Family: wife Geraldine, two children.

Mogoba, Stanley Mmutlanyane In his role as presiding bishop of the Methodist Church, and as vice-chairman of the National Peace Committee, Mogoba came up, at a South African Council of Churches' annual conference, with the idea of an armed peace force consisting of different armies which would go into trouble spots well armed and deliver peace. This germ of an idea eventually grew into the soon discredited and disbanded National Peacekeeping Force — a feather in his cap which he may wish, in time, to remove.

Mogoba, born in Sekhukhuniland, converted to Christianity while serving time on Robben Island for Pan Africanist Congress activities. He has been an eloquent force for peace, despite earlier more radical leanings.

He became chancellor of the Medical University of South Africa in 1990 and was a recipient of the human rights award of the Swiss Foundation of Freedom and Human Rights. One of his roles likely to continue into the new South Africa is that of president of the Boy Scouts movement.

Born 29 March 1933. Family: wife Johanna, four children.

Mokaba, Peter The charismatic Mokaba, voice of the radical youth, did not make it into Mandela's cabinet but did make it into *Time* magazine's 1994 list of 100 world leaders of the future. A spunky, articulate survivor of many a political battle, he can be expected to make a strong impact as a member of Parliament with potential for higher office. He is currently chairman of the Standing Committee on Environmental Affairs and Tourism.

Mokaba rose to prominence in the 1980s as the voice of the militant African National Congress-aligned youth. He hails from the Northern Transvaal, where he has a strong political base. He was founder and national president of the South African Youth Congress (Sayco), launched in March 1987. After the unbanning of the ANC, Sayco dissolved in favour of the ANC Youth League and Mokaba was elected president, a position he held until January 1994.

Mokaba has always been a controversial figure, partly because of his tough talk — such as his refusal in 1993 to stop leading crowds in the chant of 'kill the Boer, kill the farmer', despite repudiation from the ANC leadership — partly because of a run-in with Security Police at the height of repression, after which he faced accusations of having compromised himself. More recently, however, Mokaba has recast himself as a campaigner for the tourism industry and projected a more moderate, pragmatic image. He has also invested in a chain of hairdressing salons.

Nevertheless, he is likely to play an important role in retaining the support of the militant youth for the ANC. He has a taste for the cut and thrust of internal politics and was a key player in the ascendancy of Thabo Mbeki to the ANC national chairmanship and the country's deputy presidency.

Born 7 January 1958.

Mokone-Matabane, Sebeletso Mokone-Matabane is the co-chair of the powerful Independent Broadcasting Authority (IBA), a new body charged with the immense and important task of restructuring the broadcasting industry. Next to her assertive co-chair Peter de Klerk, she appears to be sometimes painfully tentative, but she is thoughtful and considered, and passionate about a new broadcasting order that will play a significant role in reconstruction and development.

She has a background in education and public broad-casting in the United States, where she received a PhD in education administration from the University of Texas in 1986. In Texas, she held senior media and administration offices at a variety of colleges, and sat on the advisory council of a public broadcasting service station in Austin. She also holds a Master's degree in television and radio from Syracuse University in New York.

Since returning to South Africa in 1992, she has been the project manager of the Tertiary Education Program Support Project, an education development project of USAid. She is also on the board of the Electronic Media in Education Forum. Her combined interests in education and broad-casting render her a firm advocate for using the SABC as a public educator. Her friendship with SABC chairperson Ivy Matsepe-Casaburri could provide for a close working relationship between the IBA and the South African Broadcasting Corporation, but it also raises fears, in some quarters, of an African National Congress domination of the broadcasting sector.

Matabane is an avowed and unapologetic member of the ANC, and although she has never held office in the organisation, she has been a board member of the ANC's Centre for Development of Information and Telecommuni-cations Policy, and has done work at the ANC's Dora Tamana Crèche in Lusaka.

Unlike De Klerk, her background is in public service rather than in the private sector, and she is particularly concerned with the ethical principles of the IBA. She is spearheading a code of conduct that will require IBA councillors to declare all their personal assets and interests, and prevent them from meeting alone with interested parties in the broadcasting world.

Born 26 October 1944. Family: husband Ntinyana William Matabane.

Molefe, Popo　If exiles and the African National Congress older guard dominate the new national cabinet, the 1976 generation of former United Democratic Front (UDF) activists took control of the provinces — and Molefe, as premier of the North West, exemplifies this.

A graduate of the 1976 uprising, Molefe moved from a black consciousness background into the non-racial movement in 1981. He learnt his politics on the Soweto Students' Representative Committee, in the Azanian People's Organisation, the Soweto Committee of Ten and the Anti-Republic Day Celebration Committee, and in 1983 became national secretary of the UDF, where he won wide respect for his organisational and mobilising abilities. He was detained two years later, became one of the Delmas treason trialists, was sentenced to 10 years' imprisonment in 1988 and released on appeal at the end of 1989.

He led the triumvirate that ran the ANC election campaign, heading the Election Department with his quiet determination and organising experience.

Now he is premier of the troubled North West province where he faces the formidable task of uniting three existing administrations — Venda, Bophuthatswana and the Transvaal — into one. Already it is clear that this cumbersome civil service is his single biggest headache. He has also been involved in a tussle with central government for control of Bop TV and Bop Air, two regional assets that were inherited from the Mangope government. And he ran into an early conflict with his rival for ANC regional leadership, Rockey Malabane-Metsing, whom he dismissed in November 1994 for allegedly failing to accept the policy of national reconciliation.

Born 26 April 1952. Family: wife Doitumelo, four children.

Molobi, Eric   In late 1993, Molobi — chief executive of the Kagiso Trust and co-chairman of the National Housing Forum — launched an attack on development consultants and parastatals in the development field. Unless parastatals are transformed, he said in a major speech, 'we run the risk of a hollow political victory'.

Molobi has spent most of the past decade in the world of non-governmental organisations: a founder of the South African Council of Churches' Joint Enrichment Project to deal with youth development, and of the National Education Crisis Committee, he was appointed chief executive officer of the Kagiso Trust in 1990. He succeeded in turning the trust, one of the Big Three funders (along with the Independent Development Trust (IDT) and the Development Bank of Southern Africa), from a struggle industry into a development agency disbursing some R240-million annually to a variety of projects. When the National Housing Forum was launched in 1992, he was named co-director.

Born in Alexandra, educated in Lesotho, Molobi trained as a technician but earned a BA from Unisa. He was a friend of black consciousness student leader Abram Tiro, moving into the Congress camp while serving five years on Robben Island in the 1970s for political offences. In the 1980s he was appointed to the United Democratic Front's national executive committee and was detained for 18 months from December 1987 under Emergency regulations. He is a member of the boards of the IDT, Telkom, the Gaming Board, and the Council of the University of the Witwatersrand.

Born 5 June 1947. Family: wife Martha, two daughters.

Motlana, Nthato The medical practitioner turned politician who turned back to medicine has created major waves on the Johannesburg stock market. He is affectionately known as the grandfather of Soweto politics; and now that the African National Congress is in government, he has turned his attention to business and black empowerment.

He earned his MBBCh degree at the University of the Witwatersrand in 1956. It was during these early years that he became involved in the struggle against apartheid, through his active participation in the ANC Youth League. He shot to prominence during the 1976 uprising; he was instrumental in forming the Black Parents' Association and the Soweto Committee of Ten, resulting in a lengthy detention. He has also served a number of banning orders.

A dedicated man always committed to capitalism and sharply critical of socialists in the ANC, Motlana is now chairman of the Get Ahead Foundation, a director of Southern Life and chairman of Prosper Africa, whose subsidiary, New Africa Publishers, agreed in 1994 to buy a controlling interest in the *Sowetan* newspaper.

His latest ventures include the purchase of Metropolitan Life and the formation and listing on the Johannesburg Stock Exchange of New Africa Investments.

He was, for the first few years after Mandela's release, the ANC leader's personal physician.

Born 16 February 1925. Family: wife Zanele Peggy, six adult children.

Msane, Thoko Angela The new deputy minister of Agriculture is an unknown quantity in politics. At 29 the youngest member of the new cabinet, she is known as a woman with an outgoing personality who 'likes laughing' and does not lack self-confidence. However, her experiences in agricultural affairs are limited to her youth when the whole community was involved in ploughing and planting activities.

She believes that women, specifically in the countryside, should be allowed access to agricultural technology to become more productive. Whether she will be able to counterbalance National Party Agriculture minister Kraai van Niekerk in looking after the interests of black small farmers remains to be seen.

Msane was born in Swaziland but grew up in Natal. She studied in Durban in personnel, training and public relations, then went to Johannesburg to qualify further in the fields of journalism and business and financial management. She is still studying towards a business administration degree.

Her previous experience includes a stint as legal secretary at Mafika Mbuli & Co, receptionist at the Diakona Ecumenical Church Agency in Durban, and national deputy general secretary of the South African Council of World Affiliated Young Women's Christian Association (YWCA).

Msane has been active in the field of Christian affairs and matters affecting the rights of women and youth, for which she has attended several overseas conferences since 1987.

Born 2 June 1965. Family: three children.

Mufamadi, Sydney   It has been a short road from Mufamadi's 1991 conviction for kidnapping and assaulting a police officer found snooping around the offices of the Congress of South African Trade Unions, where he was assistant general secretary, to his post as minister of Safety and Security, responsible for South Africa's 141 000-strong police force. His 1991 conviction followed one of seven separate arrests during the 1980s in connection with his political activism.

Mufamadi is one of a few younger African National Congress ministers who was systematically groomed for his task through the negotiations and transition period, and he is widely seen as the man to transform the paramilitary South African Police into a community policing service.

He moved rapidly after assuming office to show the direction the force would take when he appointed several committees to manage the transition to regional, community-orientated police services. Mufamadi also announced within days of taking office that the police would become more civilian in nature, shedding military rank structures in favour of titles such as 'inspector' or 'superintendent'.

Modest, thoughtful and determined, Mufamadi was born in Alexandra township. Known as 'Jomo' in his youth because of his love for soccer, he grew up in Meadowlands and Tshisahulu in Venda, where he herded his grandfather's cattle and attended school. He describes a police raid against his mother's illegal brewing operation as the beginning of his political radicalisation which led him to become a founding member of the Azanian People's Organisation, into the ANC underground, and to the South African Communist Party. In 1985 he became general secretary of the General and Allied Workers' Union, and he was a founding member of Cosatu and the United Democratic Front.

Born 28 February 1959. Family: wife Nomsa, two daughters.

Mzimela, Sipo Elijah The minister of Correctional Services is one of a string of late developers in the Inkatha Freedom Party. A former exiled member of the African National Congress who served as its deputy United Nations representative in New York, he broke ranks with the organisation in the 1980s after an 18-month spell in Czechoslovakia where he concluded that communism was 'evil'. An ordained Episcopalian priest, he settled in the United States where he worked as a prison chaplain and IFP representative before his return to South Africa in 1990. He has a doctorate in ethics.

Back home, his star in the IFP rose quickly as a hawk and a powerful orator, able to deliver tough off-the-cuff speeches. He appeared regularly on public platforms beside IFP leader Mangosuthu Buthelezi at the height of the party's anti-election campaign, lambasting the ANC and the National Party.

He has inherited a tough post, walking immediately into riots in overcrowded prisons while needing to implement President Nelson Mandela's desire for a more humanitarian approach. But early on, he opted for that approach, releasing juveniles and — weeks after he assumed office — the lonely and ill Dimitro Tsafendas, assassin of Hendrik Verwoerd, into a mental institution.

Born 19 June 1935. Family: wife Gail Spencer, three daughters.

Naidoo, Jay   Nobody can accuse Jay Naidoo, the Minister Without Portfolio, of shying away from difficult tasks. He entered the trade union movement as a youth, when it was a risky thing to do. He accepted the general secretaryship at the launch of the Congress of South African Trade Unions in 1985, at the height of state repression of opposition. Now based in the Office of the President, he has taken on special responsibility for the implementation of the Reconstruction and Development Programme (RDP). This means his name and reputation are directly linked to the success or failure of this gargantuan task — and his formidable reputation for getting things done will stand or fall on it.

Naidoo acquired a BSc at the University of Durban-Westville, where he was identified with the Black Consciousness Movement, and became general secretary of the Sweet, Food and Allied Workers' Union in 1983. When Cosatu was formed in 1985, he was elected general secretary and he carved out for the huge union federation a distinctly political role in opposition to the apartheid government. Many a campaign — including stayaways and boycotts — during the 1980s saw Cosatu in a leading position as the most organised and powerful element of the resistance movement. He led a Cosatu delegation to the African National Congress in 1985 and again in 1986.

After a Cosatu anti-VAT campaign in 1991, he called for the formation of a National Economic Forum and took Cosatu into this important body that began a tripartite (state, business and unions) relationship that laid the basis for the new labour legislation (due in 1995) to formalise this partnership.

Naidoo left Cosatu in 1993 with over a million members and as a strong member of the election alliance with the ANC and the South African Communist Party. He was one of a number of senior unionists who headed for Parliament.

He was a popular choice to head the RDP where his task is to direct special presidential projects, ensure the restructuring of all government departments towards the RDP, and the longer term redirecting of resources for the programme. All of this has to be done within the confines of fiscal discipline, to which Naidoo has committed himself. He has also pledged to implement an effective project monitoring system and a new partnership with the non-government development sector based on effectiveness and successful delivery.

Born 20 December 1954. Family: wife French Canadian television journalist Lucie Page, one child.

Naidoo, Jayendra   The executive director of the National Economic, Development and Labour Council is best known — rather unfortunately — for his joking suggestion, while Cosatu national negotiations co-ordinator, that swimming pool owners should pay a 'pool tax'. He rose to prominence as an official of the South African Commercial Catering and Allied Workers' Union (Saccawu), and first hit the headlines playing a central role in Saccawu national strikes over wages at OK Bazaars and Pick 'n Pay in 1986/87.

A key planner of the National Peace Accord and the Reconstruction and Development Programme, Naidoo declined nomination for the African National Congress parliamentary list, preferring to stay in Cosatu, even though he was trounced in the running for assistant general secretary in 1993.

He played a leading role in Cosatu during the run-up to the country's first democratic election, mostly handling policy positions of the federation in the National Economic Forum and in both the National Peace Accord and its secretariat. To distinguish him from his namesake, the former Cosatu general secretary and now minister without portfolio in the government of national unity, he was dubbed 'Baby Jay', 'Little Jay' and 'Jay Junior' by union colleagues. But he has not had the schedule that goes with the diminutive; in fact, he has been so politically involved that when asked about interests outside his job he says he has been planning for 12 years to go fishing.

He began his political career in 1977 as a South African Students' Organisation activist at the University of Durban-Westville. On entering the labour movement in 1982, he rapidly rose to become a central figure in the catering unions which later merged to form Saccawu. He was also active in the United Democratic Front and in 1990 was elected chairperson of the Durban Western Areas of the ANC.

He was formerly married to ANC parliamentarian Pregaluxmi (Pregs) Govender.

Born 5 September 1960. Family: wife Liv Torrest, two children.

Ndebele, Njabulo   It is a pity that one of South Africa's finest writers of fiction has not published a follow-up to his Noma Award-winning collection of stories, *Fools* (1984), but the loss to readers has been the gain of many students, academics and cultural practitioners in general.

Ndebele, who has enough on his hands as vice-chancellor of the University of the North, still finds time to serve on the board of the South African Broadcasting Corporation and as president of the powerful lobby-group National Arts Coalition, which has seen its programmes adopted almost wholesale by the new Ministry of Arts and Culture.

Ndebele has always been influential in the arts. A subtle and flexible thinker, known for his firm independence from party-political agendas, his critical writing took the debates around culture that were a product of the 'struggle' years and moved them to a new level. Opposing the broadly instrumentalist view, work such as his book *Rediscovery of the Ordinary* insisted that 'society is the content of politics' and argued against the reduction of complex social realities to a few political shibboleths.

He has impeccable academic qualifications — a Master's degree from Cambridge, a doctorate from the University of Denver in the United States — but it is as an administrator that he has made his most indelible mark on education. An indefatigable worker, he has been responsible for major changes at one of the country's largest universities since he took over as vice-chancellor at the University of the North. He introduced a strategic planning programme that has seen numerous innovations in the areas of curriculum, administration, and student programmes. He is recognised as a key figure in the 'new wave' in higher education, and no doubt his influence will spread as his programmes meet with success.

Ndebele has also set up a Business School in Pietersburg, and is planning a School of Fine and Performing Arts and a School of Broadcasting Journalism.

Born in Charterston township near Nigel — the setting for many of his brilliant stories — Ndebele was involved in the black consciousness inspired students' movement. He first studied at the National University of Lesotho, where he later became pro-vice-chancellor. He has been president of the Congress of South African Writers since 1987.

Born 4 July 1948. Family: wife Mpho Ndebele, three children.

Nemadzivhanani, Maxwell   The Pan Africanist Congress national organiser relinquished his National Assembly seat — he was among the top five on the PAC list — 'to concentrate on building the party for the 1999 elections'. After the humiliation of the 1994 elections, a party shake-up seemed on the cards but PAC president Clarence Makwetu held on to power despite serious challenge — making the job of strengthening the party more difficult for Nemadzivhanani. He is sharp-witted, articulate, popular and cleverer than most of his colleagues in the National Executive Committee of the PAC, and his support is overwhelming among the young and militant sections of the party.

Two months before and during elections in 1994, Nemadzivhanani disappeared from the scene and maintained a monastic silence, sparking criticism that he did very little to improve the PAC's election prospects.

He convened an urgent 'soul-seeking' summit a month after the election, at which he criticised his party's lateness in both suspending the armed struggle and entering the race. He branded the PAC's election co-ordination 'a non-starter', and remarked that people 'had no confidence in an organisation that was seen to be undecided and with discordant voices who did not abide by its decisions'.

He lambasted the 'one settler one bullet' slogan as inappropriate. 'To the masses the party was not psychologically ready. It wouldn't have made any difference even if it was Karl Marx who was leading it,' he said.

Nemadzivhanani left the country in 1977 for Botswana, and later went to Australia. In 1983 he abandoned his economics degree at the Australian National University to become chief representative of the PAC for Australia and the South Pacific, during which period he met his 'settler' wife with whom he had two children. They later divorced.

In his travels he acquired a love for tennis and ice-skating; and he learned to enjoy radio broadcasting. In 1991 he was transferred to Nigeria, but later that year was recalled to become the party's national organiser.

Born 20 August 1956. Family: wife Neliswa Simuku, four sons.

Netshitenzhe, Joel Khathutshelo   President Nelson Mandela's communications director looks back on many years spent at the heart of the African National Congress's propaganda effort, first on Radio Freedom and then as editor of the organisation's monthly journal, *Mayibuye*. As a member of the ANC's national executive, national working committee and negotiations commission, Netshitenzhe was involved in formulating the policies which created the new board of the South African Broadcasting Corporation and the acts governing the Independent Media Commission and the Independent Broadcasting Authority.

He grew up in the far-northern Transvaal where he was involved in what he terms 'tiffs' with the school administration during student efforts to oppose the establishment of the Venda homeland. As local branch secretary of the South African Students' Organisation at the University of the North, he attended workshops with Steve Biko before making contact with underground ANC structures. Feeling they were living in an ivory tower after the beginning of the 1976 uprising, Netshitenzhe and friends left the country in September of that year to join Umkhonto weSizwe. He became one of the first MK cadres to train in Angola as a member of the June 16 detachment.

Two years later he moved to ANC headquarters in Lusaka where he edited *Mayibuye* and contributed to Radio Freedom, the ANC broadcaster. While working as an ANC journalist under the *nom de plume* Peter Mayibuye, he was sent to the Social Sciences Institute in Moscow, where he studied from 1982 to 1984. On his return he became a member of the Politico-Military Council responsible for internal propaganda and was also an occasional speech writer for Oliver Tambo.

Born 21 December 1956. Family: two children.

Ngcukana, Cunningham   Long-limbed, almost painfully slim, draped in suits that are not usually the best or the latest cut, the general secretary of the National Council of Trade Unions (Nactu) does not immediately come across as what he is: the articulate and assertive leader of the country's second largest labour federation.

Ngcukana is one of Nactu's brightest talents, although controversy marred his elevation in 1989 to the post of general secretary. An Africanist by inclination — he cut his political teeth in the Pan Africanist Congress-aligned Azanian National Youth Unity — he took over from Piroshaw Camay, who had resigned as general secretary in protest against what he perceived as the politicisation of Nactu by an Africanist faction and its opposition to a closer relationship with the Congress of South African Trade Unions.

Ngcukana has, however, proved himself to be a pragmatist rather than an ideological purist. He is now in the vanguard of moves to establish a single labour federation in the country, one of the reasons he decided to stay in the union movement and declined a place on the PAC national candidates' list in the national elections in April 1994. He says he would not mind if a new all-in federation were called Cosatu: 'I'm not interested in names, but in what we achieve under that name.'

Born 28 August 1960. Family: wife Thoko Ngcukana, one son.

Ngubane, Baldwin Sipho ('Ben') The new minister of Arts and Culture, Science and Technology has added an interest in ballet and opera to his CV — interests that were not there when he was kwaZulu minister of Health. But he has taken to his new cabinet post with enthusiasm and shown an inclusive approach which, combined with his soft-spoken and rational manner, has won him early respect. He has placed a strong emphasis on 'consultation' and 'multiculturalism', and included some notable independents in his departmental offices. In the Arts and Culture portion of his portfolio he has been beset by continual challenges from his deputy, Winnie

Mandela, who seems, however, to be tending to leave the Science and Technology section to Ngubane.

Ngubane holds a Master's degree in family medicine and primary health care from the University of Natal Medical School and has a background in community health care and tropical medicine, running a practice before entering home-land government.

A moderate in the Inkatha Freedom Party, he supported election participation long before it was fashionable in his political circles to do so. He headed the kwaZulu govern-ment's negotiations team at the World Trade Centre talks, where his contribution was largely of an intellectual nature. He commands enormous respect among IFP moderates who touted him as a potential successor to Buthelezi when the IFP president threatened to quit in 1993.

Born 22 October 1941. Family: wife Sheila, four children.

Nhlanhla, Joe   Appointed to take charge of the African National Congress's security services after the Angolan camps human rights debacle in the 1980s, Nhlanhla has always been seen as more of a politician than an intelligence technocrat. Now he is in the running for a new and powerful cloak-and-dagger position — state secretary for intelligence in the President's Office. His brief would be to ensure the democratisation of South African intelligence operations, directing them away from dirty tricks and into a role as protectors of the constitution, operating within the confines of the law.

Nhlanhla wanted to retire after a lifetime of political struggle, but quickly warmed to the idea of the new task. He is described as a man of integrity and political savvy, even though his ANC Security and Intelligence Department has never had a good reputation. This department has been compared to Swiss cheese, with Nhlanhla time and again the dairyman tasked with plugging the holes, or at least explaining how they got there. Nevertheless, Nhlanhla has won the respect of the department as a clear strategic thinker, despite his lack of formal intelligence training.

Since returning to South Africa in 1990, he has been involved in negotiations on several fronts, most recently on the future of the intelligence services.

Nhlanhla was born in Sophiatown, the son of a priest, and grew up in Alexandra. He was active in the 1957 bus and potato boycotts and left the country in 1964 to join Umkhonto weSizwe. Between 1973 and 1978 he was ANC representative in Egypt and the Middle East.

Born 4 December 1936. Family: wife Mmabatho, one son.

Nkondo, Sankie Nkondo was a surprise choice in January 1995 to succeed Joe Slovo as minister of Housing, thus assuming the central and most difficult task of the Reconstruction and Development Programme. The shoes of the formidable Slovo could be hard to fill — although Nkondo has inherited a strong infrastructural and policy framework.

Born in Sophiatown, Nkondo wrote matric in 1970 but is very much a graduate of the 1976 political emancipation; she left the country at the time of the youth revolts, shortly after completing her BA degree at the University of the North, to join the African National Congress in exile. She worked as a radio journalist and as editor of *Voice of Woman* (VOW), a journal of the ANC's women's section.

In 1989, after secretarial stints in the ANC mission for Nigeria and West Africa and in Sweden, she assumed duties as the organisation's chief representative for Germany and

Austria. She only returned to the country in October 1993, to serve as deputy head of the ANC's Department of International Affairs. In May 1994 she was named deputy minister of Welfare before being promoted on Slovo's death.

Nkondo, one of only five women in a ministerial post in the government of national unity, is also a poet. Her work has been published by the Congress of South African Writers in *Flames of Fury* in 1990, and she has also been published in *Malibongwe*, *Poets to the People* and *Kultur*.

Born 23 March 1951. Family: one child.

Nkuhlu, Wiseman Lumkile   Wiseman Nkuhlu is the director of choice for non-governmental organisations with a great deal of money to spend: early in 1993 he became chief executive of the Independent Development Trust and chairman of the board of the Development Bank of Southern Africa (DBSA).

In July 1994 the need for change at the DBSA was made manifest in a series of leaks by disaffected staff members: that a board member had devised a plan for undermining the Reconstruction and Development Programme (the member denied the charge, but resigned); that the bank was planning to favour the National Party-controlled Western Cape with its largesse; that some DBSA staff were paid up to 50 per cent above market rates; that black staff were becoming impatient at their alleged invisibility.

Nkuhlu's response to the rumours was an even-handed view that staff sensitivities needed to be addressed, but that at the same time a fair amount of misunderstanding had been involved.

The first black chartered accountant in the country, Nkuhlu founded the University of Transkei's Department of Accounting a year after he qualified in 1976. In 1983, he was named vice-principal of Unitra; in 1987, he began a five-year term as vice-chancellor. Throughout his career, he has concentrated on black empowerment through the accounting profession, management and commerce.

He holds an MBA from New York University and is national president of the Black Management Forum. Chairman of the National Electrification Forum, he serves on a number of boards, including the Standard Bank Investment Corporation and Old Mutual.

Born 5 February 1944. Family: wife Hazel Nondima.

Nqakula, Charles   In contrast to his high-profile predecessor, Chris Hani, the general secretary of the South African Communist Party has remained in the background since taking over the party reins after Hani's assassination in 1993. A journalist by training, he has preferred to work quietly behind the scenes.

A sign of his self-effacing modesty was his decision upon election to the top SACP job not to move into his predecessor's office. Yet this quality has given the party a headache as it has worked to reclaim the public ground so convincingly occupied by Hani, who gave the party a major profile.

His biography parallels Hani's in many ways. Both were born into devastatingly poor backgrounds in the Eastern Cape, and both attended mission schools. Later, Nqakula took over the African National Congress underground built by Hani in Lesotho.

But to see Nqakula as a carbon copy, unable to leave Hani's shadow, is to underestimate him. Of intense, quiet passion, he has come a long way from a rural background as the son of an illiterate labourer and a washerwoman, one of 10 children. His simple, forceful advocacy of economic and political justice for ordinary South Africans has the ring of authenticity. Challenged on socialism's realities, Nqakula, who spent time in the USSR and East Germany, says: 'We believe it was bureaucracy which killed socialism. Which is why we feel that democracy must be the focus of our party. We are drawing on the experiences of the trade unions, which are steeped in democracy.'

SACP membership must continue to come primarily from within the labour movement, strengthening its watchdog role now that the ANC is in government, argues Nqakula. But first comes party building. His true passion lies in grassroots organising: 'Our future depends on solid party structures.'

Although firmly locked into an alliance with the ANC, and with several communists in government, the SACP has not held back from criticising individual cabinet ministers. Defence minister Joe Modise came in for withering flak from the party when he tried to interdict publication of details of previous Military Intelligence activities by the *Weekly Mail & Guardian*.

Yet there are those who believe the party has an uncertain future. It will, no doubt, continue to debate the exact nature of the difference between Marxist-inspired socialism and reformist social democracy, but the truth is that most party members — many of whom suffered through years of illegality, exile, imprisonment and torture for their beliefs — are unlikely to allow the organisation to fold. Their emotional attachment alone will ensure the party's continued survival at least as a ginger group within or on the fringes of the ANC.

Born 13 September 1942. Family: wife Nosiviwe Mapisa, three young children.

Nyanda, Siphiwe   Like all of Umkhonto weSizwe's senior cadres, for MK's former chief of staff politics came before soldiering. But, unlike most of MK's top brass, he has adopted a decidedly military bearing, the product perhaps of several training spells in East Germany and the USSR. Nyanda — whose MK name is Ghebuza, after Shaka's legendary general — has been appointed to the second most senior job in the South African National Defence Force, that of SANDF chief of staff, at the rank of lieutenant-general. Despite the delay in his appointment, apparently caused by establishment reluctance to accept his qualifications for the job, he clearly has the confidence and at least some of the conventional military background he will need for a senior staff career. With time and some fast-track adaptation training, he could be the first black chief of the Defence Force.

Through his close involvement in the integration talks with representatives of the South African Defence Force and the armies of the former homelands, Nyanda has gained insights into the workings of the standing armies in South Africa.

Born in Soweto, the son of a traffic inspector, he grew up in an African National Congress household, making early attempts to join the underground. He was commanding guerrilla activities in the PWV region within just a few years, rising to become MK's Transvaal chief of staff at the age of 33. Together with Mac Maharaj, Nyanda was infiltrated back into South Africa in mid-1989 as one of the commanders of Operation Vula, the ANC's effort to beef up the underground struggle against apartheid by sending senior cadres to run it from within the country. Nyanda remained underground until July 1990.

Born 22 May 1950. Family: wife Sheila, four children.

Nzimande, Bonginkosi Emmanuel ('Blade')   The chairperson of the National Assembly's select committee on Education, who has spent much of his life as an academic, has in the past few years built up a background more relevant to this critical field than many of the bureaucrats working in it: he was a member both of the principles and framework committee and the editorial group of the National Education Policy Investigation (Nepi), a massive, nationwide research project published in the early 1990s by the National Education Co-ordinating Committee (NECC) and designed to come up with a plan for post-apartheid education. He was also director of the Education Policy Unit (EPU) at the University of Natal from 1989 until May 1994, when he left to take up his seat in Parliament.

Born in Pietermaritzburg, Nzimande earned a BA from the University of Zululand and BA Honours and a Master's degree from the University of Natal (Pietermaritzburg). His field in the 1980s was industrial psychology, but in the late 1980s, he began shifting his main focus of interest to education, and the lecturer at the University of Natal's Department of Psychology became the director of the University's EPU.

He has published on a wide variety of subjects, however, from the role of civics to the experience of black students in 'white' universities, the crisis in black universities, political violence in Pietermaritzburg. On both the Natal Midlands executive of the African National Congress and the central committee of the South African Communist Party, he is also a member of the University of Transkei Council.

Born 14 April 1958. Family: wife Phumelele, four children.

Nzo, Alfred   Last year, the former secretary-general of the African National Congress did not make the *A-Z of South*

African Politics because he had been written off as a political figure. He had never been popular, so it was with some relief that the return from exile saw him replaced in this critical post.

It was with some surprise, then, that he emerged in the important and senior cabinet post of minister of Foreign Affairs. He brings to this job formidable experience in the international arena on behalf of the ANC in exile; but he also brings much baggage as the man who, in Lusaka, never really brought the ANC administration into the modern world. He is a dour and often surly character, making him an even more unlikely choice for the country's key diplomatic post.

This appointment can probably be explained by the desire of deputy president and super-diplomat Thabo Mbeki to keep a close hand on the Foreign Affairs portfolio with an incumbent who owes his appointment to him.

Nzo joined the ANC Youth League in 1950 and was active in the campaigns of that period. In 1958 he was elected to both the Transvaal and National Executive Committees of the ANC. After being repeatedly detained, he left the country in 1964 and worked as the ANC's deputy representative in Cairo and chief representative in India. In 1969, he was elected ANC secretary-general, a position he retained for 22 years. He was also a South African Communist Party member and received the USSR Order of Friendship in 1985.

On his return home, and removed from the protective cover of exile, he was voted out of office in 1991. He maintained his position on the NEC, however. In 1992, he took over as deputy head of the ANC's Security Department and then headed the Directorate of Intelligence. Questions were raised in the Motsuenyane Commission of Inquiry into abuses in ANC camps in exile about what he should have known and done about conditions in these camps.

Born 19 June 1925. Family: wife Regina Vuyelwa, one adult son.

Ogilvie Thompson, Julian   The quintessential colonial, the chairman of the Anglo American Corporation strikes the British as having a manner and accent more English than the English. As befits possibly the most powerful businessman in South Africa, his charm hides a steely temper.

In the tradition of Anglo, JOT, as he is commonly known, is a Rhodes scholar who went into Anglo soon after graduating from Oxford. His progression to the top seat of the giant conglomerate's 44 Main Street headquarters in 1990 after his predecessor Gavin Relly retired was a smooth one, though he is seen to represent the more conservative strain in the liberal Anglo. He has vigorously defended the group's size against those who think it is the epitome of the over-concentration of economic power that exists in South Africa.

Both Ogilvie Thompson and Relly were professional managers, in contrast to previous chairman Harry Oppenheimer and his father, Sir Ernest Oppenheimer. But Ogilvie Thompson fits into the Anglo corporate mould as well as Relly did. A golfer and trout fisherman, he is articulate, intelligent and impervious to criticism from the hoi polloi. He is also quite comfortable with the Anglo family business set-up, which may yet see third-in-line Nicholas Oppenheimer take over the chairmanship.

Born 27 January 1934. Family: wife Tessa, four adult children.

Olivier, Pierre Johannes   One of the most widely published members of the Bench, Judge Olivier spent 12 years as an academic, at the universities of Pretoria, Port Elizabeth and the Orange Free State, before being appointed to the Orange

Free State Bench in 1985. He has written on delict, family law and legal fictions, but there is nothing fictional about his contribution, through the South African Law Commission, to the development of a Bill of Rights for the country.

Judge Olivier was seconded to the commission in 1986 as vice-chairman, to work with its chairman, Appeal Court Judge JJ van Heerden. Since then he has spent most of his time with the commission, although he has assisted on the supreme court when needed.

During his term on the commission, he and Judge van Heerden helped move the National Party government towards accepting the need for a Bill of Rights. Judge Olivier was asked to study this question, and became convinced that a radical shift was needed away from the then commonly held view that apartheid and separate development could be justified through the application of group rights. Instead, he pushed for a charter to safeguard individual rights.

Much of the groundwork in preparing the government psychologically and ideologically for negotiations was done by the commission through its reports, which had a great impact on the outlook of the Pretoria establishment.

Judge Olivier has been a strong defender of the commission's independence, and his thinking — as seen through the work of the commission — outstripped that of the previous government on many issues.

He was appointed as an acting Appeal Court judge in 1993.

Judge Olivier graduated from the University of Pretoria, and has a doctorate from Leiden in the Netherlands. He was a member of the Bloemfontein Bar from 1973 to 1985.

Born 11 August 1936. Family: wife Helene, four adult children.

Omar, Abdullah Mohamed ('Dullah')   Unlike many of his new cabinet colleagues, Justice minister Omar's courtroom experience has always been outside the dock, and his political experience always inside the country. Born in Cape Town in 1934, one of 11 children, he has a BA LLB from the University of Cape Town. He was admitted as an attorney in 1960 and as an advocate in 1982.

His political career began at school when he joined the boycott of the Van Riebeeck Festival in 1952. His work as a civil rights lawyer began almost the day he opened the doors of his first legal practice, when the Pan Africanist Congress executive asked him to act for them. Next day, they were all arrested, and he was immediately plunged into political legal work.

This was the start of a legal career in which he acted for accused from almost every anti-apartheid tendency, and visited Robben Island several times a week to see his clients, one of whom was Nelson Mandela.

In 1985, while a member of the Cape Bar, he was detained twice. The first detention, under Section 29 of the Internal Security Act, lasted two months. Just 10 days after his release he was detained again, this time under Emergency regulations. Omar brought an unsuccessful supreme court action for his release, and the resulting Appellate Division decision on the rights of detainees, Omar v the State President, proved one of the most important, and most depressing, of the Emergency years.

Omar is a long-time opponent of the death penalty. From his vantage point of experience as both an attorney and an advocate, he supports fusion of the professions. He is a comparatively recent convert to the African National Congress: he was a staunch member of the Unity Movement until this organisation refused to join the United Democratic

Front. Then, at least partly influenced by his client, Mandela, he switched parties.

Although sitting behind the Justice desk in the capital represents something of an achievement for him, he readily admits that the women of his family beat him to Pretoria: his wife, Fareda Ally, comes from a strongly political clan, and her sister, Rahida, was one of the leaders of the women's march to Pretoria in 1955.

Born 26 May 1934. Family: wife Fareda Ally, two sons and a daughter.

Oppenheimer, Harry Frederick　　Harry Oppenheimer took over the reins of Anglo American from his father Sir Ernest Oppenheimer in 1957 and brought the family company to even greater heights, still reputedly controlling the giant empire with only an eight per cent shareholding, a stake enhanced by a web of cross-holdings.

Now in his 80s, Harry O, as he is known, bowed out of direct management around 13 years ago, but still commands respect in the business world and liberal circles.

With his cultured mien covering an iron will and razor-sharp business sense, he came to personify the Anglo aristocratic style, the steel hand in the velvet glove.

An active politician himself, serving as United Party MP for Kimberley for nine years, he has been a long-time supporter of the Democratic Party and its predecessors, and brokered the meeting that led to Zach de Beer taking over the party leadership.

He also set up the Urban Foundation in 1976, in response to the gathering political crisis, to lobby for reform and improve living conditions in the townships. That Oppenheimer failed to intervene to stop the closure of the *Rand Daily Mail* in 1985 remains a blot on his copybook, and Anglo's.

Born 28 October 1908. Family: wife Bridget, two adult children, five grandchildren.

Oppenheimer, Nicholas   Diffident and unassuming, Oppenheimer is the heir apparent to the Anglo American throne, and living evidence of the dynastic family culture that lies at the heart of the Anglo empire.

Aside from evincing a passionate interest in cricket — to the extent of having his own private cricket ground built — Nicky Oppenheimer is an enigma. He is quiet and private but clearly no empty suit. Having gone the usual top Anglo executive route of a PPE at Oxford, he is now deputy chairman and executive director of Anglo American, chairman of Amgold, deputy chairman of De Beers, and chairman of the London operation of the Central Selling Organisation diamond cartel.

Will he slide into the chairmanship of Anglo when Julian Ogilvie Thompson retires? It seems highly probable, but not absolutely certain.

Born 8 June 1945. Family: wife Orcilia, one son.

Otto, Reginald   Lieutenant-General Reginald (Reg) Otto was appointed chief of the Army in January 1995.

A career soldier with a background in armoured warfare applications, Otto is fluent in Zulu.

Born in Krugersdorp, he was first commissioned in 1963 while serving in 1 Special Service Battalion, an armoured unit. In 1976 he became commander of the unit. From 1980 until 1983 he served as commander of the armoured training school.

Otto served as staff officer, projects, at Army Headquarters from 1983 until 1986, when he became commander of the Orange Free State Command. Before being appointed as chief of the Army he was commander of the Eastern Transvaal Command.

Born 9 July 1943. Family: wife Jacoba Wilhelmina (Kowie) Kleynhans, two sons and two daughters.

Pahad, Aziz   The contrast between Aziz Pahad and his brother Essop could not be greater: the latter is a large man who wears the leather jackets and checked shirts romantically associated with the Communist Party, of which he is a leader. The former — a slim, trim man two heads shorter — is more frequently seen in the dark blue suit which is the diplomat's trademark. Prior to his appointment as deputy foreign minister, he was one of the African National Congress's most senior diplomats under former international affairs head Thabo Mbeki.

Aziz Pahad's appointment is a reflection of the deputy president's faith in his ability to be his own link-man and watchdog over Foreign minister Alfred Nzo. Pahad is widely seen as the man who will drive the ministry in a crucial time when South Africa is re-establishing its place in international forums.

Born in Schweizer-Reneke in the Western Transvaal, Pahad grew up in a politically active family which soon moved to Johannesburg, where he attended school. His father was a Transvaal Indian Congress activist, and his mother and other family members participated in passive resistance and defiance campaigns from his early childhood.

Following a banning order before the Rivonia treason trial, Pahad left South Africa in 1964 because he felt he could work more effectively against apartheid from outside the country. 'We believed freedom would come in five years,' he recalls. 'It was always five years, for years and years.'

Following a stint at Sussex University, where he earned a Master's degree in international relations, Pahad worked full time for the ANC, responsible for building solidarity organisations in Europe. On the road for weeks at a time, he would often travel hundreds of kilometres to address groups of two or three people. 'It was all worth while,' he says, 'because those organisations grew into powerful lobbies against the South African government.' He found the solidarity movements in support of Vietnam and Angola inspiring, and names Bishop Trevor Huddlestone and Canon Collins as significant figures in his life in exile.

As a member of the ANC's Politico-Military Council, Pahad was involved in all of the early meetings with South African academics, journalists and business people in Dakar, Paris, and Leverkusen, and in the briefings prior to the Groote Schuur meeting.

The widely travelled diplomat faces the task of reshaping foreign policy to serve South Africa's broad economic and political interests after four decades as the international face of apartheid.

Born 25 December 1940. Family: wife Sandra Black, one son, one stepdaughter.

Parsons, Raymond   An economist by training, the director-general of the South African Chamber of Business (Sacob) is the official voice of organised, white South African business, formed through the merger of the Association of Chambers of Commerce and the Federated Chamber of Industries in 1990. As a long-time professional business lobbyist in a country where business has been seen both as too close to apartheid and to the left of government, Parsons has had to maintain an acrobat's balance in treading the tightrope between political pressures and economic desires — not to mention handling the conflicting interests of various business groups, large and small.

Criticism has been that Sacob is over-confident of its own clout and Parsons 'too concerned with public image', but he has acquitted himself well in a difficult job.

Personal details are not available.

Phosa, Mathews   Of the African National Congress's regional premiers, Mathews Phosa is the least likely to have difficulty in matching Western Cape supremo Hernus Kriel when it comes to brash self-confidence. Secure in the knowledge of his overwhelming election victory in the Eastern Transvaal, the former ANC legal eagle is likely to be a leader in testing the limits of regional independence and room to manoeuvre under the constitution.

Phosa and Kriel have locked horns several times in the recent past, with the ever-smiling Phosa rarely bettered in arguments about such sensitive issues as joint South African Police/African National Congress investigations into the April 1993 murder of South African Communist Party leader Chris Hani and the September 1993 shootout between policemen and Walter Sisulu's bodyguards. But ANC constitutional experts intent on solidifying the centralist aspects of the new dispensation could find the two men joining forces in championing regional powers.

Phosa lists the law and business among his long-standing interests, and he has lost no time since being elected Eastern Transvaal premier in announcing a number of ambitious business projects for the region, most of them tourism-related. He appears to have particular faith in the gambling industry's potential to generate the resources he will need for implementation of the Reconstruction and Development Programme in his region.

After graduating from law school at the University of the North, Phosa made a name for himself among jurists when he fought the South African government's intention to hand over kaNgwane to Swaziland in the 1980s. He also won respect for his role in ANC underground operations: after military training in East Germany, he ran MK structures in the Eastern Transvaal.

But he is first and foremost a politician, a man who enjoys the limelight and the rough and tumble of crossing swords with his adversaries. He opted for the premiership of his home region rather than take his chances in the race for a position in the national cabinet.

Born in Mbombela township, Nelspruit, Phosa gained his political education from his mother, a nurse, but spent his early years with his grandfather in Potgietersrus, learning traditional skills such as hunting, fishing and tilling. He has since developed other interests, ranging from classical to Zairean music and karate.

Born 1 September 1952. Family: wife Yvonne, four children.

Radebe, Jeff Thamsanqa   Despite his moderate reputation, the minister of Public Works has been described by kwaZulu/Natal militant Harry Gwala as having 'one of the best political brains in the country'. He cut his teeth helping form a youth organisation in Durban's kwaMashu township before heading for exile where he served the African National Congress in several fields, including the information and international departments. The South African press declared him dead after the South African Defence Force's raid into Matola. In fact, he was in East Germany at the time, acquiring a Master's degree in law from Leipzig University.

He became involved in the ANC's underground structures and undertook a mission back into the country in 1986, was arrested and sentenced to 10 years on terrorism and other charges, reduced to six on appeal.

In 1990, he co-ordinated a hunger strike on Robben Island, forcing the government to release a batch of political prisoners. Shortly afterwards, he was elected ANC Southern Natal deputy chairman, and later chairman.

His star rose with Nelson Mandela when he became a strong proponent of peace talks with the Inkatha Freedom Party, though he also defended ANC guerrillas who were arrested in 1992 with a huge arms cache.

This is typical of the man — a master of sitting in all the pews of the ANC's broad church. He can be heard spouting militant rhetoric to township youths, touting to South African Communist Party members his political credentials as a student of the legendary Moses Mabhida, and promising market-orientated policies to businessmen. He makes a point of wooing the different ethnic elements of his constituency, appearing in a Nehru suit at samoosa functions, in a tuxedo at cocktail parties and in leopard skin at Zulu rallies.

Now holding an important 'delivery' portfolio, he has pledged to rid the kwaZulu/Natal region of its 'Cinderella status' in the national budget allocations.

Born 18 February 1953. Family: two children.

Ramaphosa, Cyril   The real surprise in the choice of the first cabinet in a democratic South Africa was the omission of Ramaphosa, secretary-general of the African National Congress. Ramaphosa had played a leading role in ANC and related politics for at least a decade, and in particular had been central to the success of the negotiations, so he was thought to be a certainty for a senior cabinet post. But, having lost the race for deputy president to Thabo Mbeki, he turned down the Foreign ministry and asked to stay out of the cabinet in order to rebuild the ANC organisational structure. He was at least partly brought back into the system by his appointment as chairman of the Constitutional Assembly: the two houses of Parliament, sitting together, to write the country's constitution.

Ramaphosa quickly set about restructuring the ANC and, with his usual super-efficiency and utter determination and drive, soon had it down to a lean structure, ready to start preparing for 1995's crucial local government elections. But there were those who resented his strong hand and rumours began to surface of concerted opposition to his re-election as secretary-general, but this challenge never materialised at the 1994 congress. Part of the problem appears to be the weight of his two formidable tasks in the ANC and the Constitutional Assembly.

Like so many of his generation, Ramaphosa came from a black consciousness background. Born to modest beginnings in Soweto, he studied law at the University of the North and later Unisa and held positions in the South African Students' Organisation, the Black People's Convention and the Students' Christian Movement. He spent long periods in detention in 1974 and 1976.

The Council of Unions of South Africa plucked him from relative obscurity to form the National Union of Mineworkers (NUM), where he quickly proved his organisational and strategic abilities. He broke with black consciousness when he led the NUM into the Congress of South African Trade Unions and played an important role in union-liberation movement relations thereafter. In 1987, he led mineworkers in one of the largest strikes in the country's history.

Plucked out of the unions in 1991 when he was elected ANC secretary-general, he played a crucial role in reorganising the ANC and in steering negotiations towards success, where his personal ability to relate to government negotiator Roelf Meyer was an important factor in achieving the necessary breakthroughs. This made him a hot favourite for the deputy presidency, but the matter was in the hands of President Nelson Mandela and he had never shown much affinity for Ramaphosa.

Wherever he may end up in the political hierarchy, Ramaphosa's experience, skill and drive will ensure that he remains a major influence in national politics.

Born 17 November 1952. Family: three children.

Ramatlhodi, Ngoako   Northern Transvaal premier Ramatlhodi does not believe the mystique of political leaders requires a closed office door. This is not because he is unused to power or responsibility: he served as personal assistant to two African National Congress presidents, Nelson Mandela and Oliver Tambo, and was deputy registrar at the University of the North before leaving the position to head the party's election list in the region.

Genuinely unassuming, he sought a career as an academic and a poet, not as a politician. A distinguished career in the ranks of the ANC's Umkhonto weSizwe does not receive much mention in his curriculum vitae, while his academic achievements are listed.

Expelled from the University of the North for political activity, he joined the ANC in 1978. Two years later he joined MK and by the mid-1980s was head of its political military council in the northern Transvaal — a border area of great strategic importance for the insurgent army.

In 1988, he received a Master's degree in law from the University of Zimbabwe and he joined the ANC president's office, where he worked as a speech writer and administrative secretary until 1992, returning to South Africa with other exiles after the unbanning of the ANC. In 1992 he left to take up the position of deputy registrar at the University of the North.

The ANC has 96 per cent support in the Northern Transvaal, which is one of South Africa's least developed provinces. The region's premier will have to show wisdom beyond his years to deal with the high expectations of its people.

Born 21 August 1955. Family: wife Ouma Mathuding, one son.

Ramphele, Mamphela   As someone who has been an activist and a community worker since the repressive days of the 1970s and who has made a name for herself in three different academic fields, Dr Ramphele is a redoubtable figure.

Ramphele is both the first black person and the first woman to have been appointed to her present post as deputy vice-chancellor of the University of Cape Town. While holding this position, she has continued to research and to write. Her most recent book is *A Bed Called Home: Life in the Migrant Labour Hostels of Cape Town*. Earlier publications include *Restoring the Land*, which she edited, and *Bounds of Possibility*, a book on the Black Consciousness Movement, which she co-edited. Together with Professor Francis Wilson, she co-authored *Uprooting Poverty*; this book grew out of their research for the second Carnegie Inquiry into Poverty and Development in South Africa and won several awards, including the prestigious Noma Award for Publishing in Africa.

She is chairman of the board of the Independent Development Trust. She is also a member of the boards of

Anglo American, the Old Mutual Foundation and the Open Society Foundation.

Ramphele qualified as a doctor in the mid-1970s. Shortly afterwards, her work with the Black Consciousness Movement resulted in her banishment to the Northern Transvaal, where she founded the Ithuseng Community Health Programme.

She enrolled at UCT when the banning order was lifted and completed diplomas in tropical health and public health and a BComm in administration before starting a PhD in social anthropology. She was appointed deputy vice-chancellor in 1991.

As a powerful intellectual with a long record of community service, her voice and influence carry far.

Born 28 December 1947. Family: two sons, the eldest born some weeks after the death of his father, Black Consciousness leader Steve Biko.

Reddy, Govin   Reddy's appointment as chief executive of the South African Broadcasting Corporation's radio section provoked a storm of criticism, based on his alleged links to the African National Congress. The timing — he was one of three senior appointments announced simultaneously, two of them of ANC members — probably had a great deal to do with the criticism, for Reddy's links with the organisation have never been particularly strong; in fact, he is not a member. Suspicion that he might be biased all the same may have been provided by his 10-year stint in exile from 1981.

Prior to being appointed to the SABC, Reddy was deputy director of the Institute for the Advancement of Journalism. Although fully qualified in 'struggle credentials' with a stint in detention in 1976 and a banning order, he is not considered ever to have been a hard-core activist.

The chief executive for radio was born in Durban and has held a variety of media positions in and outside the country, ranging from a post as head of current affairs on the Zimbabwe Broadcasting Corporation's Radio 4 to editor-in-chief of *Africa South*, a regional magazine.

Since his appointment, he has been pursuing his stated plan of making Radio South Africa a truly South African public broadcaster, especially in the news services. He has moved quickly: a substantial number of black people have been hired for the audible posts of radio journalists, previously the preserve of white employees.

Born 16 June 1943. Family: wife Tessa, four children.

Rupert, Anton   In his 70s, but still fit enough to play an active role in the affairs of Rembrandt, the Afrikaner conglomerate he founded, this legendary Afrikaans entrepreneur uttered the oft-quoted phrase about black workers during the dark years of apartheid: 'If they don't eat, we don't sleep.'

Rembrandt has long been identified with the rise of Afrikaner capital. It is famous for, among other things, its partnership approach to business and its regime of secrecy. The partnership concept Rupert once summed up as 'he who covets all will lose all', and Rembrandt prefers buying a stake in businesses rather than outright control.

The secrecy has lessened over the years, but Rembrandt, like Rupert, likes to keep a low profile, an approach which aided its overseas expansion during the sanctions years. At the same time it has diversified from its base in tobacco and alcohol products into every nook and cranny of the economy. It has also expanded overseas, and then hived off rand-hedge stock Richemont, which owns luxury brands like Dunhill and Mont Blanc.

Rupert has paid a great deal of attention to conservation and his company has been prominent in funding fine arts. He has also played a key role in the Small Business Development Corporation, and although he was not one of apartheid's most outspoken business opponents, his preaching of internationalism and modernisation contributed to the change of thinking which led to apartheid's demise. Nevertheless, the company's secretiveness, the boost it is supposed to have got from Afrikaner nationalism, and its sinful birth from liquor will not endear it to the politically correct.

Born 4 October 1916. Family: wife Huberte, three adult children.

Rupert, Johann   Johann Rupert has more or less taken over the reins of the Afrikaans conglomerate Rembrandt, which his father Anton built up from a small tobacco company. He made his mark in business before going into the family group in 1985, working at Chase Manhattan and Lazard Freres in New York for five years after finishing his degree and national service. Using that experience he returned to South Africa to take over the then bankrupt Rand Merchant Bank, spruce it up and sell at a profit what is now one of South Africa's most successful merchant banks.

He oversaw the splitting of the Rembrandt empire into South African and foreign assets by forming Richemont, of which he is managing director, and was key in the diversification of the group out of tobacco products into luxury goods such as Cartier, Dunhill and Mont Blanc.

Johann Rupert was one of the first leading Afrikaners to come out publicly against apartheid in his student days, and he supported then president FW de Klerk's reform initiatives.

Like his father before him, he thinks globally, is reticent to the point of secrecy and tends to take the long view of events.

Born 1 June 1950. Family: wife Gaynor, three children.

Sack, Steven Joseph   The director of the Johannesburg Art Foundation is the newest and most junior of that loose affiliation of cultural polydactyls who have fingers in more pies than most people have fingers. Often and with some justification referred to as the 'fine arts mafia', the group in question — whose membership includes Johannesburg director of culture Christopher Till, the South African National Gallery's Marilyn Martin and the University of the Witwatersrand's Alan Crump, among others — decides most of what happens in the fine arts, from museums policy to the awarding of major prizes and senior appointments in the public sphere and community arts.

Sack is pre-eminently the new South African designate member of the 'mafia'. His background is left wing; he was a resident of long-standing in the Crown Mines community, an active participant in the United Democratic Front-aligned Johannesburg Democratic Action Committee (Jodac), and a founder member of the Junction Avenue Theatre Company, as much a bold socio-cultural experiment as a producer of dramatic arts. In 1985 and 1986 Sack served as director of the African Institute of Art at Funda Centre in Soweto. Even today the energies he brings to the numerous committees on which he sits are largely directed towards development and community programmes.

He qualified as an art and English teacher at Wits University before studying for a BA (Fine Arts) at Unisa, awarded with distinction, and lectured in fine arts at Unisa during the 1980s. On the death of the Johannesburg Art Foundation's founder director, Bill Ainslie, Sack was appointed to replace him in the largely city council-sponsored institution. He has taken it in a more professional direction but continued to be active in fields related to community cultural development. Since 1992 he has sat on the committees of the National Arts Coalition and the Art Educators' Association, holding the treasurer's portfolio.

He continues, though infrequently, to make artworks himself, participating in group exhibitions, has written numerous academic and other articles and delivered papers, many on the subject of 'people's parks' built by community youths in strife-torn township areas during the 1980s. Among the exhibitions he has curated is The Neglected Tradition: Towards a History of South African Art, 1930-1988, at the Johannesburg Art Gallery.

Born 11 December 1951. Family: wife artist and critic Ruth Jacobson, a teenaged son and daughter.

Schutte, Danie   The National Party's new leader in kwaZulu/Natal and previous minister of Home Affairs is known to have strong sympathies with the Inkatha Freedom Party, and is also popular in white right-wing circles. With only nine members in the provincial Parliament, however, his once mighty party has been all but obliterated in its former provincial stronghold.

Schutte — who has been demoted to just another MP in the National Assembly — now serves as the NP's chief spokesman on justice. The man he replaced as Natal leader, George Bartlett, is the only NP minister in the provincial cabinet of kwaZulu/Natal.

Schutte was born in Pretoria and obtained his BComm Honours degree and LLB at the University of Stellenbosch, where he was a member of the Afrikaanse Studentebond executive.

Born 13 June 1947. Family: wife Alphia, three daughters.

September, Connie   Such a committed trade unionist is September that she lists 'Cosatu and mountain climbing' as hobbies — in that order. She was born into a working-class Cape Town family and learned activism in civic associations working on electricity and other campaigns on the Cape Flats.

She started her working life at the Rex Trueform factory in 1980 and continues to work there even though she is the second deputy vice-president of the Congress of South African Trade Unions and the federation's only woman national office-bearer. September was elected to that position while serving as the national treasurer of the South African Clothing and Textile Workers' Union (Sactwu). She has risen steadily through trade union ranks since 1980, honing her skills in the series of mergers which led to the formation of Sactwu in 1989.

She is at the forefront of the new generation of second and third-tier Cosatu leaders to whom many are looking to fill the gap left by the departure of the federation's best strategists to Parliament. More unionist than political activist, she is known to favour greater distance between Cosatu and the African National Congress.

Born 26 June 1959. Family: one teenaged daughter.

Sexwale, Gabriel ('Tokyo')   As premier of Gauteng, by far the most important province, Sexwale will play an enormously important role in the overall success or failure of the Reconstruction and Development Programme. So far, the reviews are mixed: Sexwale has impressed with his leadership and energy, but dismayed some with rash statements that pander to populism and often appear out of step with the central government's pragmatism. In particular, he has promised 150 000 houses in his first year in office — an almost certainly unachievable goal — and rejected notions that these should be anything less than full-service, four-roomed homes.

Sexwale is probably the first South African leader whose career was built on television. It was his spontaneously tearful on-camera response to the assassination of his close friend, South African Communist Party chief Chris Hani, in April 1993 that shot him into national consciousness. He went on to play an important role in calming mass emotions and replaced Hani as the voice of the ANC militants urging support for negotiation compromises. With his sonorous voice and powerful military bearing, he is one of the most telegenic of ANC leaders.

An ANC member since students days and a specialist in conventional warfare — he was trained in the Soviet Union, specialising in army engineering — he has gained a reputation as a cross between a fiery populist and a skilful negotiator.

He went underground in the 1970s after matriculating in Soweto and completing a short spell in the Black Consciousness Movement, and in 1975 went into exile.

On his return, he was arrested and convicted of terrorism and conspiracy and jailed on Robben Island, where he spent 13 years and met his wife, lawyer Judy van Vuuren. Four months after his release from prison under the amnesty agreement, he was elected to the ANC's executive committee in the PWV region. His popularity was confirmed when he took the position of PWV chair and a seat on the ANC national executive. He was a natural choice to lead the ANC election campaign in the region.

Since his election, he has spent much of his time fighting fires. Rushing from problem to problem, he has impressed many with his willingness to dirty his hands in difficult and tense situations. His long-term problem, however, will be to move the provincial bureaucracy from Pretoria to his

Johannesburg headquarters and put it to work on long-term projects.

Much depends on him: if he fails in South Africa's financial and industrial hub, the rest of the country will fail with him.

Born 5 March 1954. Family: wife Judy, three children.

Shaik, Moe As the strategic thinker and de facto number two of African National Congress Intelligence and Security, Shaik looks back on years as an underground cadre and a leading Vula operative in Natal, but he claims that optometry remains his abiding interest. And indeed, his CV shows him graduating cum laude with a Master's degree in 1993 from the University of Durban-Westville where he also lectures, an achievement all the more impressive because most of his time has been spent on intelligence work.

Now Shaik is among those in the ANC who are feeling increasing pressure to give up their civilian careers for a future in the bureaucracy or security forces. There is a greater need for his clarity of vision within national intelligence structures, argue his compatriots, than in the Optometry Department at Westville. Weeks after the April 1994 election, Shaik still professed a preference for 'the indulgences and the irresponsibilities of academic life'; and he hoped to learn to sail. At the same time, he promised he would 'keep a special eye' on intelligence matters no matter where he was. Should he give in, and go into government, he is most likely to be number two to Intelligence head Joe Nhlanhla.

Involved in negotiations over the integration of the armed forces and intelligence services before the elections, he is destined to remain intimately connected with the country's security matters for decades to come, whether as a policy-maker outside the services, or as a senior operative. As someone who believes in transparent government and the need for clear direction of the intelligence and security services by a democratically elected Parliament, he will work to prevent the creation of a new, secretive and all-powerful securocracy.

Born 26 August 1959. Family: wife Suraya Jacobs and two collies.

Shilowa, Sam General secretary of the Congress of South African Trade Unions, once a security guard and shop steward of the Transport and General Workers' Union (T&GWU), Sam Shilowa has had a meteoric rise within the labour movement.

Articulate and ambitious, he is seen by some unionists as being too close to the African National Congress, and to a lesser extent the South African Communist Party. His newfound taste for expensive designer suits and silk ties has also excited comment. Rumour has it that he filled his wardrobe when he seemed bound for the new Parliament, but was later persuaded to remain with the federation when Jay Naidoo — then general secretary, with Shilowa his deputy — topped the ANC list. He denies this.

Shilowa began his career by recruiting security guards for the T&GWU in the early 1980s. With incredible speed he rose to the vice-chairmanship of the Transvaal branch, the second vice-presidency and presidency of the union within two years. In 1993 he was elected Cosatu assistant general secretary and later that year general secretary.

Independent socialists and working-class ideologues in Cosatu fear that his outspoken support for the ANC-SACP-Cosatu alliance may prove increasingly problematic in the new era, as labour's interests diverge from those of the government. He insists, however, that the alliance will not be maintained at the expense of labour's independence. He points out that Cosatu criticised the Melamet Committee's recommendations on salaries of parliamentarians, that it opposed increased defence spending in the budget, and that when Defence minister Joe Modise tried to interdict the *Weekly Mail & Guardian* to prevent publication of reports about top ANC officials who might have been agents for the former government, Cosatu was among the first to criticise Modise.

Shilowa has interests outside the trade union movement: soccer and mbube music.

Born: 30 April 1958. Family: wife Wendy Luhabe, a human rights consultant, and one son from a previous marriage.

Simpson-Anderson, Robert   Despite the name, the chief of the Navy is an Afrikaner, which becomes evident whenever the vice-admiral greets even the most distant acquaintance with the warmth of *mense van die plaas*. As if to prove the Navy's claim to be the senior service, he also speaks Dutch and German — and, of course, the language of naval tradition, English.

Born in Pretoria, he grew up in the Alexandria district of the Eastern Province before volunteering for the military after matriculating. He holds a BMil degree and an MBL.

The Air Force Gymnasium doesn't seem to have been to his liking, and by 1962 Simpson-Anderson was well on his way to a naval career which has spanned ocean-going command as well as several shorebound stints. Besides completing the Royal Navy's specialist navigation course, he has commanded the South African Naval Academy and the generals' kindergarten, the Military Academy at Saldanha Bay.

Simpson-Anderson is anything but a desk sailor. He proudly wears the strike craft commander's badge, having been the first naval officer to take charge of one of the 450-ton vessels which today are the backbone of the Navy's fighting capability. The admiral would like to see this change: he rarely misses an opportunity to argue the case for a new flotilla of corvettes, battleships five times the size of the strike craft and with the blue-water capability the smaller boats lack. He is dismissive of suggestions that South Africa, with its long coastline, should downgrade the Navy to a coastguard service, arguing instead for better anti-submarine, fisheries protection and long-distance capabilities within the fleet.

Born 4 July 1942. Family: wife Geesje.

Sisulu, Max   As chairman of the National Assembly select committee on the Reconstruction and Development Programme, Sisulu will play an important role as the parliamentary watchdog on the implementation of the government's central programme.

Born into the Sisulu dynasty, he had most of his education abroad, beginning with a pre-university preparatory course in Moscow. He earned a Master's degree in economics at the Plekhanov Economic Institute in the former Soviet Union. That was followed by a research fellowship at the University of Amsterdam to look into transnational corporations and South Africa's electronics industry, and a course in industrial restructuring at the University of Sussex's Institute of Development Studies.

He rose rapidly through ANC ranks, as deputy head of the Youth League, unofficial African National Congress representative in Hungary and, in 1986, head of the ANC's Economic Planning Department. On his return from exile in

1990, he became involved in setting up the Macro-Economic Research Group (Merg). He spent some time as a fellow at Harvard University on an MA in public administration.

Born 23 August 1945. Family: wife author Elinor Batezat Sisulu, four children.

Sisulu, Zwelakhe   When Zwelakhe Sisulu was appointed in November 1993 as assistant to the then CEO of the South African Broadcasting Corporation, Wynand Harmse, talk was that he was being groomed to take over that post. The SABC dismissed the rumour, but when Sisulu finally did take over several months later, it came as no surprise.

Sisulu, son of African National Congress stalwarts Walter and Albertina Sisulu, is a graduate of both the mainstream and the alternative press — he worked for the *Rand Daily Mail*, *Weekend World* and *Sunday Post*, and in 1984 was awarded a Nieman Fellowship at Harvard University. Soon after his return he was appointed founding editor of *New Nation* — a post he could fulfil only part of the time, in between detentions and restriction orders.

A few weeks after taking over the post as CEO of the SABC Sisulu had a different sort of baptism of fire when he had to deal with the furore raised by Chief Mangosuthu Buthelezi's unscheduled appearance on a television actuality show, Agenda; the chief allegedly threatened an interviewee, unaware that the cameras were rolling, capturing and transmitting the drama as it unfolded. Sisulu's response was to institute an inquiry into the incident.

He has had to encourage change within the corporation while ensuring an influx of new talent. He has also had to carve out a place for the public broadcaster as the Independent Broadcasting Authority (IBA) re-apportions access to the airwaves.

At the time of going to press Sisulu had unveiled plans to reorganise the SABC into 11 radio stations — one for each official language — and three television stations: a fully fledged public broadcaster, a fully blown commercial channel and a hybrid channel with two components, one devoted to public service and the other component, commercial.

This move was criticised from some quarters as unfairly consolidating the position of the SABC before the IBA had finished its inquiry into the role of the state broadcaster.

Born 17 December 1950. Family: wife Zodwa, three children.

Skosana, Peter   The credentials of Gauteng's MEC for Arts and Culture, Sport and Recreation lie more obviously in the field of 'struggle' than they do in any of the areas he is now responsible for. But his own involvement in such matters — he is both a balletomane and an enthusiastic member of the Orlando Pirates supporters club — belie the raised-fist image that observation might conjure.

Like many another member of his generation in the townships, in his case Sharpeville, Skosana was involved in liberation politics full time before he completed his education, and was expelled from the Northern Transvaal Technikon in 1984 as a result of his political activities. Deputy president of the Southern Transvaal branch of the South African Youth Congress between 1987 and 1990, Skosana has since served as chairperson, treasurer and secretary for education in the African National Congress Youth League for the PWV region.

He is described by those who know him well as quiet, thoughtful and considered, but formidable on points of principle. He indicated the priorities he would be pursuing at a meeting of the ANC's Gauteng Department of Arts and Culture in June 1994, shortly after his appointment. He stressed a need to rehabilitate traditional forms of African culture at the same time as developing Western modes among the disadvantaged sectors of the community, thus moving towards a viably national culture. He committed himself to pursuing education in the arts and to making facilities, like community arts centres and libraries, available in areas where they previously had not existed.

At the same time, he has come out strongly in favour of freedom of expression and has stressed that while his ministry seeks to support the arts, 'we do not intend to control them' and, as guarantee, supports an independent system of arts councils to administer the arts.

Born 29 March 1961. Family: three children.

Skweyiya, Zola Sydney Themba   Among Skweyiya's early moves as minister of Public Service and Administration has been the announcement of plans for affirmative action in the civil service, dominated at the moment by white males.

He is a quiet 'backroom' worker, unused to the limelight and glare of publicity under which some of his cabinet colleagues have worked. Skweyiya was born in Simonstown into an impoverished community. His family moved to Port Elizabeth and he went to primary schools in New Brighton and in Retreat in Cape Town. His view of the world was broadened by tours run by the Catholic Church to show children the peninsula, and by a love of reading.

When his family moved back to Alice in the Eastern Cape, he went to Lovedale, a Methodist missionary educational institution. He took part in school boycotts against the introduction of Bantu education in 1953 and three years later joined the African National Congress. By the time he matriculated from Lovedale and enrolled in Fort Hare

University he had met and worked with ANC stalwart Govan Mbeki.

Skweyiya helped mobilise support among young people for Umkhonto weSizwe when Mandela went abroad to seek military training facilities. In 1963, fearing arrest, he fled to Tanzania and began working for the ANC in exile.

In 1978 he received a doctorate in law at the University of Leipzig. He is highly respected for his knowledge of constitutional law and has held several positions within the ANC; he has headed the Legal and Constitutional Department and chaired the constitutional committee. He helped set up the Centre for Development Studies and the South African Legal Defence Fund, both at the University of the Western Cape. He is also on the board of trustees of the National Commission for the Rights of Children.

His task now is one of the most formidable in the government of national unity: transforming the civil service without allowing the powerful 'old guard' to impede progress. Change in every other single department depends on his policies since all civil service appointments pass through the hands of his Commission.

Born 14 April 1942. Family: one adult child.

Spicer, Michael Wolseley   Spicer has slowly graduated from propagandist of the giant Anglo American conglomerate to policy-making itself. He was recently elevated to the board of the Anglo American Investment Trust (Anamint) as well as appointed a director of Anglo's long-term insurance company Southern Life and a member of the Anglo scenario forecasting team. He has been personal assistant to former Anglo chairman Gavin Relly, and has done time in various Anglo public affairs positions. He also served a spell as deputy director of the South African Institute of International Affairs.

An education at Johannesburg's elite St John's College was not followed by the studies at Oxford typical of Anglo's head honchos, but at Rhodes, where he obtained an MA with distinction. None the less, Spicer's views are Anglo's views, and he defends them with vigour.

Born 24 February 1953. Family: wife Irene, two sons.

Steyn, Pierre   When the South African National Defence Force decided to re-establish a defence secretariat with responsibility for financial control and fiscal administration, Lieutenant-General Steyn was a natural choice to head it. Part of the purpose of the new secretariat, says the SANDF, is to 'ensure more transparency, increase legitimacy and make the military more accountable' — and Steyn, before his retirement in 1993, was considered the 'Jesuit' of the former SADF: intellectual, incorruptible, an upholder of the highest principles of the service.

The new secretary of Defence joined the Air Force in 1960. A Mirage jet pilot, he moved rapidly through the ranks after taking top honours at the Military Academy and a Master's degree in business leadership through Unisa. As the SADF's number two — chief of Defence Force Staff — he was expected to move on to the top military job, but was passed over — probably because he accepted former President FW de Klerk's mandate in late 1992 to clean up Military Intelligence. The police seconded to him, however, failed to produce any hard evidence.

Steyn took early retirement and began a career in the private sector — a career now curtailed in favour of continuing government service.

Born 25 November 1942. Family: wife Fiona, three children.

Sunter, Clem   With casual demeanour and a disregard for sartorial niceties that borders on the eccentric, intellectual Sunter fits the description of the absent-minded Oxford don rather than that of a top executive. But Sunter is more than Anglo's chief soothsayer. He is chairman of Anglo American Property Services and Anglo's gold and uranium divisions.

Indeed, in the Anglo tradition Sunter read politics, philosophy and economics at Oxford before joining Charter Consolidated as a management trainee, moving in 1971 to Lusaka to work for Anglo, thence to be transferred to Anglo's head office in 1973.

Sunter shot to fame in South Africa for his part in Anglo's 'high-road, low-road' scenario exercise that probably played a role in influencing the then Nationalist government and National Party sympathisers to ditch then President PW Botha's iron rule and embrace change. Since then he has been a popular public speaker and has published, among other big-selling simple guides to life and business, *Pretoria Will Provide*, a little book which displays a neo-conservatism that matches the *laissez-faire* of his choice in ties and in interests: he plays golf, but he also plays folk guitar.

Born 8 August 1944. Family: wife Margaret Rowland, three children.

Terre'Blanche, Eugene   Despite court cases in London, unruly horses, purges of his organisation and continuous brushes with the law, Terre'Blanche has by now proved himself to be the true survivor and arch opportunist of the far right.

His fortunes may have waned considerably after the April 1994 elections, but Terre'Blanche has in the past proved that he cannot be disregarded for too long. With the Afrikaner Weerstandsbeweging (AWB) inextricably intertwined with the mixed fortunes of its leader and vice versa, the movement and the leader have moved quickly to try to claw their way back to their former stature as the most prominent right-wing belligerents of the transitional era. But Terre'Blanche this time around has had to contend with significantly more hurdles than in the past.

The AWB received what amounted to a near-death blow when a force consisting of about 500 AWB 'troops' mounted an excursion into Bophuthatswana during an uprising in March 1994, presumably to support the homeland government. A photograph of two members pleading for their lives — they were shot dead by an enraged Bophuthatswana Defence Force member — was flashed round the world, as were reports of AWB troops shooting residents at random.

The second blow to the organisation came when 30-odd members were taken into custody for their alleged involvement in a pre-election bombing spree. And many supporters left the organisation after the election, blaming Terre'Blanche for failing to deliver on his promise that an African National Congress government would never come to power.

Apart from a dwindling political power base, the economic future of the AWB does not look good, as the movement has always depended on new members joining to fill the coffers.

The post-election situation is a far cry from the period at the end of 1993 when the AWB had finished a three-year restructuring exercise to become the South African private army with the highest profile and possibly largest membership. Membership figures had risen from about 8 000 at the end of 1989 to an estimated 18 000 at the end of 1993, and the AWB and Terre'Blanche had for a time also found a broader acceptance in mainstream right-wing circles. But this has come to an end post-election, with all the mainstream parties of the right shunning Terre'Blanche and his movement.

Born 31 January 1944. Family: wife Martie, one daughter.

Tshwete, Steve Tshwete has taken to his job as minister of Sport with obvious relish. Characteristically, he was one of the first cabinet ministers out of the starting blocks and has taken a keen interest in the development plans of the different sports groups. Within the first two months of assuming office he released development blueprints that, if successful, could see the construction of sporting facilities in disadvantaged communities within the first year of the government of national unity.

He has been known since the early 1990s as 'Mr Fixit' for his crucial role in the unification of previously racially divided sporting bodies, and his cabinet appointment seemed a mere formality. But plans by President Nelson Mandela to offer the post as an olive branch to the National Party nearly put paid to that. Only frantic lobbying by the African National Congress Youth League and the National Olympic Sports Congress led to his inauguration day appointment.

An ANC national organiser before the party's decisive electoral victory, Tshwete was imprisoned for 15 years for Umkhonto weSizwe activities. Four years after his 1979 release he played a major role in the formation of the United Democratic Front, becoming one of its most visible spokesmen in his home region of the Eastern Cape. He eventually had to flee into exile for his activities in the UDF and clandestine ANC structures.

According to Tshwete, were it not for apartheid he would have preferred to represent South Africa in either cricket or rugby. It is largely a credit to him, and the acumen of the cricket board's Ali Bacher, that cricket has one of the best

development programmes already functional in the townships. And although unity in South African tennis is still
fragile, it was his intervention that made any kind of merger
— even a shaky one — possible. Tshwete's performance has
won him wide support among his parliamentary colleagues,
and he managed it even while filling in for two months for
Education minister Sibusiso Bengu when Bengu fell ill shortly
after his appointment.

Born 12 November 1938. Family: wife Pam, two children.

Turok, Ben   The appointment of fiery socialist Turok in
charge of the Reconstruction and Development Programme
in Gauteng initially perturbed business, but Turok has gone
out of his way to ask publicly for consultation and advice
from business to implement the RDP. In any case, it is a
fitting task for Turok, as one of the framers of the Freedom
Charter, forerunner of the RDP, and the speaker on its
economic clause at the Congress of the People in 1955.

Turok left South Africa on 10 February 1966 and came
back on 5 February 1990, three days after FW de Klerk's
famous speech unbanning the political opposition.

Turok is known for his fierce opposition to the International Monetary Fund and World Bank in Africa, and
headed the Institute for African Alternatives before being
elected to the regional authority.

Born 26 June 1927. Family: wife Mary Elizabeth Turok
(an MP), three adult sons.

Tutu, Desmond Mpilo   The Anglican archbishop of Cape
Town, the Most Reverend Desmond Tutu, always said that
he would put aside his political work when the politicians
were released from prison and returned from exile. He did so,
but appears to have assumed the role of unofficial court

chaplain, one of a number of religious leaders who, in the new mood of multiculturalism, officiated at the presidential inauguration and the opening of Parliament and the role of moral guardian, quick to criticise the government where he feels it necessary.

Tutu was born in Klerksdorp. He originally wanted to study medicine but the family couldn't finance it, so he pursued a career as a priest, being ordained in 1961 after studying at St Peter's Theological College in Rosettenville. He worked as a part-time curate in London and returned home in 1967 to become chaplain at Fort Hare University in Alice. After lecturing in Lesotho he worked for the World Council of Churches in London and in 1975 returned permanently to South Africa, where he was named dean of Johannesburg. Rising rapidly in church structures, he became bishop of Lesotho, general secretary of the South African Council of Churches and bishop of Johannesburg before being named archbishop of Cape Town in 1986.

His oratorical and political skills, his moral leadership, his powerful intellect and his administrative skills − not to mention his wicked sense of humour − thrust him to the fore during the 1980s when he filled the leadership gap in the black community.

He is a modest man; the Nobel Peace Prize he was awarded in 1984 does not appear on his CV.

Tutu, a statesman of some stature guided by an absolute sense of ethics and justice, is a great conciliator with a knack for getting it right politically. He has managed to rise above the demonic image cast on him by the conservative white media in the 1980s. Not afraid of controversy, he forbade his priests and bishops from participating in party politics before and during the April 1994 elections − a move appreciated by many of the clergy but defied by many others who, with

Tutu's wife, Leah, arranged for an advertisement during the campaigning proclaiming that the African National Congress's policies were compatible with the Gospel.

More recently, Tutu expressed outrage against high salaries for parliamentarians, charging that those now in government had promised to stop the gravy train, but they had stopped it only long enough to climb on. He has also been strongly outspoken against attempts to bolster the country's arms industry.

Born 7 October 1931. Family: wife Leah, four adult children.

Tyamzashe, Mthobi   Experience gained first as general secretary, then executive director of the National Sports Congress (NSC) will stand Tyamzashe in good stead in his new position as director-general of sport.

His years with the NSC saw him deeply involved in developing sports policy, administration, managing staff, organising meetings and conferences and representing the organisation at international conferences.

Born in East London, he matriculated from St John's College in Umtata, where he was general secretary of the Students' Christian Movement. He worked in the Ciskei Department of Agriculture as a personnel clerk before a government-sponsored bursary enabled him to go to the University of Fort Hare, where he majored in psychology and computer science, earning his BSc degree in 1978.

He returned to government service to work back his bursary and then joined an East London manufacturing company where he was to spend eight years, broken by a two-year sojourn in the United States where he did an MBA at Bowling Green State University in Ohio. Returning to East London in 1983, he oversaw the computerisation of the company. On completing the project, he joined a multi-national pharmaceutical company as a marketing assistant.

He was promoted to market research officer and then put in charge of personnel administration and employee and community services. This saw him responsible not only for recruitment, job evaluation and other aspects of personnel administration but also the company's affirmative action programmes and social responsibility projects. He also had to track the company's progress in terms of the Sullivan Code.

When the company was restructured, it was mutually agreed to make his post redundant; he already had his hands more than full as general secretary of the NSC. In 1993 he was promoted to executive director of the NSC.

Born 26 November 1954. Family: wife Queeneth, two children.

Valli Moosa, Mohammed   Valli Moosa has political experience and skill that belies his age. As deputy minister of Constitutional Development and Provincial Affairs, he will take much responsibility for the all-important and tough task of preparing local government structures for elections due in 1995.

He studied for a BSc at the University of Durban-Westville where he became active in black consciousness politics. He turned thereafter to the politics of local civic associations and played an important role in the revival of the Congress tradition in the Indian community.

He rose to prominence through the Anti-South African Indian Council Committee and later the United Democratic Front, where he was Transvaal general secretary, taking over the national office after the detention of Popo Molefe. He served as the co-ordinator and secretary of the African National Congress's negotiations commission, in which role he was an important ANC talks strategist and therefore a natural choice to serve as deputy to minister Roelf Meyer.

Born 9 February 1957. Family: wife journalist Elsabe Wessels, one daughter.

Van Graan, Michael   Van Graan is the commissar who isn't. Appointed in June this year as one of four special advisers to Arts and Culture, Science and Technology minister Ben Ngubane, Van Graan can be expected to play a crucial role in framing cultural policy in the new society. Nevertheless, in many ways his own cultural politics are those of the maverick, and his best efforts will be directed towards ensuring the independence of the arts and culture from state control.

Van Graan's own persona is anything but that of the dour Stalinist stereotype of the cultural worker. For some years he contributed a notably irreverent column to *South* newspaper; he has written a number of satirical plays, debunking the pretensions of cultural politicians; and was the driving force behind a nationwide Festival of Laughter, designed to poke fun, one week before the April 1994 elections, at all parties, politicians and platforms.

The political platform Van Graan occupies — that of the National Arts Coalition, where he serves as general secretary — was built largely out of disgruntlement with perceived attempts by the African National Congress's Department of Arts and Culture to direct and control cultural infrastructures and expression. Beginning as the Arts for All Campaign in early 1992, the initiative — largely driven by Van Graan throughout — led in December that year to a National Arts Policy Plenary and culminated a year later in formal consolidation as a National Arts Coalition (NAC).

The central goal of the NAC — to take culture and politics out of the party political arena while still working towards reconstruction and development — is one which enjoys widespread support. But Van Graan will be going against the bureaucratic grain in arguing for the dissolution of the old provincial performing arts councils — to date recipients of the lion's share of government funding in the arts — and their replacement by more broadly based distribution of funding via a national arts council.

Van Graan earned a BA at the University of Cape Town, majoring in English and drama. In 1986, with a strong background in activist Christian organisations, he served as organising secretary for the Institute for Contextual Theology's Kairos Document. Later that year he was on the executive of the Towards a People's Culture Festival, which the government banned as a security threat the day before it was to begin. In 1987, he was elected to the national executive of the Congress of South African Writers (Cosaw). In the following year he joined the Community Arts Project (Cap) in Cape Town as theatre co-ordinator, before being appointed director of Cap, a post which he held with some distinction until 1991 when funding dried up.

After a brief stint with the Human Sciences Research Council — 'the section in which I worked had not progressed to the post-apartheid era' — Van Graan left to work with Cosaw, first on a policy formulation project, then as national projects co-ordinator, before administrative crises again led to his resignation. At this point he started the ball rolling that would become the NAC. He serves on various arts and cultural committees. In 1994, he was appointed director of the newly established Bartel Arts Trust.

Born 31 August 1959. Family: wife Janet Purcell, one child.

Van Niekerk, Andre Isak ('Kraai')   The National Party's Northern Cape leader, now a senator, is one of the very few

NP ministers to keep their posts in the government of national unity. Van Niekerk was made minister of Agriculture in 1991 under FW de Klerk, and President Nelson Mandela has kept him in that job.

Born in Natal, Van Niekerk was a part-time merino sheep farmer who embarked on a political career when he was elected MP for Prieska in 1981. He was made deputy minister of Agriculture in 1986, and became minister of Agriculture and Water Affairs in the all-white House of Assembly in 1989.

He was widely expected to become Northern Cape premier, but the NP was unexpectedly beaten into second place by the African National Congress, putting paid to his ambitions. Although in his post he must concentrate on South Africa and its land, his major outside interest — stamp collecting — encourages an international outlook.

Born 7 October 1938. Family: wife Theresa, three sons.

Viljoen, Constand   Thrust into prominence from relative obscurity and subsequently cast as the prime symbol of the right wing's resurgence before the April 1994 election, Viljoen has seemingly come to terms with his new political role as leader of the Freedom Front and the driving force behind the Volkstaat Council.

In early 1993 he regarded his initial involvement in right-wing politics as a short-term affair. This view was soon overtaken by events and the cut and thrust of right-wing politics before the elections.

Finding himself on a runaway train of others' making, Viljoen soon emerged as his own man, eventually alienating a large part of his constituency by deciding at the last moment to participate in the elections. This decision was all the more remarkable as, more than anyone else, he had succeeded in uniting the broad right wing during the preceding months.

He has won the grudging respect of his adversaries as well as the admiration of his followers. Nevertheless he made some serious errors of judgement in the period leading up to the election. The ill-fated excursion of right-wing forces into Bophuthatswana in March 1994 and his initial association with the Afrikaner Weerstandsbeweging are some examples.

He was born in Standerton where he matriculated in 1951. He started his studies in agricultural engineering at the University of Pretoria, but a lack of funds saw an unplanned switch of career to the South African Defence Force, and with the SADF footing the bill, he obtained a BSc (Mil) in 1955. The following year he was commissioned as an artillery officer.

In 1976 he was appointed chief of the Army and it was while holding the post that he personally took part in several military incursions into Angola. This gave birth to his reputation as a soldier's general.

In 1980 Viljoen was appointed chief of the SADF. He retired five years later. Breeding cattle in the Ohrigstad area ever since, he only recently became active in right-wing politics.

Born 28 October 1933. Family: wife Risti, five children.

Wessels, Leon   Personal disappointment at not being nominated for a ministerial position in the cabinet of national unity turned into joy for the amiable Wessels when he was unanimously elected by MPs to the post of vice-chairman of the powerful Constitutional Assembly. He had been Manpower minister in the cabinet of FW de Klerk, and his election to his new post was not without controversy: the African National Congress caucus wanted one of its own members — and preferably a woman — as assistant to chairman Cyril Ramaphosa. Frantic behind-the-scenes negotiations preceded the election, and the fact that he made it is seen as an indication of the high esteem in which Wessels is held in ANC ranks.

The first National Party cabinet member ever seen on TV lifting a clenched fist and calling 'Viva!' ('Viva negotiations!' he shouted while addressing demonstrators outside the World Trade Centre), Wessels has embraced the new South Africa wholeheartedly. Early in the sitting of the new Parliament, he burst into song, singing some lines of Nkosi Sikelel' iAfrika on the floor of Parliament.

Wessels' positive predisposition goes back even further: during the previous dispensation he became the first senior Nationalist to apologise publicly for his party's racist past.

Born in Kroonstad, Wessels was president of the Afrikaanse Studentebond in one of its most conservative phases, from 1971 to 1973, while earning his law degree. But after joining the cabinet in 1988 as deputy minister of Law and Order, he became progressively vocal in his rejection of racial discrimination. After the failure of Codesa II, he joined Roelf Meyer in the tricameral government's negotiating team, bringing debates back on track when negotiators wandered off on side issues.

Born 19 April 1946. Family: wife Tersia, two children.

Williams, Abe   The controversial minister of Welfare and Population Development was nominated to the cabinet by the National Party as a token of appreciation to the Western Cape's coloured voters for their support in the first democratic elections. Coloured support was a major factor in handing power in the province to the NP.

Williams is a veteran of tricameral politics, which were clearly rejected in previous elections by coloureds when most of them refused to vote. His appointment in the Mandela cabinet was met with strong opposition from African

National Congress members in Cape Town, many of whom have not yet forgiven him for the role he played in supporting the government during the United Democratic Front's years of extra-parliamentary struggle against apartheid.

White Nats, on the other hand, welcomed him with open arms. One of the first coloured politicians to leave the Labour Party and join the NP, Williams was soon promoted to minister of Sports in the last white-dominated Parliament.

The jovial Williams was born at Saldanha and qualified as a teacher at Athlone Training College in Paarl, before obtaining a BA degree from the University of the Western Cape and a BEd from Stellenbosch University.

He became known as a sportsman and sports administrator, particularly in the rugby sphere. For many years he was organiser and secretary of the South African Rugby Federation, and in the early 1980s acted as assistant manager to the last official Springbok rugby team to visit New Zealand before the country's sportspeople were finally isolated by the rest of the world.

In the 1984 elections for the first tricameral Parliament, Williams won the Mamre seat in the House of Representatives (HoR). Five years later he was appointed the HoR's deputy minister of Education and Culture, and in 1991, HoR deputy minister of National Education and Culture; he also held the Welfare portfolio.

In April 1993 he joined former President FW de Klerk's cabinet as Sports minister.

Born 12 December 1940. Family: wife Esme, two adult children.

X, !Khoisan   X, a member of the Gauteng legislature, was an excellent choice to head the committee to choose a new name for the province formerly called PWV. Known for most of his life as Benny Alexander, he announced in mid-1994 that he was rejecting his 'settler name' and giving himself a temporary designation until he could trace his ancestry.

Last year's *A-Z of South African Politics* described him as flamboyant and a political streetfighter. Born in Kimberley, he was schooled in pan-Africanism by Pan Africanist Congress founder Robert Sobukwe. His background is in trade unionism: while working for a pharmaceutical company in Johannesburg he helped form the Black Health and Allied Workers' Union of South Africa and, in 1986, left his job to work full time for the South African Black Municipal and Allied Workers' Union.

A member of the PAC underground through most of the 1980s, he was instrumental in forming the movement's legal front, the Pan Africanist Movement, in 1989. He resigned as PAC general secretary in December 1994.

His fortunes have waned — perhaps temporarily — with the PAC's since the April 1994 election; but he has retained his flair for gaining media attention.

Born 4 March 1955. Family: wife Iman, three children.

Yacoob, Zakeria ('Zak')   Yacoob has been a member of the Durban Bar since 1973, taking silk in 1991. He was educated at the Arthur Blaxall School for the Blind in Natal and graduated with a BA LLB from the University of Durban-Westville in 1972.

Apart from his professional work, Yacoob has been active in political and welfare organisations including the Natal Council for the Blind and the Natal Indian Congress, and was an executive member of the United Democratic Front in Natal.

He was part of the legal team in the Delmas Treason Trial; his practice tends to concentrate on commercial work and cases involving administrative law, particularly human rights work. During the multiparty negotiating process at Kempton Park he was part of the technical committee to draft the chapter on fundamental human rights in the constitution. During the 1994 elections, he served on the Independent Electoral Commission.

Born 3 March 1948. Family: wife Anoo, two children.

Yengeni, Tony Sithembiso   The former head of Umkhonto weSizwe in the Western Cape made a post-election political comeback with his appointment as head of the parliamentary joint committee on Defence. The appointment came shortly after Yengeni withdrew from the race to become provincial chair of the African National Congress in the Western Cape — a position which eventually went to Chris Nissen.

Since his release from prison in 1991, Yengeni has been a champion of the poor and the homeless within the ANC and South African Communist Party. From 1992 to 1993 he served as general secretary of the ANC in the Western Cape, losing this position at the 1993 regional congress — apparently owing to fears that his militant image could cost the ANC votes in a province that has a relatively conservative electorate.

Born in Cape Town, Yengeni was involved in the Black Consciousness Movement before joining the ANC underground in 1976. He received training in ANC camps in Botswana, Zambia and Angola, and studied for a social science diploma in Moscow.

Returning to Southern Africa, he served as regional secretary of the South African Council of Trade Unions based in Lesotho. He was arrested in 1987, shortly after taking up his MK duties in the Western Cape, and became accused number one in a protracted trial in which he was never convicted, and which ended with his indemnification in 1991.

Born 11 October 1957. Family: wife Lumka, two sons.

Zuma, Jacob Zuma, who could have commanded a major national post, fought a bruising battle to be the African National Congress's premier candidate for kwaZulu/Natal against two other candidates, only to see the province go to the Inkatha Freedom Party and find himself relegated to the position of MEC for Economic Affairs and Tourism.

Although he has a reputation as a moderate with deep respect for Zulu traditionalism, Zuma's political tutor was hardliner Harry Gwala.

A dour man who avoids the public eye, Zuma comes from a poor background and is entirely self-educated. He was born to a domestic worker in rural Natal and joined the ANC in 1959 aged 17, even though the ANC constitution required a minimum age of 18. He was arrested in 1969 while leaving the country for military training, and served 10 years on Robben Island. On his release he left for exile and was based in Mozambique and Zambia, rising to head the ANC Intelligence Department and to the position of deputy secretary-general in the head office.

After the April 1994 elections, he took some of the blame for the ANC's defeat in his province, having taken a soft approach to the IFP, but won much respect for his key role in wooing King Goodwill Zwelithini away from the Inkatha Freedom Party. His name was tarnished by the Motsuenyane Commission of Inquiry into atrocities in ANC camps, where as head of intelligence he was responsible for some of the activities at the camps.

He is married to the current minister of Health.

Born 12 April 1942. Family: wife Nkosazana Zuma, 10 children.

Zuma, Nkosazana During the first weeks of the new administration, the minister of Health signalled her intention to bring about profound and adequate changes to the health system. She proposed new anti-smoking regulations; that children under six, whose parents were not covered by insurance and medical aid, receive free health care at all state hospitals and clinics; and promised that some form of national health system would be introduced to give basic health care to as many people as possible.

The minister of Health was the oldest of eight children, brought up in an environment where racial and gender discrimination were anathema. At the University of Zululand she completed a BSc in zoology and botany and in 1972 became a research technician for the dean of the University of Natal's Medical School.

For the next four years she studied medicine at Natal University. During this time she was also working underground for the African National Congress. In 1976 she fled into exile, moving from Botswana to Tanzania to England, and completed her medical studies at the University of Bristol, working in her spare time for the ANC youth section.

Between 1980 and 1984 the ANC sent her to Swaziland where, using the cover of her job as a doctor at Mbabane government hospital, she worked underground for the movement. In 1980 she met fellow ANC activist Jacob Zuma, who was also in exile; they were married in 1982. In 1985 and 1986 she was back in the United Kingdom, studying successfully for a diploma in tropical child health from Liverpool University's School of Tropical Medicine. This qualified her for the regional health committee of the ANC in the UK.

Before coming home, Zuma held the job of director of the Health and Refugee Trust, a British non-governmental organisation, and from 1991 she has chaired the Southern Natal region's health committee.

Within public health circles she is held in very high regard and said to be capable of carrying out her job as minister of Health better than any who have held the post for some years.

Born 27 January 1949. Family: husband Jacob Zuma (an ANC MEC in kwaZulu/Natal), five children.

Zwelithini, Goodwill   The King of the Zulus would not have featured in an A-Z of political profiles a few years ago, and it is the hope of his current circle of advisers that he won't again. For the moment, however, the status of his shifting position is important for winning the loyalties of many Zulu voters.

Zwelithini has been involved in a 25-year battle — since his investiture — with Inkatha leader Mangosuthu Buthelezi for control over the throne, a battle between a nominal king who wants to be a real monarch, and an ambitious politician wanting to use the monarchy for his own ends. The result has been a messy, sometimes ugly reign, exacerbated by the fact that the inheritor of the title of Shaka and Cetswayo is a weak and ineffectual man, particularly when faced with a formidable politician like Buthelezi.

Their differences date back to Buthelezi's differences with the regent who held the throne until Zwelithini came of age. Buthelezi elbowed the regent away from the king, shut down the royal council that surrounded the monarch and opposed Buthelezi, and became the king's 'traditional prime minister'. The king and his advisers now claim that Buthelezi appointed himself to this position, but in fact Buthelezi and Zwelithini were often side by side.

In the intervening years, Zwelithini did try to assert an independent political power from time to time, only to be swiftly and ruthlessly slapped into place by Buthelezi who, as chief minister of the kwaZulu homeland, had control of the royal purse-strings. At one point the king, summoned to account for his behaviour in the kwaZulu Legislative Assembly, fled the chamber.

He was also barred from talking to the media without the permission of the kwaZulu authorities.

It may be an apocryphal story, but Zwelithini is rumoured to have sympathised with Nelson Mandela at their first meeting after the ANC president's release, saying he knew what it was like to be a prisoner since he himself had been one for 24 years.

Having gained control of the monarch, Buthelezi used his traditional power and the loyalty of his subjects to the full in a bid to strengthen his hand in constitutional negotiations and the elections.

But the change of government in 1994 and the dis-appearance of the kwaZulu homeland freed the king and allowed him to reassert his independence. The African National Congress played a cautious and skilful game, using traditionalist Jacob Zuma to wean the king away from the IFP over a four-year period.

Now the king has revived his circle of advisers, who are determined to keep him independent of political parties. The king, however, may have other ambitions: he has shown signs of wanting to go further in re-creating the Zulu kingdom and re-establishing his political authority. At present, he is locked in battle with Buthelezi for the loyalty of the backbone of traditional power: the chiefs, most of whom proclaim loyalty to the king but are dependent on the regional, IFP-controlled government for their stipends.

The king is a renowned Nguni cattle breeder and enjoys hunting, though ironically he does not eat beef. He is rumoured to be by far the country's best-paid traditional leader, and has five 'palaces' built at a cost of almost R7-million.

Born 14 July 1948. Family: wives Sipongile Dlamini, Buhle Mathe, Mantombi Dlamini, Thandi Ndlovu and Nompumelelo Mchiza, many children.

2

ISSUES

Broadcasting

Public hearings for a new board for the South African Broadcasting Corporation in May 1993 were an early sign of transformation in a new South Africa — not only because selection panel co-chair Ismail Mahomed used the opportunity to excoriate representatives of the old apartheid order, but because the event promised to take broadcasting out of the hands of 'His Master's Voice' (the SABC) and to put into place a new broadcasting dispensation of openness, fairness, diversity and quality.

Over a year later, the process of re-regulating the South African broadcasting spectrum had proven to be messier and more complicated than ever anticipated, and a veritable industry of lobby groups had been spawned: broadcasting, after all, is big business.

The Independent Broadcasting Authority (IBA) Act, tabled by the Transitional Executive Council early in 1994, was intended to 'promote the provision of a diverse range of sound and television broadcasting services on a national, regional and local level which, when viewed collectively, cater for all language and cultural groups and provide entertainment, education and information'.

The IBA Act calls for a three-tiered system, with public, private and community broadcasting services. Most importantly, it takes broadcasting out of the hands of the government and puts it under the control of seven independent councillors, who are responsible for issuing licences and maintaining the spectrum — and who are thus the most powerful people in broadcasting. Appointed in 1994 were co-chairs Peter de Klerk and Sibeletso Mokone-Matabane; media lawyer William Lane, journalist John Matisonn, former unionist Frank Meintjies, African National Congress telecommunications expert Lyndall Shope-Mafole, and former SABC chairman Christo Viljoen.

In mid-1994, the IBA began putting into place an operating staff of over 100 people. But before it can even consider issuing new licences, it is required to undertake several public hearings: into how the public broadcaster will be financed, into local content quotas, and into cross-media ownership regulations. Only after it has drawn up a frequency plan, and Parliament has approved a new Broadcasting Act to govern the SABC, can it begin the actual process of re-regulation. This is expected to happen towards the end of 1995.

Already, the IBA has come under fire for moving too slowly. Part of the problem was a political crisis sparked by the far-right Radio Pretoria which continued to broadcast early in 1994 despite the lack of a licence. The then minister of Home Affairs, Danie Schutte, mishandled the crisis by issuing temporary licences to Radio Pretoria and several other private stations. So before it could even begin its other public hearings, the IBA had to sort out the temporary licence mess. The whole month of July 1994 was taken up with public hearings on this issue — which did, however, have the positive side-effect of defining 'community broadcasting', since only community broadcasters are entitled to apply for temporary licences.

IBA councillors have claimed that the Act is deficient and that Parliament needs to amend it to expedite the process. Meanwhile, several key issues need to be addressed: will the

SABC continue to be financed by advertising revenue, or will it receive a state subsidy? What will happen to the TBVC broadcasters, such as Radio Bop and Bophuthatswana TV? Is public broadcasting a national or a regional responsibility? How much local content will services be obliged to provide? And will private broadcasters have public broadcasting responsibility?

One positive sign for a new broadcasting dispensation is that the minister for Posts, Telecommunications and Broadcasting, Pallo Jordan, was one of the architects of the IBA, and is a firm advocate of independent regulation and public broadcasting. There is uneasiness, however, about the pro-ANC bias of the current SABC board. An important future watchdog role will be played by organisations like the Media Monitoring Project and the Freedom of Expression Institute.

Ministry of Posts, Telecommunications and
  Broadcasting: (021) 462-1632/3/4/(012) 326-1110
Association of Broadcasters: (011) 788-7910
Broadcasting Association of South Africa: (011)
  435-3445
Film and Television Federation: (011) 838-6275/
  836-4425
Freedom of Expression Institute: (011) 29-4355
Independent Broadcasting Authority: (011) 447-6180
Media Monitoring Project: (011) 838-7522
National Community Radio Forum: (011) 982-7003
South African Music Content Alliance: (011) 886-1342
Independent Broadcasting Committee: (011) 789-8200

Commissions

The new constitution sets up several new commissions to deal with problems left over from the apartheid era, or to ensure that such problems do not arise again.

Perhaps the most important is the public protector's office (usually known as the ombudsman in less gender correct constitutions). The public protector will have wide powers to make sure that bureaucrats do not ride roughshod over the public as they have done so often in the past. The person holding this office will have to be a judge or someone with at least 10 years' legal experience. He or she will be given the task of investigating any alleged maladministration of government affairs, abuse or unjustifiable exercise of power, or even 'unfair, capricious or discourteous or other improper conduct or undue delay' by a civil servant. A wide range of other possible improper conduct may also be investigated and the public protector may try to resolve the situation by mediation, advising the aggrieved person on what other action to take, or bringing the problem to the attention of the prosecuting authorities.

The provinces may also decide to have their own provincial public protectors, but so far none of them has opted to do so.

- The Human Rights Commission will, like the Constitutional Court, consist of 10 members and a chairperson. All must be 'fit and proper' persons who broadly represent the South African community.

Their brief is to make up for years of oppressive state brainwashing, by promoting respect for human rights, developing an awareness of human rights and making recommendations to the state authorities about what laws should be passed to promote fundamental rights.

It must act as a watchdog body, and if it believes that any proposed legislation might contradict any of the fundamental rights guaranteed in the constitution, it must draw this to the attention of Parliament. Some experts believe it will even be able to initiate legal action of behalf of such complainants.

- The Commission on Gender Equality is the most vaguely worded of the new bodies and most of its mandate must still be finalised by Parliament. Its object is to promote 'gender equality' and to advise Parliament on any proposed legislation which might affect 'gender equality and the status of women'.

- The Commission on Restitution of Land Rights must also be set up to deal with any claims about land dispossession before a still-to-be-fixed date. Among its tasks, the commission will have to investigate the merits of the claims, mediate and settle disputes about these claims and draw up reports to submit to court as evidence.

Constitutional Development

It is widely accepted that the transitional constitution agreed to during the multiparty negotiating process in Kempton Park will survive the interim period largely unscathed. But the final constitution, in terms of which the next elections scheduled for April 1999 will be held, will be decided by the Constitutional Assembly — combined sittings of the National Assembly and the Senate, under the chairmanship of African National Congress secretary-general Cyril Ramaphosa.

The present minister of Constitutional Affairs is the National Party-nominated Roelf Meyer, who played a crucial role in the negotiations. He is assisted by the ANC's Mohammed Valli Moosa. According to agreements reached at Kempton Park, decisions regarding the constitution must be taken on a consensus basis. This means that both Meyer and Moosa are pivotal in identifying problems of governance resulting from the present untested constitution and relating to local, provincial and central government.

Another important role player is Public Service and Administration minister Zola Skweyiya, who has to oversee the transferring of powers jointly exercised by the provinces and central government — including policing and education — to the provincial legislatures.

The Commission on Provincial Government, under chairman Thozamile Botha, is an extra-parliamentary body which also plays a crucial role in identifying problems and in proposing the distribution of powers and functions to the various levels of government. Botha — one of the ANC's key strategists during the negotiations — will probably have a direct hand in drafting the final constitution.

But while the Constitutional Assembly will decide on the final document, the government is already bringing about changes to the transitional constitution as problems arise. Four amendments have been brought about by Parliament since the transitional constitution was accepted at the end of 1993, among them changes to accommodate demands by the Inkatha Freedom Party before the April elections. Additional changes were necessary to enable the appointment of Chris Liebenberg as minister of Finance on a non-party base. The transitional constitution only allows members of political parties to serve in the cabinet, but it was agreed that Liebenberg would be appointed without having to join any party.

The Constitutional Assembly is expected to follow closely the changes brought about by Parliament to ensure efficient governance, but it will also introduce more substantial changes to accommodate grassroots demands relating to land issues and ensuring more equitable distribution of resources and wealth. Whereas the present cabinet has the decisive say in changes to the transitional constitution, the ANC caucus will without doubt be the driving force behind the stipulations of the final constitution. However, the ANC, despite its huge majority in Parliament, will be restricted severely in drafting the constitution by a set of principles adopted by the negotiators in 1993 (see pages 320-328). These principles are 'written in stone' and the Constitutional Court will have the final say on whether the new constitution complies with the criteria.

Ministry of Provincial Affairs and Constitutional
    Development: (021) 462-1441/(012) 341-1380

Crime

A steady rise in crime throughout 1994 has threatened government attempts to build a stable and violence-free country.

By the second half of the year, a serious crime was being committed every 17 seconds: a murder every half hour, a housebreaking every two minutes. A car was stolen and a robbery committed every five minutes, while an assault took place every three minutes.

Before the elections in April, political crimes which claimed the lives of thousands of people in areas like the East Rand and Natal posed a serious threat to the stability of the country. But, with the peaceful transition and the willingness of South Africans to put aside their political differences and opt for reconciliation, the country experienced a decline in political crimes.

Yet crime soared out of control.

In the first eight months of 1994 over a million cases of serious crimes were reported. Murder was on the rise: over 50 murders for every 100 000 people in the country, most of the killings in kwaZulu/Natal, where political tension between the African National Congress and the Inkatha Freedom Party could have played a significant role.

Other areas where murder was rife during that period were the Witwatersrand (over 60 people killed for every 100 000 population) and the Western Cape (over 40 people killed for every 100 000).

Police, no longer political targets, were also being murdered at an alarming rate for their weaponry. According to police statistics, in the first 10 months of 1994, 196 policemen were killed, 88 of them in the Witwatersrand area. Police unions have demanded that the Safety and Security Ministry provide them with tactical training specific to urban policing; they want permission to draw and point their guns while conducting searches and arrests.

Not only have police been killed, but the number of those killing themselves has increased. There were 142 police suicides in the first eight months of 1994, compared with 65 in 1991, 106 in 1992 and 134 in 1993.

Although police psychologists say the triggers were failed relationships, financial problems and alcohol abuse, work-related problems also played a role — non-satisfactory transfers and, especially, the problem of being targets of community anger because of their profession.

Crimes against women were also a great concern: a rape was committed every 18 minutes countrywide. Topping the list were Natal and Eastern Cape, where over 100 rapes were reported for every 100 000 people.

With more publicity being given to the issue of child abuse, reported incidents increased dramatically after April. In the first eight months of 1994, there were 13 508 cases reported — almost as many as in the whole of 1993.

The Child Emergency Services found its calls rising from 62 000 to 72 000 a month — about 2 500 a day. This prompted organisations like the Soweto Child Protection Unit to talk to youths in schools and churches and create awareness of the problem.

Crimes on the rise also included vehicle hijacking, which rose by over 50 per cent nationwide in the first eight months of this year. Between July 1993 and July 1994, the total value of cars stolen in the PWV area was R95 950 954, while in other regions it was R33 608 422.

Meanwhile, attacks on freight-laden trucks were on the increase — mostly in the PWV area, where over 400 trucks were hijacked in the first nine months of 1994.

White collar crime also rose significantly.

Crime could be one problem that money could alleviate. The institution of Reconstruction and Development Programme projects to improve social conditions could make a difference. The once violence-torn East Rand was well on its way to stability towards the end of 1994, after the injection of one tranche of over R600-million in RDP funds promised for the next five years in Katlehong, Thokoza and Vosloorus. The money will be used to develop the area by restoring services, repairing streets and houses and improving living conditions in the hostels and squatter camps. The project is also aimed at providing employment for local residents because part of the reason for the increase in crime is attributed to unemployment.

There will also be an SOS phone-in service throughout the townships, where residents can call in to report crimes immediately and any other complaint pertaining to their lives. The success of this project will depend on the community working together with the police, army, civics, business people and all political formations to create a crime-free community. If it succeeds, its architects see it as the yardstick for other areas countrywide.

Ministry of Safety and Security: (021) 45-7400/
    (012) 323-8880
Nicro (National Institute for Crime Prevention and
    Rehabilitation of Offenders: (011) 336-5236
Police and Prisons Civil Rights Union (Popcru):
    (011) 337-3970
South African Police Union (Sapu): (012) 328-4192
Correctional Officers' Union of South Africa:
    (011) 913-1770 ext 2267

Culture

Arts and culture are, so to speak, *sub judice* in the new South Africa. They are likely to remain so until a permanent advisory body to the minister of Arts and Culture, Science and Technology, Ben Ngubane, has been appointed. By late 1994, Ngubane's temporary Arts and Culture Task Group (Actag) was considering policy submissions. The best estimate for any arts and culture legislation is the middle of 1995.

Nevertheless, certain policy directions are clear. The minister has strongly underlined his commitment to an arts and culture sector located primarily within civil society, and a policy as far as possible removed from party politics. Thus it is almost certain that an independent national arts council will have responsibility for the distribution of government funds within the arts.

The role to be played by Ngubane's ministry is essentially one of facilitation, of developing infrastructures and the formulation of broad principles; as the terms of reference for

Actag — and the interim constitution — make clear, primary responsibility for the nitty-gritty of culture falls on provincial legislatures.

Perhaps the most persuasive of the submissions to be considered by Actag is a draft policy developed by the National Arts Coalition (NAC). The NAC, which boasts a membership of around 120 000 practitioners, proposes a system of arts and culture development based at local level on community arts centres administered by national and regional government. Equipped with rehearsal spaces, teaching areas, studios, libraries and other facilities, these can be used to promote and develop artistic and cultural expression.

The NAC envisages a tiered system of arts festivals built around community arts centres to promote and professionalise the work done at grassroots level. Work would be selected from sponsored arts festivals at local level for inclusion first at regional festivals of the arts and, after further selection, at national festivals.

Alongside, the NAC envisages the formation of national companies working within specific arts — theatre, dance and other disciplines. But, apart from the community-based infrastructure, funding in the arts would be strictly at the discretion of national and regional arts councils.

The structure would require the phased dissolution of the previous government's four provincial performing arts councils — one for each of the former provinces — which in the past received nearly all the direct subsidy central government made available for the arts: around R90-million in the past financial year. The performing arts councils could survive as private managements, with no more claim on government funding than any other arts practitioners.

Such a radical step, entailing the redistribution of the councils' assets and facilities among community arts centres, has not proved popular with the old guard. The newly formed Foundation for the Performing Arts, representing both audiences and performing arts council employees, proposes instead that suitably transformed and democratised councils be developed as the core of a new cultural infrastructure.

The issue of the future of the performing arts councils is certain to be divisive and difficult, but it is not the only issue that will engage the major players. Equally ominous is a bizarre rift which developed between the minister and his deputy, Winnie Mandela, within weeks of their appointments. Mandela criticised the minister's choice of director-general, regularly failed to arrive at meetings called by Ngubane, and announced unilaterally, with neither consultation nor official sanction, an advisory committee of her own, tasked with working up an arts policy. Ngubane had by this stage appointed his own (officially mandated) committee of advisers, and for some months the two bodies worked in an absurd and counter-productive parallel. Though, by November 1994, a compromise joint committee with representatives from both the Ngubane and Mandela factions had been cobbled together with Deputy President Thabo Mbeki, by December it already showed signs of falling apart.

By the end of 1994 a third power grouping was consolidating around the Parliamentary Select Committee on Arts and Culture. With the ANC's discredited Department of Arts and Culture dissolved earlier in the year, former DAC head Wally Serote appeared to be consolidating his power base as chairperson of the new select committee, whose membership also included onetime DAC boycott hardliner and spokesperson Mewa Ramgobin. By November 1994 the select committee was, astonishingly, calling for its own proposals on arts and culture policy; at the same time, there were moves in government to extend the powers of the select committees to include that of initiating legislation.

Meanwhile, cultural workers in the Western Cape banded together as the Arts and Culture Development Network to lobby for the creation of provincial and national arts forums as alternatives to Actag's proposed open hearings.

Though far from unified, the various counter-initiatives could well sow enough confusion to jeopardise the effectiveness of the new Arts and Culture ministry, and thereby create opportunities for the old-style cultural commissars to hijack a department whose top post is occupied by an Inkatha member and whose key advisers — among them the NAC's Mike van Graan — are avowedly politically non-aligned.

Ministry of Arts and Culture and Science and
    Technology: (021) 45-4850 / (012) 324-4096
National Arts Coalition: Michael van Graan (031)
    25-2369. PWV: (011) 836-6028/6036
Foundation for the Performing Arts: Sheena Hart
    (011) 442-7676
Performing Arts Councils:
    Pact (012) 322-1665
    Pacofs (051) 47-7931
    Napac (031) 304-3631
    Capab (021) 21-5470
Arts and Culture Development Network: Interim
    Steering Committee: Mario Pissaro (021) 45-3689
    or Omar Badsha (021) 761-5440

Customary Law

The interim constitution calls for the establishment of a national council and provincial houses of traditional leaders. However, these institutions cannot meet the desire of the

Council of Traditional Leaders of South Africa for the power to veto legislation at local and national level that conflicts with traditional practices.

The term customary law refers to practices and traditions which have historically regulated communities, especially in the areas of marriage and family. The paying of lobola or a dowry, customs surrounding marriage, birth and death, and the duties of individuals to their families all fall within the ambit of customary law, which varies for different communities and from region to region.

Traditional leaders feel strongly that customary law should be recognised in South Africa but many women's groups are opposed to giving customary law too much power, arguing that some customs and local laws restrict women's rights. They refer to laws which prevent women from owning land, inheriting their husband's property or from having a say in the community decision-making body, which is composed of male elders.

The Bill of Rights guarantees women the right to equality before the law and entrenches it in a clause which specifically states that no right may be limited by common law, customary law or any other legislation.

This is not the end of the matter, however. Customary law has not been codified and placed on the statute books, but it has found its way into formal legal structures through the law of contract. Customary law is also dealt with in the Black Administration Act which is still on the statute books and regulates the way in which magistrates and legal officials deal with so-called tribal practices.

Some legal commentators argue that until the Black Administration Act is repealed or replaced, customary law will still have legal force. Black women are designated minors in this Act and, although this conflicts with the Bill of Rights, the status quo will prevail until it is challenged in the Constitutional Court.

There is a strong argument for recognising customary practices in law, however, because in many cases they protect people or reflect a contract that has been made between two individuals, like marriage. The way in which custom and the law interact is an area that still needs to be clarified.

Council of Traditional Leaders of South Africa:
    (011) 838-5802
Women's National Coalition: (011) 331-5958
African National Congress Women's League:
    (011) 330-7119
African Women's Organisation: (011) 838-2702

Defence

Perceiving a serious threat to the funding and functionality of the country's armed forces as they compete with the reconstruction and development ministries for state resources, South Africa's new defence establishment has followed legendary Prussian strategist Karl von Clausewitz in its attempt to stave off inevitable budget cuts. Attack is the best form of defence, Clausewitz said, and the generals and politicians — now a collection of hawks from across the political spectrum which includes African National Congress Defence minister Joe Modise and his deputy Ronnie Kasrils — have gone on to the offensive, demanding expensive new weapons systems as they are told to cut costs. The Navy needs Corvettes, the artillery the big G-6 gun, the Air Force the new Rooivalk attack helicopter and Pilatus trainers, they claim, mentioning just a few big-ticket items.

Some capital investment will be unavoidable: the Pilatus will replace the ageing Harvard trainers which are becoming increasingly costly to keep in the air, and the Air Force is under irresistible pressure to buy the Rooivalk as an expression of faith in the South African product which should help it sell elsewhere. But given the demands on the country's resources in the areas of housing, health and education, it is difficult to imagine that the Navy's wish to buy four expensive 25 000-ton Corvettes will get beyond the planning stage. The 1994/95 budget foresaw an increase in military spending to R12,124-billion to accommodate the integration of up to 30 000 Umkhonto weSizwe (MK) cadres, around 1 500 members of the Azanian People's Liberation Army, and the armies of the former Bophuthatswana, Transkei, Ciskei and Venda. Currently 91 000 strong, the South African National Defence Force (SANDF) aims to be back at this manning level within three years.

A civilian Secretariat of Defence, whose tasks were taken over by the South African Defence Force more than two decades ago, has been restored and Lieutenant-General Pierre Steyn, a highly respected Air Force officer who retired in 1993, placed at the helm, both to impress the primacy of politics on the generals and to increase the legitimacy of the military. The secretariat, responsible for financial control and fiscal administration, is expected to be operational by April 1995.

A services brigade under former MK commander Lambert Moloi will absorb those who fail to make the SANDF grade. Moloi has been named a lieutenant-general along with former MK chief of staff Siphiwe Nyanda, now in the military's number two job as chief of Defence Force Staff. Several other senior black officers have been named, including minister Modise's wife Jackie Sedibe, who is a brigadier in the personnel department with special responsibility for women.

Integration poses the greatest single mid-term challenge for the defence force. It will affect the military's ability to project the force both as part of its peacekeeping role within South Africa and during potential international missions beyond the country's borders, such as to Rwanda or Bosnia.

It is understandable, therefore, that the SANDF leadership has been extremely cautious in responding to demands for an early deployment of large-scale elements on humanitarian missions, advising against committing forces to the United Nations or the Organisation of African Unity. Also holding them back is the absence of a doctrine governing troop deployments. To do so before the ground rules have been discussed thoroughly could be disastrous, particularly if South African forces were to get bogged down prematurely in the kind of situation which cost the United States so dearly in Somalia.

The integration task alone is indeed massive: a former guerrilla army with a strong tradition of political education but little grounding in the tactics of conventional forces is to be melded with a conventional military that has spent the past four decades as the partisan force of a racist, expansionist regime − and with homeland armies made largely in the image of the old SADF. Still recognisably organised on the British model despite efforts over the last 30 years to 'Afrikanerise', the core defence force went into action against the National Party's political foes and South Africa's neighbours.

The year 1975 saw the forces in Angola in a desperate attempt to prevent the MPLA from taking power. The result was the internationalisation of the conflict and the stationing of Cuban troops in the former Portuguese colony. Content to hold the line for many years, the Cubans finally gave the SADF a thrashing a decade later at Cuito Caneval, sometimes called the SADF's Stalingrad. Army officers deny having lost the battle to this day, but South Africa's withdrawal from Angola and Namibia — and some say the end of apartheid — can be dated to that battle.

Conventional warfare was only part of the SADF's fight against anti-apartheid forces. In a series of bloody cross-border raids in the 1970s and 1980s which affected Botswana, Lesotho and Mozambique, SADF commandos killed and maimed ANC guerrillas, their families and, often, innocent locals. The misnamed Civil Co-operation Bureau, formed as a unit of the SADF's special forces, specialised in the assassination of apartheid's opponents both within and outside the country.

Despite battle honours gained in faraway places such as North Africa and Italy during the century's world wars, the defence force has always been first and foremost an instrument of domestic policy, from its role in ending the 1922 miners' strike to its deployment on patrols in the East Rand townships in support of the South African Police. This role is unlikely to change in the foreseeable future, because the army will be needed as the police forces go through massive change.

But in order to serve what is likely to be a less than perfect democracy, the SANDF will have to resist the common third-world temptation to take the country over, promising to give it back to the politicians once order has been restored.

Only a culture change within the military, argue critics, can ensure that it remains the servant of democracy and individual human rights. The SANDF must make the transition from a technically proficient army which still sees itself as a separate caste to an organisation integrated into the mainstream of society, ready to defend the values upon which a democracy is based.

The integration of the non-statutory forces will help democratise the SANDF, making it a force representative of the nation in terms of both its ethnic and political origins. In the mind of the South African public, it is already well on the way to true legitimacy. Peacekeeping activities in many Reef and Natal townships have won the hearts and minds of many. And the Air Force flypast during President Mandela's inauguration in May seemed to symbolise change for many in the crowd, who cheered the jets that 'now belong to us'.

At the end of 1994, the cabinet was debating a request to contribute peacekeeping troops to Angola, and seemed likely to comply.

Ministry of Defence: (021) 469-6045/(012) 428-1912/3
South African National Defence Headquarters: (012) 428-1913
South African Army: (012) 291-9111
South African Air Force: (012) 312-2911
South African Navy: (012) 317-3911

Economy

South Africa approaches the mid-1990s with an economy damaged by mismanagement and the political disaster that was apartheid. Behind protectionist walls of high tariffs and under an inward-looking economic strategy bolstered by fierce international disapproval — manifested by trade and financial sanctions and disinvestment — the etiolation of the economy was encouraged. This in turn led to the tightening of exchange controls, which created a hothouse effect for the stock exchange and allowed the big conglomerates to spread their tentacles into every cranny of the economy.

The economic legacy of the Nationalist government can be shown up in many different statistics. One is unemployment, estimated to be more than 40 per cent of the economically active population. A population growth rate of 2,7 per cent means economic growth must exceed that rate just for the country to stand still. More pessimistically, Unisa's Bureau of Market Research reckons that if the labour-capital ratio of the late 1980s is maintained, an annual economic growth rate of eight to nine per cent will be needed just to absorb the expected increase in the labour force.

Another legacy is the disparity, still largely racially based, in income. This is among the greatest in the world. In the most common measure of income equality, the Gini coefficient, perfect equality equals zero and perfect inequality equals one. According to recent research by the Human Sciences Research Council, South Africa's Gini coefficient of 0,68 heads the list of 36 developing countries.

Black empowerment has been given a boost by the transition, in a few particularly high-profile exercises. The National Sorghum Brewery was the first privatisation exercise to put shares in black hands, and in August 1994 a consortium of black businessmen — National African Investment Limited, or Nail — headed by Dr Nthato Motlana was listed on the Johannesburg Stock Exchange. The two major trade union federations, Cosatu and Nactu, announced they were considering buying a stake.

But no real entrepreneurial threat has emerged to loosen the white business grip on the economy, although in the corporate world there has been a late rush to employ blacks, especially on boards of directors. The haste to change the profile of white corporations has enabled qualified black applicants to command an affirmative action premium over their white counterparts, said to be up to 30 per cent.

The new government faces the conundrum of trying to achieve greater economic equality and at the same time maintain high rates of growth. Its grand economic plan, the Reconstruction and Development Programme, is designed to solve the first part of the equation, in focusing on meeting basic needs; it does not really provide any answers to the second, though it does at least promise not to make matters worse through fiscal indiscipline. The government will struggle to contain its spending as the bureaucracy grows through affirmative action not accompanied by wide-scale retrenchment, but it has committed itself to containing consumption spending in real terms. And it has acknowledged the overall tax burden at 25 per cent of Gross Domestic Product cannot be increased.

Business will battle, too, with the expectations of the labour movement, which accepts the need for growth but so far has been unwilling to accept the trade-off for world competitiveness: lower wages. The National Productivity Institute finds the country's wage rates too high compared with other developing countries and productivity too low. High wage increases could also undermine the successful if painful efforts of South Africa's central bank, the Reserve Bank, to cut inflation down to size.

There is hope that the reality of reduced tariff barriers negotiated under the General Agreement on Tariffs and Trade will be faced by both labour and government, which co-operated through the National Economic Forum on South Africa's most recent GATT submissions.

The big challenge that has not received enough attention is encouraging both domestic and foreign investment. Gross domestic fixed investment recently fell below 15 per cent of GDP, compared to an average of 24 per cent in the 1960s. So far, aside from promises of aid, international response to the brighter political outlook in South Africa has been slow.

Ministry of Finance: (021) 45-7594/(012) 323-8911

National Institute for Economic Policy: (011) 403-3009
South African Chamber of Business (Sacob): (011) 482-2524

Education

If the African National Congress's education policy is
implemented, education and training will be integrated into
a new, radically restructured system that allows for flexibility
in acquiring and accrediting learning. The system will
recognise prior learning and experience and will have
multiple entry and exit points. A national qualifications
and certification framework will give cohesion to the system.

Adult basic education and early childhood educare will be
given high priority. A preschool year will be included as part of
10 years' free education provided by the state (up to Standard
Seven). The system will have three major exit points: the first
10 years of schooling will be accredited with a general
education certificate, further education will result in the
further education certificate, and higher diplomas and degrees
will also be issued.

Any education system takes years to change and South
Africa's will be no exception: real change is likely to be
exceedingly slow. A myriad bureaucratic structures stand in
the way of early restructuring. Eighteen education departments
must be consolidated into one department. The ANC envisages
that four statutory councils involving all stakeholders will
assist the Education ministry and provincial departments by
devising policy which the latter will implement.

Although expenditure on education remains high compared with other countries — 22 per cent of the 1994/95
budget — change is not likely to be dramatic or very visible.
The education component of the Reconstruction and
Development Programme will have some impact, but the

daily hardships of township scholars and teachers won't disappear.

The sector is likely to remain volatile for some time. With increasing numbers of black children entering schools ill-equipped to cope with them, an eroded culture of learning and a still-militant teacher sector, schools are liable to remain flashpoints.

So, too, are universities where the funding crisis — particularly in the historically black universities — is intense. A national loan scheme to enable students to pay fees is a matter of urgency if volatile disruptions in these institutions are to be averted.

While the very organisations at the forefront of resistance to the apartheid state are now close to government, relations are likely to become more strained over time. Frustration at the slow rate of delivery became apparent within a few months of the new government taking office. Education minister Sibusiso Bengu is perceived to lack the dynamism and energy required to steer the ministry. He has also remained outside the process of policy formation.

With former ANC education head John Samuel — who steered the policy debates — no longer in the picture, there are fears that many of the policy initiatives will fall by the wayside during the restructuring process. As it is, any national plans to revise the education system will be hamstrung by regional considerations, with a distinct possibility that each of the regions will have different needs and different political agendas.

Although a single national education department has been announced, restructuring had not begun by the time of going to press. Meanwhile, each province had been given the go-ahead to form its own department.

Ministry of Education: (021) 45-7350/(012) 326-0126

Department of National Education: (012) 314-6911
Key education organisations:
  National Education and Training Forum (NETF):
     (011) 403-5500
  National Education Co-ordinating Committee (NECC):
     (011) 836-4726
  South African Council for Early Childhood Development
     (SACECD): (012) 322-0601/2
  National Literacy Co-operation (NLC): (011)
     711-2341/2874
  South African Democratic Teachers Union (Sadtu):
     (011) 331-9586
  Union of Democratic University Staff Associations
     (Udusa): (011) 403-2870
  Congress of South African Students (Cosas): (011) 836-
     5984/5 or 333-0624 (regional office)

Environment

The term 'rainbow alliance' was first coined in South Africa
about four years ago when a group of factory workers, white
farmers, black peasants and university students banded
together outside a company called Thor Chemicals to
protest about high levels of toxic chemicals in the firm's
workplace and the rivers of Natal.

It is fitting that those words are now used as a generic
description for the diverse groups who are building a new
South Africa. The basic motto of the motley group that
gathered outside the gates of Thor's factory — that economic
growth should take place without threat to the health of
nature and people — now runs through the new government's Reconstruction and Development Programme. That
message also signifies a fundamental shift in the meaning of
environmentalism in contemporary South Africa — away

from the protection of threatened plants, animals and wilderness areas to the conservation of the natural resource base on which all economic activity depends.

Traditional green activities, such as protection of the white rhino or the use of unbleached toilet paper, are being supplemented by campaigns to counter brown hazards like air pollution and the dumping of toxic waste near residential areas. Environmentalism is being linked to issues of health and development and broadened to include programmes that aim to improve the quality of life for urban as well as rural people.

While historically in South Africa nature conservation was the other side of land dispossession as many rural people were forcibly removed to create game parks and game reserves, it is now recognised that the residents of neighbouring settlements should be involved in and obtain concrete benefits from wildlife-based projects. Nature-based tourism, farming with game instead of cattle and the harvesting of wild resources such as honey, thatch and palm wine are receiving new attention as strategies for rural development.

It is estimated that by the year 2000, two-thirds of the South African population will live in the cities. Instead of focusing primarily on the protection of species like the big five — lion, leopard, elephant, rhino and buffalo — environmentalists are now also looking at the big five of the urban environment: housing, electricity, water, sewage and refuse removal.

There is no mass-based environmental movement in South Africa, but local campaigns are taking shape as organised labour, civic groups and environmentalists try to deal with these issues in a co-operative way, empowered by a clause in the country's transitional constitution that guarantees the right to a healthy environment. Various efforts are under way to co-ordinate these small 'rainbow alliances' and it is possible that a national organisation along the lines of Greenpeace will develop.

The social diversity of those involved in local environmental initiatives is ensured by the fact that South Africa experiences a mix of first-world environmental problems, such as acid rain and air pollution, and third-world ecological crises including soil erosion and deforestation.

The Eastern Transvaal highveld, for example, is one of the most polluted areas in the world; coal-burning power stations produce annual emissions of sulphur dioxide, the main ingredient of acid rain, that equal between 31 and 57 tons. A recent government report estimates that as much as 400-million tons of topsoil are washing off South Africa each year — the fifth worst rate of erosion in the world.

South Africa has a legacy of inadequate environmental legislation and governmental agencies to implement it. In the apartheid era, insensitivity towards social security translated into shoddy environmental safeguards. Military campaigns used up vast resources that could have been channelled into the development and rehabilitation of nature. The exigencies of defying sanctions defined an adventuristic nuclear programme that produced Koeberg nuclear power station, outside Cape Town, and a clutch of atomic bombs.

The new government has inherited many of these inadequacies. Ecological protection is still splintered between several different government departments. The inspection and monitoring of environmental abuse is fragmented and under-resourced. Some green organisations have complained that, after the elections, environmental portfolios in the new cabinet were not given strategic priority but instead were placed in the category of political horse-trading.

Ministry of Environmental Affairs and Tourism: (021) 45-7240/(012) 21-9587

Council for the Environment: (012) 310-3528 or
   310-3534
Environmental and Development Agency: (011)
   834-1905
Earthlife Africa (ELA): (021) 761-0938/(031) 94-2565 or
   86-1750/(011) 837-5365/(0331) 42-3983 or 64303
Environmental Justice Networking Forum (EJNF):
   (0331) 65410
Group for Environmental Monitoring (Gem): (011) 838-5449
   or 838-7702
Institute of Natural Resources (INR): (0331) 68317
National Environmental Awareness Campaign (Neac):
   (011) 988-1089 or 728-2255
National Parks Board: (012) 343-9770
Southern Africa Nature Foundation (SANF): (02231) 72801
Trees for Africa (TFA): (011) 803-9750
Wildlife Society of Southern Africa: (011) 482-1670

Freedom of Speech and Censorship

The South African media are having the time of their lives —
with more freedom and more protection than they have ever
enjoyed. The pendulum has swung from the severe censorship
of the 1980s to an almost complete *laissez-faire* policy. The shift
from a society in which nipples caused public outrage to one in
which medium hard-core porn is freely available at corner
stores has been a swift and dramatic one. This comes, however,
after a long and arduous battle for freedom of speech.
   South Africa has a long tradition of individuals and
organisations fighting against attempts to silence them. The
years of National Party rule saw the government steadily
winning the battle to silence its critics through a battery of
legislation, the closure of newspapers, the detention, banning

and harassment of journalists, direct control over broadcasting and pre-censorship of films.

The 1990 unbannings of the African National Congress, Pan Africanist Congress and other political organisations brought a 'Prague spring' when media enjoyed an unprecedented freedom to publish as they saw fit, political debate opened up and magazines such as *Playboy* and *Hustler* appeared on the streets. The tragedy of this period was the gradual decline and even demise of some of the lively anti-apartheid publications that had maintained an independent opposition voice during the years of repression. Eventually, it was increasingly hard-core porn magazines manning the frontline of anti-censorship activity.

The question being asked now is whether this spring will turn into a summer or a winter. The signs are contradictory. On the one hand, the Bill of Rights – Chapter 3 of the Constitution, titled Fundamental Rights – protects freedom of speech and information, and the government has shown an early commitment to its policy of increasing government transparency and accountability. The Bill of Rights also recognises a limited right to access to information. The government has begun a process of reviewing the censorship legislation on the statute books, including the Publications Act which rules over films, books and magazines. At the moment, these laws are respected only in the breach thereof.

On the other hand, the freedom of speech clause in the constitution is less protected than other rights; some government departments, such as the military, started early campaigns to limit press probing and access to information, and some individual leaders were soon attacking the media for their attitude to government policies.

There have also been individuals and groups campaigning for legislation to prevent race hate speech. This is an issue likely to be decided in the Constitutional Court.

Freedom of the airwaves, promised by the new government, has yet to come to fruition as a new Independent Broadcasting Authority delays issuing licences and opening up access to this medium.

Recently, a host of anti-censorship organisations joined together under the umbrella of the Freedom of Expression Institute. Other relevant bodies for media freedom are the Media Defence Trust, which has provided support for newspapers under legal attack, and the Independent Media Diversity Trust, a body which has attempted to keep alive and promote new independent media voices.

Freedom of Expression Institute: (011) 403-8309
Media Defence Trust: (011) 403-8359
Independent Media Diversity Trust: (011) 447-1264

Gay Rights

South Africa is the first country in the world with a constitution that protects, explicitly, the rights of gay people. According to Section 8(2), Chapter III of the interim constitution, South Africans may not be discriminated against on the basis of 'sexual orientation'.

The existence of the clause is astonishing, given South Africa's social conservatism and its history of homophobia both in the law (where a range of homosexual acts and activities remain illegal) and on the left, where there is a pervading African Nationalist notion that homosexuality, in the words of the Pan Africanist Congress's !Khoisan X, is 'un-African', a decadent bourgeois colonial import.

Responsible for the clause is a small group of gay activists within the African National Congress, and several enlightened ANC constitutional lawyers, most notably Albie Sachs and Kader Asmal. Certain ANC leaders have openly supported the clause: in his victory speech at Cape Town's Grand Parade after the April 1994 elections, President Nelson Mandela mentioned it, and, opening South Africa's first annual Gay and Lesbian Film Festival in Johannesburg three months later, Gauteng MEC for Safety and Security Jessie Duarte called, loudly and publicly, for an end to discrimination against gay people. 'Not only are there legal injustices to be done away with,' she said, 'but mindsets and cultures have to be done away with too. It is one thing for you to have your rights and equality in the law. It is quite another to have them each day in the street, at work, in the bar, in public places where you socialise and where you cruise.'

Duarte has since become the patron of Gays and Lesbians of the Witwatersrand (Glow), but her enlightenment is by no means shared by members of her own party. For this reason, perhaps, the gay non-discrimination clause was quietly and unobtrusively slipped into the interim constitution. It remains little known and little publicised, perhaps deliberately so, for a conservative coalition of right-wingers and African National-ists could well see it being dropped from the final constitution.

This presents certain critical strategic dilemmas for South Africa's budding gay liberation movement, and opinion remains divided, within the gay community, over whether the gay rights issue should become more or less strident. The potential implications of the clause are profound: gay people can use it not only to challenge anti-gay legislation but to establish legal partnerships, tax equity, rights to adoption, and a range of rights that could fundamentally alter the nature of this society.

Organisations such as Glow and the Association for Bisexuals, Gays and Lesbians (Abigale) in Cape Town have been growing over the past few years. Gay Pride marches staged annually through downtown Johannesburg since 1990 have attracted over one thousand people and resulted in unprecedented media coverage of the gay issue. An important new organisation, spearheaded by prominent lawyers Edwin Cameron and Kevan Botha, is the Equality Foundation: it has been set up expressly to find strategic ways of challenging homophobic laws and practices in the Constitutional Court.

Glow: Simon Nkoli (011) 648-5873/982-1016.
    Beverly Ditsie (011) 939-1190
Abigale: (021) 24-1532

Gender Equality

One important social consequence of the African National Congress's passage to power is the party's commitment — on paper at least — to gender equality. This concept is to be found in Chapter 3, Fundamental Rights, in the interim constitution, which explicitly outlaws discrimination on the basis of gender, and in the Reconstruction and Development Programme which, largely due to the work of the ANC Women's League and RDP drafter Cheryl Carolus, has integrated gender equity provisions into all aspects of reconstruction and development.

As important, the ANC made the decision that 30 per cent of all elected officials at a national and regional level must be women. The effect has been palpable: Parliament is no longer an oak-panelled boys-only club. But, perhaps because of South Africa's own history of denying women access to the corridors of power, very few women are actually to be found in senior parliamentary positions. Veteran women's rights activist Frene Ginwala is speaker (and she has vowed to use her position to advocate female empowerment), but many believe that she was offered this position — which is largely ceremonial — to keep her (and her troublesome ideas about women) away from real power.

There are only three female cabinet ministers — Health minister Nkosazana Zuma, Housing minister Sankie Nkondo and Public Enterprises minister Stella Sigcau — and three female deputy ministers — Winnie Mandela in Arts and Culture, Science and Technology, Geraldine Fraser-Molekete in Welfare, and Thoko Msane in Agriculture. There are also no female regional premiers, and scarcely a handful of female regional MECs.

At the time of writing, only one woman had been in line for a director-general's post: Olive Shisana at the Health Department, joining Independent Broadcasting Authority co-chair Sibeletso Mokone-Matabane and SABC chair Ivy Matsepe-Casaburri as the country's ranking female public officials.

None the less, there are several powerful new feminist parliamentarians who are beginning to make their voices heard. They include Pregs Govender, Brigitte Mabandla, Baleka Kgositsile and Mavivi Manzini. And, even though Gill Marcus has never formally aligned herself with the feminist movement, it is significant that she is chairperson of the powerful parliamentary standing committee on Finance, traditionally male territory.

Already Govender is working for minister without portfolio Jay Naidoo on gender issues, and the women's lobby in Parliament — having won the battle against a separate women's ministry because it might ghettoise women's issues — is now advocating a formal gender issues post within Naidoo's Reconstruction and Development

Programme (RDP) office. As well as this, the interim constitution calls for a Gender Commission to monitor and drive the process, and legislation is currently being prepared by Cathi Albertyn of the Centre for Applied Legal Studies at the University of the Witwatersrand to institute it. The Women's Charter, a broad-based document compiled earlier this year by the Women's National Coalition, has been accepted as the foundation for all future gender equality programmes.

Several issues threaten to become touchstones for the budding South African women's movement. Perhaps the most controversial is the abortion issue. While the constitution is deliberately ambiguous on the issue of reproductive rights, the ANC — both in the RDP and in its electoral campaign — has come out firmly in favour of legal abortion on demand. In all likelihood, this issue will only be resolved by the Constitutional Court.

Realising the potential divisiveness of the abortion issue, feminists inside and outside Parliament plan to find easier common ground in the shared agenda of fighting violence against women. Meanwhile, female parliamentarians and lobby groups are beginning to compile a dossier of discriminatory laws and practices that the new constitution can be used to overturn. These are likely to include tax and salary inequities.

Perhaps the cutting edge of South African feminism will be found, in the next few years, in the battle over customary law, wherein gender discrimination is most severe and notable. Already women from across political affiliations have found common ground in this issue: it was, in fact, a shared outrage against constitutional provisions exempting customary law from the non-discriminatory clauses of the Bill of Rights that brought the women at the constitutional negotiating forum together into an ad hoc women's forum. They won the battle at the World Trade Centre, thereby transforming their 'token' status into meaningful representation. In the battle against sexist customary law, an important figure to follow will be ANC backbencher MP Lydia Kompe, long a lone and powerful advocate for the empowerment of rural women.

Women's National Coalition: (011) 331-5958/9
People Opposing Woman Abuse: (011) 642-4345
Abortion Reform Action Group: (021) 762-1846
Transvaal Rural Action Committee (Rural Women's Movement): (011) 833-1063

Government of National Unity

The beast known as GNU, the government of national unity, is the one which will shape the South African polity for the next five years. The concept emerged from a proposal by Joe Slovo, South African Communist Party and African National Congress leader, in 1993 to break the logjam of negotiations. Seeing the need to placate the fears of the National Party and its largely white constituency that they would be swamped by majoritarianism, Slovo proposed that a transitional constitution should give minority parties entrenched positions for a set period in the new government. A radical version of this notion of power-sharing was included in the interim constitution.

The concept of a government of national unity is thus written into political structures at almost every level for a period of five years. It starts with the vice-presidencies: the two largest parties, or any other party that got more than 20 per cent of the vote, were entitled to nominate someone to one of these posts. It is also entrenched in the cabinet, with any party holding more than 10 per cent being entitled to ministerial and deputy ministerial positions in proportion to their success at the ballot box. The same principle applies at a provincial level, with membership of executive councils being divided in proportion to parties' regional votes.

Thus, the cabinet of 27 seats (excluding the president and vice-presidents) automatically included both of the two significant minority parties, the National and Inkatha Freedom parties (with six and three seats respectively). At a provincial level, this sometimes went further, with ANC premiers offering some position to parties that did not get even the minimum proportion of votes, such as the Freedom Front in the Northern Transvaal province.

It was agreed that the cabinet would make decisions by simple majority. However, entrenched in the constitution is the principle that the cabinet will operate 'in a manner which gives consideration to the consensus-seeking spirit underlying the concept of a government of national unity as well as the need for effective government'. Only time and practice will determine the exact meaning of this phrase.

There is some debate over how far this principle extends. Does this mean that Parliament should also share out powerful committee chairmanships in the same proportions? Are other parties entitled to demand ambassadorships as part of the deal? The NP and IFP are naturally pushing the principle to the limit, though this is being resisted by ANC rank and file.

The GNU is an unusual animal in that it does not take the ordinary form of such governing arrangements. Unity is not voluntary, as has been common in some divided societies, but is enforced by the constitution and entrenched for five years.

It makes for interesting politics: the NP and IFP are the leading opposition parties, yet they are also members of government and share responsibilities and burdens inherent in that position. This gives them the bargaining power of being able to threaten a walk-out if they disagree with decisions; yet, they would also have to bear the political cost of being seen to damage the concept of national unity.

It has also enforced the ANC policy of reconciliation: the ruling party has no choice but to work alongside its erstwhile enemies if the government is to survive.

Health

South Africa's health services face a radical shake-up. With separate health departments for the state, each of four provinces and each former homeland, the government is to bring health under one department which, unlike its predecessors, will aim to serve all the country's people. Current policy buzz-words are primary health care — by which health administrators mean getting appropriate and affordable health care to as many people as possible, with an emphasis on preventing disease rather than curing it.

South Africa's health profile mirrors its demography and serves as a sad testimony to the damage done by decades of discrimination. The divide between rich and poor, black and white, extends to diseases and disabilities; while the incidence of poverty-related disease is high among blacks, as is the rate of early childhood mortality and death in childbirth, whites show a high rate of affluence-related ailments such as cardio-vascular disorders and various types of cancers.

Cardio-vascular diseases cause 12 per cent of deaths among blacks but 40 per cent among whites, while infectious and parasitic diseases cause 14 per cent of deaths among black people but only two per cent among whites. Infant mortality rates brutally display these disparities: 130 infants per 1 000 in the Transkei (as an example of rural poverty), while among urban whites the figure is closer to 15 per 1 000.

The maternal morbidity rate — women who die as a result of pregnancy and childbirth — reflects the lack of health services and the poor health status of women. In 1989, the rate was eight per 100 000 for whites and more than 58 per 100 000 for blacks.

South Africa's tuberculosis rates are among the highest in the world — a problem which is growing and not abating. In 1990 in the worst-hit area, the Western Cape, there were 229 cases reported per 100 000 population.

Meanwhile, 28 per cent of the hospital beds in the country are private and in urban areas. Many are 'fee for service' with the private sector growing rapidly over the last decade. Ninety-three per cent of dentists work in the private sector.

While hospital beds in affluent urban areas are empty, in some black urban areas overcrowding forces patients to sleep on the floor. Doctors, pharmacists and others in the medical sphere are concentrated in affluent urban areas, leaving black urban and rural areas under-supplied.

There are an estimated 35 000 traditional healers in South Africa who are likely to be brought, in a limited way, into the organised health services.

About R21,6-billion is spent on health services annually, which is about six per cent of the GNP. The new Health ministry hopes to use the same amount of money but spread differently to ensure a more equitable distribution of care.

Although the Aids epidemic is still in its early stages (there only 10 000 reported cases of full-blown Aids), the HIV-infection rate shows that South Africa is following African trends set in countries like Zambia, Malawi and Uganda: there are an estimated 500 HIV-infections a day. Most of these are in the economically active sector of the population. At Baragwanath Hospital in Soweto, eight per cent of all pregnant women attending ante-natal clinics test HIV-positive. Given the latency period of the HIV virus, South Africa can expect a serious crisis in five to seven years' time, with up to a million seriously ill people and between 500 000 and 1,3-million orphans. Projections show that HIV infection in South Africa will most likely plateau at 20 per cent of the population by 2020.

But despite the fact that this country has been in the fortunate position of being able to plan ahead with Aids prevention and awareness programmes, there has been astonishingly little political will to tackle the impending crisis head-on. The old National Party government all but ignored it, and the African National Congress has not paid much attention to it. This is partly because of the stigma attached to Aids — which is still seen as something shameful and sinful because it is transmitted through sexual activity — and partly because the latency period means that, although the virus is already rife in South Africa, there is not much sign of it. Because Aids is perceived to be a 'gay disease', there is still very little public consciousness of the fact that the vast majority of infections (an estimated 95 per cent) are heterosexual.

In July 1994, however, minister of Health Nkosazana Zuma gave her stamp of approval to a R256-million Aids programme, developed by the National Aids Convention of South Africa, a coalition of state, non-governmental and political organisations. The programme will have a heavy bias towards public awareness and in-school education, and will also tackle discrimination against people with HIV/Aids, which is seen as a major inhibitor towards Aids education programming. At the time of writing, however, Zuma had not yet got the programme approved by cabinet.

South Africa is back in the World Health Organisation, which means it will receive research data and infrastructural help from the WHO. This body has already stated its hope that South Africa will play a helpful role on the continent in exporting aid and vaccines — an interesting view, as South Africa has one of the lowest immunisation rates in Africa.

Ministry of Health: (021) 45-7713 / (012) 323-5466
South African Institute for Medical Research: (011) 725-0511
Institute for Virology: (011) 882-9910
South African Medical and Dental Council: (012) 328-6680 /
    324-1626
Medical Association of South Africa (Masa): (012) 47-6101
Nursing Council: (012) 343-0121
South African Nursing Association: (012) 343-2315
South African Optometric Association: (012) 322-1310
Progressive Primary Health Care Group: (011) 333-5486

Housing

It is a theory almost universally acknowledged that housing lies at the core of the government's Reconstruction and Development Programme. With the ability of housing schemes to create employment — an estimated 200 jobs for every rand spent — and training projects, plus their potential to encourage similar benefits in related sectors such as electricity and water supply, one need not be a developer, service organisation or shack-dweller to believe that the RDP will fly or crash according to its success in housing the homeless.

The urban housing backlog, currently estimated at 1,4-million units, grows every year as new families join the queue. The RDP promise of one million houses within five years, with 300 000 to be built in the final year, has not yet put corrugated iron roofs over the heads of enough families to stop homeless people from occupying land earmarked for low-income housing development, as they did in June 1994 in

Johannesburg and in August 1994 in Cato Manor — or low-cost houses whose occupants have not yet moved in, as they did in July 1994 in Lamontville.

The current national housing budget is R2,2-billion. That figure was matched in July 1994 by developers' applications for subsidy in the four Transvaal provinces alone.

Until early in 1994, there were only two major forms of subsidy: the first-time homebuyers' scheme financed by government, and the Independent Development Trust's capital subsidy scheme, paying developers R7 500 per site to install running water, water-borne sewerage, streets and stormwater drainage. The new subsidy scheme — R12 500 per beneficiary — was negotiated before the election by the National Housing Forum. Initially it was available only for projects and applicants — nearly all of them developers — had to prove a 'social compact' involving the community for whom they are building. Slowly it is being extended to individuals; to those who want to improve their serviced site; to people in need of bridging finance, and to renters. There is also an intention to accommodate new forms of ownership, such as collective ownership.

A crucial component of the RDP, housing was the first sector confounded by tension over whether the power to make policy lies at the centre or in the regions. Some premiers haven't waited for recommendations from the ministry, preferring to devise their own housing schemes. Only two months after the election, Gauteng premier Tokyo Sexwale announced his plan, worked out by developer Stocks and Stocks, to build 150 000 homes in a single year with loans made by a regional community bank for Gauteng, financed by the Life Offices Association of South Africa, with participating construction companies ploughing five per cent of turnover back into housing.

The reaction of Housing minister Joe Slovo was not favourable. Among other issues, a national Community Bank which would liberalise access to credit had been on the cards for close to two years; in fact, weeks after Sexwale announced his plan, the first branch of the national bank was opened in Benoni. Eventually, the two men agreed to a compromise, and Slovo said he had no problem with regions finding their own funding to supplement their allotment from the national budget.

While Gauteng plan was hitting the headlines, Eastern Transvaal premier Mathews Phosa quietly got on with it. Days after Sexwale laid the first brick of a R40 000 house in Rooikop, Phosa handed over the keys to over 200 houses, each costing about R20 000. Fairly basic four-room houses with inside bathrooms but no ceilings, they had been built by local labour working with established developers.

The difference between the two schemes points up a crucial debate that began when the South African National Civic Organisation criticised informal housing and site-and-service projects; the national Housing ministry and regional governments have followed suit, pointedly announcing they will build only 'decent homes'. Critics point out that housing funds are limited, and ambitious schemes even targeted at R20 000 houses close out the poorest — the 75 per cent of all homeless families who cannot afford a bond for any sort of 'decent' house, not even one built as a shell, lacking ceilings and interior finishes.

End-user finance is a major problem. Bankers continue to be wary of granting bonds to low-income applicants, partly because the cost of servicing the bonds cuts deeply into profits but largely because of a legacy of bond boycotts during the late 1980s and early 1990s, plus the impossibility of repossessing homes in townships whose buyers have defaulted on their bonds. The legacy of Slovo, who died in January 1995, is the scheme he announced in October 1994, wherein the government would offer private lenders mortgage indemnities in areas where foreclosure is impossible and the banks would make mortgage loans as low as R10 000. At the same time he urged an end to rent and bond boycotts, pointing out that the scheme would not work if the boycott continued.

Meanwhile, the Housing ministry had announced disbursements of the first slice of housing subsidy — about half the national housing budget.

The amounts for each province underlined how little has actually been allocated to housing nationwide. kwaZulu/Natal, favoured with the largest amount, or 22 per cent, wound up with R291-million. Gauteng was next, with R272-million. Other allocations were: Eastern Cape, R173-million; Western Cape, R164-million; Northern Transvaal, R130-million; Eastern Transvaal, R90-million; North West, R89-million; Orange Free State, R81-million; and Northern Cape, R39-million. Initial grants were made according to, inter alia, population, parliamentary seats and the proportion of households living in poverty.

Future distribution of funds will address such criteria as urbanisation and the housing backlog.

Ministry of Housing: (021) 45-7295 / (012) 44-7875
National Housing Forum: (011) 838-2822
South African National Civic Organisation: (011) 333-2106
Regional housing boards:
  Transvaal: (011) 339-4061
  Orange Free State: (051) 405-4911
  Natal: (031) 327-0509
  Cape: (021) 45-6577

Provincial housing departments:
    Gauteng: (011) 836-5060
    Northern Cape: (0531) 81458
    Eastern Transvaal: (01311) 53051
    Western Cape: (021) 483-4226
    Orange Free State: (051) 405-5809
    Northern Transvaal: (0152) 291-1907
    Border: (0401) 99-2000
    kwaZulu/Natal: (0331) 95-2013
    North West: (0140) 29-2203

Intelligence

Like the more visible security forces, South Africa's intelligence services face a period of transformation likely to affect both personnel structures and thinking. Largely white, male and Afrikaner-dominated institutions used to operating with immunity in the grey areas on the far side of the law now face a process of integration and change which is liable to include public and parliamentary control.

A complete reorganisation of South Africa's intelligence services — consisting of the National Intelligence Service, Military Intelligence, an intelligence arm in each of the Army, Navy and Air Force and the former Security Police, all previously co-ordinated by the State Security Council — will require some time.

But whatever form the new services take, they will find themselves on a much shorter leash than before. Parliamentary control via a senior government official who carries political responsibility for their doings seems certain, as policymakers show determination to avoid the past pattern in which a single agency dominated government thinking by virtue of its direct access to the state president. There is also likely to be a parliamentary standing committee on intelligence which will oversee the services.

Senior government officials are squaring up for a battle over control of the intelligence services ahead of a presidential proclamation integrating state cloak-and-dagger organisations with those of the African National Congress and the former homelands. To be called the National Intelligence Agency (NIA), the service will operate for an interim period prior to a fundamental reorganisation of South Africa's spook services designed to democratise and streamline them. A parallel effect of the reorganisation will be the opportunity it affords the government to rid the services of operatives, practices and traditions associated with South Africa's dirty war against the enemies of apartheid, in which many government opponents were killed or maimed.

The high-level political tug-of-war comes in response to claims that President Nelson Mandela had agreed to cede control of intelligence matters to his second deputy, FW de Klerk, in an apparent barter for ANC control of the police and the South African National Defence Force. Mandela is officially minister of Intelligence and is still studying the implications of delegating his authority. Intelligence officials familiar with the integration plans for the services are understood to have advised Mandela against including Intelligence in the national unity trade-off. They fear that unless the intelligence services report to the president, they could continue to function in a partisan manner.

Senior ANC officials have indicated that structures currently being finalised will ensure presidential control over the shadow services. The new intelligence dispensation is likely to include four agencies.

Military Intelligence, long at the forefront of the dirty war, will return to its classic role of information gathering and analysis of potential threats to the sovereignty and integrity of the country. It seems likely to be headed by General Dirk Verbeek after the early retirement of Joffel van der Westhuizen, implicated in the 1985 murder of Eastern Cape activists Matthew Goniwe, Sparrow Mkhonto and others. Police intelligence could be restricted to information gathering on criminals, including international gun runners and drug dealers.

The militant ultra-right wing is likely to be a major target of the internal intelligence service in the future.

The ANC Department of Intelligence and the party's VIP protection wing will be integrated into the NIA and the police bodyguard service respectively. ANC intelligence looks back on a patchy history, the result of its inability to prevent major penetration of the underground movement by the apartheid state, and of its human rights abuses during the 1980s when dissidents were manhandled in Umkhonto weSizwe's Angolan camps.

A national intelligence co-ordinating mechanism, most probably a committee made up of the heads of all the agencies, will report to a state secretary for intelligence in the president's office. This is likely to be a political appointee. The current premier political intelligence agency, the National Intelligence Service (NIS), is to be broken up into two agencies, one responsible for domestic surveillance and analysis, the other involved in international work. It is as yet unclear whether any or all of the agencies will have any police powers, such as the right of arrest, or whether the German model of a strict separation of powers will be followed.

Much of the new structure is likely to revolve around a core provided by the NIS. It has managed to craft an image of itself as the country's intellectual intelligence service, a sort of ivory tower think-tank wisely advising enlightened politicians on how to abolish apartheid and unban the enemies of old. The truth is more complex. Those familiar with the agency say that the NIS has not achieved its potential, despite the enormous resources available to it. But it was an important adviser to the last government, both under founding director Neil Barnard, an academic brought in from the University of the Orange Free State, and under Mike Louw, a career intelligence officer trusted by NIS staff because of his intimate knowledge of the service. Louw is likely to continue as a senior operative, joined by ANC figures such as Joe Nhlanhla, Moe Shaik and Billy Masetla.

In his first public appearance before Parliament, Louw told MPs this year that the NIS had a budget of R410-million and argued that South Africa was increasingly becoming a target for foreign intelligence services. Numbers are a closely guarded secret, but the NIS is believed to employ between 5 000 and 10 000 operatives in a full- or part-time capacity.

Modelled on British and American intelligence agencies, NIS has a wide network of informers inside the country and an active, if smaller, group of cloak-and-dagger operatives outside, often based at South African embassies and hitherto involved in keeping tabs on anti-apartheid activists. Their role is likely increasingly to become that of gatherers of economic and technical information, supplying the NIS's analytical staff.

Justice and the Courts

With the new constitution, public perceptions of the legal system seem likely to improve. No longer will the courts be required to uphold and mete out laws which oppress the majority. However, although those grounds for holding the justice system in disrepute have gone, the lack of an established civil rights culture means it could be some time

— if ever — before respect for the law becomes a way of life in South African society.

The court at all levels will be drawn in to help create this culture, through upholding the new constitution, but in a special way it is the task of the new Constitutional Court to be the guardian of the new constitution and Bill of Rights. The new court has the duty to weigh the final constitution, which must be drafted by both houses of Parliament sitting as a constitution-making assembly, against the set of principles agreed to at the Kempton Park negotiations. The final constitution may only become law once the Constitutional Court declares that it passes this test.

The Constitutional Court, the first in this country, seems to have emerged because negotiators felt a new court, untainted by association with the previous order, should be given the task of protecting and interpreting the new constitution. As the law now stands, this court will be the final appeal on all matters relating to the constitution. In certain cases it will also be the only court to hear a constitution-related matter. This has caused some concern as critics feel there should always be a second forum to appeal to, which will look at the dispute afresh.

The new court has 11 members. Its president, prominent civil rights lawyer Arthur Chaskalson, will sit with all the other members to hear each case scheduled for the court. This has raised fears about backlogs building up, but it was intended to avoid any suggestion that particular members of the court are chosen to hear particular issues — an allegation made often in the past about the Appeal Court, especially when it was required to hear politically sensitive cases.

The Appeal Court will be the highest court on all non-constitutional issues. However, because most dramatic legal developments are sure to happen in the Constitutional Court, there are fears that top legal brains will not want to 'disappear' into the Appellate Division, and that it will come to be seen as a legal backwater.

The supreme courts will continue rather as before. However, they will have to deal with constitutional issues along with their previous work.

One of the major changes brought about by the new constitution is the method of choosing judges. Previously this was done informally and secretly. Now, however, all judges will be appointed by the president from a list of candidates prepared by the new Judicial Service Commission (JSC). The only exceptions are the president of the Constitutional Court, and the four members of that court who must be already sitting judges.

The new JSC will be a powerful body, able to shape the courts around the country, and thus indirectly the kind of judgments they will hand down. Already the JSC has made a great difference, with its decision to hold public interviews for the six posts on the Constitutional Court for which it had to make recommendations. This decision, taken in the name of transparency, makes South Africa one of very few countries in the world to hold open hearings for judicial posts.

Ministry of Justice: (021) 45-7506/(012) 323-8581
Judicial Service Commission: (051) 47-2769

Labour

In the aftermath of the April 1994 election, the most important issue in the South African labour field is the relationship between the Congress of South African Trade Unions and its alliance partners — the African National Congress and the South African Communist Party — now in the government of national unity.

Cosatu released more than 20 of its top unionists to serve the new government at national and regional levels to ensure that worker rights would be high on the new government's agenda. Given that they are tied to an ANC mandate and have to take broader issues into account, these MPs cannot merely implement union demands, and this could bring them into conflict with the federation.

Sam Shilowa, Cosatu's general secretary, has asserted that despite its partnership in the alliance, the federation will act independently. This has been borne out by its threat to stage a general strike over inclusion in the interim constitution of an employer's right to lock out workers. Cosatu also refused to agree to the ANC's proposal for a moratorium on strike action over the election period, following widespread public sector strikes over wage demands and job security in five homelands. It has also indicated that it will fight vigorously against the government's watering down of the Reconstruction and Development Programme (RDP).

Militant demands by union members for higher wages could also lead to conflict with a government committed to fighting inflation. Commenting on the upsurge in strikes in the months after the election — more than double the number over the same period in 1993 — Shilowa said that workers believe that democracy does not mean elections every five years, but meeting their expectations now. The beginning of the economic recovery also fuelled their demands for higher wages.

There are divisions within Cosatu over its future role in the alliance. Some affiliates, notably the Southern African Clothing and Textile Workers' Union (Sactwu), believe that in order to serve the interests of workers effectively, Cosatu should be independent of the government — requiring it to pull out of the alliance. Others, such as the National Union of

Mineworkers (NUM), argue that Cosatu should remain in the alliance to safeguard the implementation of the RDP. Cosatu's partnership in the alliance is also seen as a stumbling-block to plans for the merging of Cosatu, the National Council of Trade Unions (Nactu) and the Federation of South African Labour Unions into a mega-federation of over two million workers.

Issues at the top of Cosatu's agenda are a drive to establish centralised industrial bargaining as a major feature of South Africa's labour relations system; the introduction of a programme of legislative and institutional reform to strengthen the building of stronger institutions of collective bargaining and industrial democracy; a revamping of the industrial councils framework; promotion of co-determination in the workplace; the amalgamation of different social security funds; and the development of human resources.

The minister of Labour, Tito Mboweni, has indicated that he intends to take an independent stance in the labour arena and that his department is not an extension of the trade union movement. His non-partisan approach has been welcomed by employers, who believe that his background in economics — he has a degree in development economics from the University of East Anglia and served as deputy head of the ANC's economics department in exile — will stand him in good stead in making changes to the labour portfolio. He also has credibility with leaders in the union movement who believe that his lack of experience in the labour field can quickly be overcome.

Mboweni has stressed the importance of a social partnership between labour and business as a means of achieving economic growth and implementing the reconstruction process. He has announced a five-year plan for the development and implementation of labour market policy in a new South Africa which will dovetail with the RDP. It will stress, among other things, the importance of job creation and skills development to ensure South Africa can compete in the world economy. After discussions with unions and business, Mboweni has called for a white paper as a basis for devising a labour market policy and intends appointing a core team of labour, business and government representatives to oversee the process.

Mboweni and Cosatu have agreed that the government's reform agenda should include the rationalisation and reform of labour legislation, including the harmonisation of labour laws to incorporate the former homelands (the Public Service Labour Relations Act has already been extended to the homelands); the drafting of a new Labour Relations Act to bring labour law in line with the interim constitution; an urgent investigation into policies and laws which inhibit the right to strike; and the drafting of labour law amendments to bring legislation in line with international standards.

Mboweni has said that the department will also look into expanding the social security net and improving the efficiency of service delivery, as well as the possible amalgamation of the National Manpower Commission (NMC) and the National Economic Forum (NEF), tripartite think-tanks on labour and macro-economic affairs respectively.

There is an overlap in their work and a lack of co-ordination between the two. The NMC is currently working on the harmonisation of homeland labour legislation and the restructuring of the Labour Relations Act, in particular the regulation of collective bargaining at industry and workplace levels. At the same time, the NEF has reached agreement on centralised bargaining and a commitment on the part of employers to assist in the stabilising and securing of existing industry-wide bargaining forums and the establishment of such forums where none exist.

South Africa's readmission to the International Labour Organisation (ILO) will bring South Africa's labour standards increasingly in line with international norms. In a speech to the ILO, Mboweni promised to work for the ratification of key conventions on freedom of association, collective bargaining and forced labour. The Department of Mineral and Energy Affairs, testifying before the commission of inquiry into mine health and safety, has recommended to Mboweni that he ratify the ILO's convention on health and safety in mining.

To meet these challenges and revitalise a stagnant Department of Labour, Mboweni plans, through training, retraining and affirmative action, to transform the mainly white department (only 20 per cent of 5 500 employees are black) into one more representative of South African society. He will also merge the 11 labour departments into one, with regional offices in provincial capitals.

He will be assisted by the acting director-general of the new department, Jogie Kastner (assistant director-general of the old department), who has replaced Joel Fourie — viewed by the unions as an opponent of labour reform — who resigned just before the election. In the ministry, Mboweni will be advised by labour lawyer Halton Cheadle, and the strategic planning team will be convened by ex-unionist Les Kettledas.

In the labour field, Cosatu remains the largest union federation with 1,3-million paid-up members in 17 affiliates as at March 1994, compared with Nactu which has 327 000 members in 24 affiliates. Cosatu's three largest affiliates are also the three largest unions in the country: the NUM (310 000 paid-up members), the National Union of Metalworkers of South Africa (Numsa, 170 000 paid-up members) and Sactwu (150 000 paid-up members).

At its eighth national conference in 1994, the NUM, headed by general secretary Kgalema Motlanthe, gave notice that it would press the new government for a framework for the union's participation in the running of the mining industry. It also proposed the introduction of a wealth tax on individuals to help finance reconstruction, and gave its support to the legal enforcement of affirmative action.

To combat the negative effects of unemployment in the industry — an estimated 160 000 jobs have been lost in mining in the last five years — the NUM has launched two development centres (in the Northern Transvaal and the Eastern Cape) to train retrenched miners to set up their own small enterprises. The union has criticised the mining industry for failing to develop a national approach to deal with the closure of marginal mines, stressing that the government has a responsibility to ensure that mining companies protect workers from unplanned closures.

The rise of worker leaders to take over from unionists sent to Parliament is bound to have an impact on trade union policies in the future. One example is the case of Numsa, whose new worker leader, Enoch Godongwana, has put special stress on the need to strengthen the union's grassroots support, believing that this has been undermined by the union's concern in recent years with macro-economic issues. Numsa will also concentrate on the continuing implementation of its three-year plan for the training and regrading of workers, strategies to ensure job security and higher living standards and ensuring that the union movement retains its independence. The latter is also an overriding concern of Sactwu, now led by another worker leader, Jabu Gwala. He has said that it is wrong to have a union/government alliance and that the union will have to distance itself from the government.

Ministry of Labour: (021) 461-6030/(012) 322-6523
National Manpower Commission: (012) 310-6111
Congress of South African Trade Unions (Cosatu):
    (011) 339-4910
National Council of Trade Unions (Nactu): (011)
    29-8031
Fedsal: (011) 476-5188
National Economic Forum: (011) 614-2251

Land

Between 1960 and 1982 an estimated 3,5-million people were victims of forced removals. The single largest category was labour tenants/farmworkers, who had no legal title to land; about a million people were ejected from farms. An additional 834 400 people in rural areas fell foul of the Group Areas Act.

The Reconstruction and Development Programme commits the government to settle land claims and to redistribute 30 per cent of South Africa's agricultural land within five years. Demands for land will come from people who were removed under specific pieces of apartheid legislation as well as those who have been generally disadvantaged through apartheid policies. While urban land demands will centre on housing, rural people are likely to want land for agriculture and social security.

Two months after assuming office, the minister of Land Affairs was already dealing with 90 land claims, and the Commission on Land Allocation, a body established in 1992, was fielding 20 requests a week. Once the Land Claims Commission and Land Claims Court are fully functional they will be able to pick up the commission's outstanding cases. A register of all state-owned land will be available for inspection by claimants. The budget of minister Derek Hanekom's department is R68-million, but he has indicated he will ask for another R250-million to carry out land reform for the 1994/95 financial year.

The land restitution process will allow the government to address claims on land which has passed into private ownership since removal. If property is expropriated, the state will have to compensate current owners, taking into account the history of its acquisition, its market value and the interests of the parties involved. Mechanisms to deal with specific land claims resulting from apartheid dispossession since 1913 should be in place early in 1995.

The new government will try to balance the demands of dispossessed people with the fears of current landowners. A mixture of market and state mechanisms will be used to effect redistribution. These include incentives to bring land on to the market, taking over indebted or under-used land, removal of financial and legislative obstacles to black land acquisition, strengthening existing tenure rights of people who already occupy land and state grants or subsidies. Targets for redistribution will be indebted, under-used or state-owned land. The World Bank estimates 320 000 hectares of arable unoccupied state land are available for redistribution.

The new ministry and department of Land Affairs have identified two key areas of responsibility: land reform, comprising land restitution, and redistribution. Rural development will tend to be linked to restitution cases in the immediate future.

There is an intention to strengthen the rural directorate in the department and to establish a development planning unit to help rural people decide how they want to develop the land they acquire. Among the minister's advisers on policy and strategy are Joanne Yawitch and Bahle Sibisi, both former employees of the National Land Committee, a non-governmental land rights umbrella body.

The redistribution leg of land reform is more complex. Market mechanisms, where black people simply buy land on the market, would entail removing obstacles like the Subdivision of Agricultural Land Act, which makes it difficult to subdivide agricultural land, and restructuring financial institutions to give aspirant black farmers easier access to finance.

Non-market mechanisms include a change to tenure rights, allowing various tenure forms; legislative changes; and the provision by the state of financial assistance — subsidies or grants — to disadvantaged communities.

Underpinning proposed legislation on restitution is the need to make it quick, effective and accessible and to encourage local settlement of land disputes. Two mechanisms will ensure this: the Land Claims Commission, with offices in every province, and the Land Claims Court, which will operate as a circuit court.

The restitution process has been set out clearly in the law. It applies only to persons, communities or descendants of those dispossessed by an act of the state at any time on or after 19 June 1913, or anyone whose dispossession was effected under or for the purpose of furthering the object of a law which would have been inconsistent with the prohibition of racial discrimination contained in the new South African constitution, had that constitution been in operation at the time.

The right to restitution does not apply to acts of dispossession which occurred before 19 June 1913, nor to land expropriated under the Expropriation Act whose owners are compensated according to provisions in the new constitution.

Public land includes all land owned by the various levels of government, development bodies, local authorities, the Land Bank and any company where the state is the majority or controlling shareholder.

Claims will come to the commission first; those it cannot resolve will be referred to the court, which will also ratify agreements reached at commission level. The commission will be headed by a director, appointed by the minister of Land Affairs, who will also appoint a deputy director and provincial directors.

The Land Claims Court will be able to order the transfer of state land and expropriation or purchase of land in private ownership. It may also award alternative land to claimants, just compensation or alternative remedies, depending on the case. Awards will take into account compensation claimants received at the time of their dispossession and this compensation will be deducted from the award. Attempts to evict claimants or to sell land in dispute — there was growing evidence of such incidents in 1993 and early 1994 — will result in contempt of court orders.

As a specialised court, the Land Claims Court will be able to receive any evidence which it considers relevant, even if such evidence would not be admissible in other courts. Its judge president and other judges will be appointed by the state president and must be South African citizens. There will also be a panel of assessors, who need not be lawyers, but who must have appropriate skills and knowledge. Assessors will have equal votes with judges on questions of fact but not those of law or judicial discretion. Appeals on Land Claims Court decisions will go to the Constitutional Court.

Ministry of Land Affairs: (021) 45-7690/(012) 323-5212

Department of Land Affairs: (021) 45-6363 or (012) 312-8911
Land and Agricultural Policy Centre (LAPC): (011) 339-3516
National Land Committee (NLC): (011) 403-3803
NLC affiliates:
  Association for Rural Advancement (Afra): (0331)
    45-7607/45-8318/45-8007
  Eastern Cape Land Committee: (041) 54-7879
  Farmworkers' Research and Resources Project: (011)
    487-1603
  Transvaal Rural Action Committee (Trac): (011) 833-1063
  Border Rural Committee: (0431) 42-0173/43-3611
  Orange Free State Rural Committee: (051) 30-1556/7
  Transkei Land Service Organisation: (0471) 31-1815
  Southern Cape Land Committee: (0441) 746-148/746-162
  Surplus People's Project (SPP): (021) 696-8026

Local Government

The issue of local government goes to the heart of
expectations raised in black households specifically after the
country's first democratic elections. By the third quarter of
1995, non-racial municipal councils should be in place, after
local elections at the end of a complicated process.

In terms of the interim constitution, municipal boundaries
have to be redrawn countrywide, and local government
forums have to be appointed before new municipal councils
can be elected.

Disputes about the outer boundaries of metropoles flared
up shortly after the national elections and are being
investigated by various demarcation boards, while the
debate about inner boundaries between future local governments has begun only in certain municipalities, notably
Johannesburg.

Near the end of May 1994 the portfolio of Local Government was added to the responsibilities of Constitutional Development and Provincial Affairs minister Roelf Meyer. However, by September 1994 it seemed likely that a new minister of Local Government would be appointed from the ranks of the National Party.

The Local Government minister will be responsible for overseeing the enormous task of holding local government elections, expected towards the end of 1995. The elections, to be based on newly drawn up voters' rolls, are regarded as far more complex than the elections for the national and provincial legislatures. This time, voters' rolls will include all adult residents, ending the property-based municipal franchise. However, it will only be possible to prepare voters' rolls once boundary disputes are resolved.

Changes to the Local Government Transition Act — agreed to during the Kempton Park negotiations — are expected to purge it from clauses bogging down prospects of democratic local elections during 1995. The Act sets out a process for appointing local forums which in turn will appoint metropolitan and local councils in a 'pre-interim' phase before electing transitional councils on a partly race-based roll.

Discussions are already under way for changes in local government electoral legislation to provide, among other things, for voter education. The provinces were asked by Commission on Provincial Government chairman Thozamile Botha to move urgently and identify members of executive councils (MECs) for local government. These MECs would approve structures to be recognised as local forums.

Rural development organisations have expressed their concern about the 'lack of attention paid by the new cabinet to local government', arguing for the establishment of district councils, described as critical for the co-ordination and equitable distribution of resources and skills. There was widespread community opposition to arguments from regional service councils and joint service boards that they should be 'democratised' into district councils.

The Local Government Transition Act, aimed at reforming local government, provides for local authorities to represent interest groups in their areas. In local government parlance, the various interest groups are identified as the 'statutory side' (those who have participated in local government in the past, or white councils) and the 'non-statutory side' (those who have been excluded in the past, including liberation-organisations-turned-political-parties and black-dominated civic organisations).

Negotiation forums have been established all over the country as a first step towards appointed local managements. Delimitation councils, answerable to the various provincial governments, have been appointed to look at municipal boundaries.

The right wing promised to make the issue of local authorities a battleground, but the signs are that they are accepting the inevitability of the political changes. Although by the end of May 1994 only 10 per cent of white-controlled local authorities in the North West had established negotiating forums, they were warned by premier Popo Molefe not to delay the process deliberately. Leeudoringstad in the North West became the first Conservative Party-controlled town to sign the final agreement on a transitional local council, with the council backing the move because it was 'the best thing for the town'. Other right-wing councils quickly followed suit.

Civic associations and ratepayers' organisations are still battling to find a suitable role in the new transitional municipal structures. For the South African National Civic Organisation (Sanco), a close ally of the African National

Congress during the anti-apartheid struggle and in the April 1994 elections, its relationship with central government has become increasingly problematic.

Sanco began assuming an increasingly independent stance after the national election. In May 1994 Sanco secretary-general Penrose Ntlonti said his group was concerned about the level of salaries paid to members of Parliament. In June, ANC MP Moses Mayekiso, a former Sanco president, called on Sanco to demand 'solidarity, accountability and co-operation' from officials in government, to ensure that civic interests are accommodated in the Reconstruction and Development Programme.

One of the main tasks awaiting the new non-racial local authorities is to convince residents to pay their monthly rentals and electricity bills, following boycotts assumed during the apartheid years. Six weeks after the national election, it was reported that fewer than one per cent of Soweto residents had paid their rents, contributing only R59 000 to the council coffers instead of the estimated R3-million the council was entitled to. Boycotters were warned by Soweto Civic Association president Isaac Mogase to meet their obligations in order to be part of the RDP. The call was followed by demands that rent arrears be scrapped.

Ministry of Provincial Affairs and Constitutional Development: (021) 462-1441/(012) 341-1380
South African National Civic Organisation: (011) 333-2106

Public Enterprises and Privatisation

While its value may be a matter of economic debate, privatisation remains the litmus test of the government's economic policy.

Foreign and local investors will probably see privatisation as proof that the African National Congress has not only abandoned nationalisation, but has actively embraced free market policies.

For the government, privatisation is a thorny issue. Objection to privatisation, chiefly from the union movement, is partly a hangover of the suspicion engendered by the Nationalist government's late enthusiasm for it, partly deeply ingrained socialist mistrust, and partly a real fear that jobs will be lost.

ANC and union rejection of privatisation was so bitter that the government stalled in the beginning of the 1990s at the commercialisation stage of the process where — preparatory to privatisation — state corporations are run as private companies, though still 100 per cent state-owned. There is a residual feeling in the ANC that government intervention, albeit of the Far Eastern model rather than the Eastern European, can be relied on to restructure the economy on a new dynamic growth path.

Leading businessmen have argued that privatisation of public enterprises could be seen as a means of raising revenue for the government's Reconstruction and Development Programme. Economists, however, stress that the main benefit of privatisation is increasing competition, so all participants in an industry have to be restructured at the same time, and the cost of this could cancel out the revenue gains.

Minister of Public Enterprises Stella Sigcau says her ministry is not absolutely opposed to privatisation, but does not want it just yet; the ministry is studying ways to use privatisation in order to benefit black South Africans. She cites privatisation in Malaysia, where it was used to empower the Malay ethnic group by reserving shares for them, as an example of what can be done, but stresses that each country is different.

Sigcau controls parastatals with assets worth more than R100-billion and employing about 210 000 people. Parastatals under her supervision are Eskom, Transnet, Denel, Alexcor, Safcol, Sun Air, Transkei Airways and Aventura, covering everything from transport, electricity supply and weapons to spa resorts.

Other large parastatals, or companies wholly owned by the state, such as Telkom, are accountable to other ministries; Telkom, for example, is answerable to the minister of Posts, Telecommunications and Broadcasting. Telecommunications is the first area usually privatised in the third world. What are the other likely candidates? Like Telkom, forestry has already been commercialised. Transnet, too, has been restructured.

Eskom is an efficiently run utility, but because of, among other things, its role in extending electricity to poor areas, it could be difficult to privatise now. And the government might object to the privatisation of Denel — formerly Armscor — because of the company's strategic importance.

That does not leave much, but Sigcau has earmarked as musts for privatisation the physical assets of some of the former homeland governments which are not in use now that provincial governments have taken over.

Ministry of Public Enterprises: (012) 44-2369

Public Service

'Unbundling' the apartheid civil service — with its various central and homeland components — is proving to be one of the most complicated tasks facing the new government. Almost 40 per cent of all civil servants were employed by the 10 homelands of the previous era, and the slow task has only now begun to integrate them into one central bureaucracy and nine provincial ones.

The Public Service Act, giving effect to the new constitution, makes provision for 26 national departments, six organisational components and nine provincial administrations. The organisational components include the Central Economic Advisory Service, the Central Statistical Service, the offices of the two deputy presidents, the Office for Public Enterprise and the South African Communication Service.

The responsibility for the integration of the various departments into a unified South African public service rests with the national government, which acts on the recommendations of the Public Service Commission. The man at the centre of the process is Public Service and Administration minister Zola Skweyiya.

In August and September 1994 many senior jobs were advertised, notably the jobs of the directors-general, who serve on a contract basis. Although the adverts struck terror into the hearts of the incumbents, in the end most of them reapplied and kept their jobs.

The interim constitution guarantees civil servants' jobs, although their tenure will be governed by normal labour practice only. At present there are 746 378 civil servants working for central government; the former Transkei still employs 94 664 people, Bophuthatswana 64 890, Venda 30 520, Ciskei 30 553, Gazankulu 35 125, KaNgwane 15 251, kwaNdebele 12 456, kwaZulu 82 578, Lebowa 59 617, and Qwaqwa 15 406. The already bloated civil service is set to become even more cumbersome as the government creates an additional 11 000 jobs in an effort to apply affirmative action.

No fewer than 21 laws — including a host of Public Service Acts dating back to 1984 — had to be repealed in order to untie the crow's nest of apartheid legislation providing for homeland administrations. The task of integration is made even more difficult by the fact that some of the new provinces include parts of up to three homelands.

The constitution provides for the exercise of substantial powers by provincial service commissions, which will play a central role in the administration of the provincial segment of the national public service. However, the provincial service commissions will be required to observe norms which apply nationally. The constitution and the Public Service Act aim to make the public service non-partisan, career orientated, and functioning on fair and equitable principles — a considerable departure from the previous Afrikaner-orientated approach.

Ministry of Public Service and Administration: (021) 45-5403/(012) 314-7911

Public Works

One of the first tasks awaiting the Public Works department is sorting out some of the more lavish legacies of the previous system — including the anomaly of cabinet members being paid subsidies to stay in their own homes.

The man who has inherited the problems is Public Works minister Jeff Radebe, an African National Congress-nominated cabinet member. Radebe is in charge of some of the most impressive buildings in the country, as well as overseas embassies (including the stately South Africa House on Trafalgar Square in London). It will be his task to select new embassy buildings as the international world opens its doors to the country.

The buildings under his care inside the country include the Union Buildings in Pretoria, and stately homes like King's House in Durban and Libertas in Pretoria (home of the president). Radebe's department also has the responsibility of providing homes for ministers and looking after the gardens of the buildings under its care.

Only four months after the elections, the department was running into considerable flak for what was seen as over-spending on renovations to residences: R1-million for 'essential maintenance and limited upgrading' to the Presidency in Pretoria; R1,4-million for the president's official residence in Cape Town; R5-million for deputy president Thabo Mbeki's official homes in Pretoria and Cape Town, and R3-million for Overvaal, the official Pretoria home of second deputy president FW de Klerk. The director-general, Theo Robbroeck, claimed plans for upgrading had been made by the previous government.

Less controversial but equally interesting buildings under the care of Public Works include the South African National Antarctic Expedition base in Antarctica, the Beit Bridge border post and the Delville Wood Museum in France.

During the constitutional negotiations the department accepted responsibility for adapting the Transitional Executive Council headquarters in the Saambou Building in Pretoria to the needs of the TEC. It is also responsible for the restoration of the Castle in Cape Town.

The 1993 year report states that 411 government buildings were repaired during the previous year with the allocation of R15-million from the sale of strategic oil reserves.

The department employs 6 427 people.

Ministry of Public Works: (021) 462-4184/
    (012) 324-1520

Reconstruction and Development Programme (RDP)

This is the new, improved version of the Freedom Charter, designed to right the economic wrongs apartheid inflicted. Its six chapters range widely, from telecommunications to redistribution of land and water supply, education, health, the public sector, management/labour relations, the role of civil society, transport policy, the economy − in fact, almost everything that impinges on South Africans' basic needs and the running of the country. It is now the main economic programme of the government of national unity, and the article of faith of all who believe in the new South Africa.

Luckily perhaps, because of its necessary vagueness, the initials RDP mean many things to many different people. It is possible, for instance, for the left to see the RDP as an instrument of socialism, and certainly from a distance it must look like this to some foreign investors.

It is equally possible to link the RDP to moves to kick-start the economy or to privatisation, to pay for it.

While still worried about government overspending, businessmen have abandoned their initial hostility towards the RDP. They now accept it is essential to address the underlying social problems associated with poverty and unemployment − and, more cynically, see that massive spending may prove a boost to business in general and their own businesses in particular.

With the confusion over the RDP's scope, extent and shape, however, comes some controversy over its cost. Huge figures have been bandied about, first by the National Party during its election campaign, then by the African National Congress's own economic think-tank, the National Institute for Economic Policy. The ANC has put the cost at R39-billion; the NP at double that; the NIEP at R135-billion or so.

The RDP does mean spending more on socially desirable projects like job creation, housing and health. But as envisaged by the ANC its main thrust is redirecting existing state spending, as well as mobilising private sector finance for desired programmes. So the whole of the national budget can be seen as an instrument of the RDP.

Setting the tone, only R2,5-billion has been set aside in the 1994/95 budget specifically for RDP expenditures. Along with an additional estimated R1,7-billion, it has been directed to a special RDP fund from cuts in other departments like Defence. The total destined for the RDP fund is around R37,5-billion, to be made available from the budget over five years. This money is intended for infrastructural development, while recurring costs of RDP projects will rest with the relevant departments, provinces or local governments.

While redirection of existing spending will go some way towards rectifying the inequalities left in the wake of apartheid, it will take more than that to make the necessary difference; the government undoubtedly needs to increase its spending on socio-economic projects from present, already high, levels. The World Bank puts the backlog of social investment at R46-billion, a little more than the overall amount targeted for the RDP fund.

It is also clear that these sums assume fairly high rates of economic growth. Forget, however, where the money is going to come from. The sheer size of the development task coupled with the complexity involved in spending money effectively is such that those involved in the RDP fund may find getting the money together is the least of their worries. To illustrate the problems involved in spending money on development, at the time of writing the Independent Development Trust had allocated but not yet disbursed the full R2-billion it had been given in August 1990. The reason for the delay: 'capacity constraints', or awareness of the pointlessness of simply throwing money at development problems without first laying the groundwork in research and training.

Jay Naidoo, minister without portfolio, responsible for the
    RDP: (021) 45-5541/(012) 328-4708
National Institute for Economic Policy: (011) 403-3009

Right Wing

From a relatively cohesive power bloc at the end of 1993, the
white right once again stands deeply divided and fragmented.

The Afrikaner Volksfront (AVF), formed as a right-wing
umbrella body during the negotiations stage and once the
very symbol of right-wing unity and strength, has been
virtually usurped by the Conservative Party. Under youthful
secretary Pieter Aucamp the organisation is trying to regain
the dynamic image it lost with the departure of the generals
— specifically the departure of General Constand Viljoen to
fight the elections under the banner of the Freedom Front.
But it is experiencing scant success.

Having acted out its spoiler's role during the election
period to the very end, and consequently threatened by the
danger of being sidelined, the CP/AVF grouping began trying
a month or two after the election to wriggle its way back into
the mainstream political process. To this end the grouping
submitted a set of proposals to the government concerning
qualified participation in the constitutional process.

Concurrent to this strategy is a low-key approach to the
international community, as witnessed by submissions made
to the subcommittee on Indigenous People of the Human
Rights Committee of the United Nations.

The CP/AVF's greatest fear seems to be that of being
made irrelevant by the Freedom Front (FF) and the
Volkstaat Council (VSC), the official body set up in terms
of the constitution as part of the negotiations that brought
the FF into the elections. By having participated in the
elections, the FF already occupies an important niche in the

mainstream political process; and the VSC is a statutory body, albeit with no more than advisory powers.

By late August 1994, the VSC was on the verge of submitting its final proposals and recommendations to the government regarding an Afrikaner homeland. At the same time the CP/AVF's counter to the VSC, the Volksrepubliek Werkskomitee, was ostensibly pursuing the same interests but with nothing of substance expected from its ranks until much later.

Yet indications were that the remainder of the white right was finally emerging from its shell-shocked post-election cocoon. Statements by the FF's Viljoen, for instance, caused a degree of uneasiness among volkstaat supporters and political opponents alike; they perceived excerpts from his speeches as indicating that he had become part and parcel of the government of national unity, more interested in helping to create a common South African nationalism than furthering the cause of Afrikaner nationalism.

Apart from mainstream right-wing players such as the CP, AVF, FF and VSC, even the virtually sidelined warhorses of old began showing signs of life late in August 1994, when the Afrikaner Weerstandsbeweging's Eugene Terre'Blanche embarked on a campaign to restructure his much depleted organisation. But virtually emasculated by the arrest of 30-odd of its most active members after a pre-election spate of bombings in Johannesburg and Pretoria and on the East Rand, the organisation is unlikely to regain the stature it enjoyed among the right wing prior to the raid carried out by its members in March 1994 on a Bophuthatswana in the throes of casting out its homeland government.

In an initiative of the Herstigte Nasionale Party (HNP) and like-minded tilters at windmills, a hush-hush meeting was held in early August 1994 in which the idea of a Volks Congress was mooted. The convener was theologian Professor Adriaan Pont, and allegedly representatives from more than 90 different organisations attended the meeting. The central idea seems to be to fan the flames of Afrikaner nationalism once again by concentrating on cultural initiatives at grassroots level. Once Afrikaner nationalism has been restored, it is believed, constitutional freedom will follow inevitably.

Maybe all a bit vague, but if there is one sentiment clearly discernible among the supporters of the Volks Congress initiative it is a total distrust of and aversion to Viljoen and those willing to participate in the structures of a post-election South Africa.

The Volkstaat Council is the statutory body pursuing the interests of the right-wing Afrikaner and the volkstaat ideal in a post-election South Africa. During the election period the promise of the to-be-established VSC formed the core of the Freedom Front's election ticket.

Formally established on 16 June 1994 in Pretoria under the chairmanship of Johann Wingaard — no less a personage than first deputy president Thabo Mbeki spoke at the launch — the council consists of 20 members. The council's task, and that of its study groups, is to investigate possibilities for Afrikaner self-determination and put proposals regarding these possibilities to the GNU.

It is regarded by hard-core right-wingers as an ineffective body established for the sole purpose of placating the right wing, but the Volkstaat Council also has its advocates, who hold that it is the only realistic vehicle for achieving any form of Afrikaner self-determination. VSC supporters still see a sovereign volkstaat for the Afrikaner with its own territorial area as the council's ultimate goal. However, proposals will not include a demand for the immediate establishment of a volkstaat, they note, but will contain several interim measures that they believe will eventually lead to some degree of independence.

At its second formal session held in July, the VSC decided that self-determination for the Afrikaner means eventually having 'supreme constitutional sovereignty in a geographical volkstaat'. Questioned on this statement, VSC spokesman Koos van Rensburg acknowledged that it meant a reasonable measure of independence in a specific area but that such a volkstaat would at the same time not be completely independent from South Africa.

Explaining that a symbiosis would have to be found between Afrikaner loyalty to an Afrikaner state and concurrent loyalty to a larger South Africa, he views the volkstaat of the future as a sort of additional province, with stronger regional powers than those currently accorded the nine existing provinces.

At the same time such a volkstaat would have to be acceptable to the majority of South Africans. The proposals under current review by the various working committees of the VSC will set out to meet these requirements in a white paper to be submitted to the government.

With the advent of the VSC, the Afrikaner Volksfront, perhaps the strongest and most influential right-wing pressure group during the transitional period, has now been relegated to a CP-aligned body. CP-aligned critics of the VSC have since also established their own counter to the VSC, calling it the Volksrepubliek Werkskomitee.

Afrikaner Weerstandsbeweging (AWB): (012) 323-7613
/(01480) 2005/7/(011) 403-1191/2
Afrikaner Kultuurbond and Radio Pretoria: Ds CL van den Berg (012) 543-0120
Afrikaner Volksfront: (012) 342-2872/3
Afrikaner Volkswag: (053202) 878

Boerestaatparty: Robert van Tonder (011) 708-1988
Boere Vryheidsbeweging (BVB): (012) 335-6840
Boereweerstandsbeweging (BWB): Kommandant-Generaal
   Andrew Ford (0142) 25277
Conservative Party: (012) 342-3408/7
Freedom Front: (012) 47-4387
Oranjewerkers: (012) 348-5607/8
Mynwerkersunie (MWU): (011) 403-3930
Transnet Unie van SA: (011) 403-3530
Transvaal Municipal Association: (0148) 294-6673
Volkseenheidskomitee (Vekom): (012) 86-2073
Yster en Staalwerkers: (012) 327-4914

Safety and Security

South African police officers may soon be known as
inspectors, superintendents and commanders, instead of
majors, colonels and brigadiers. Generals will be out, chief
constables may be in. Rapidly taking charge, Safety and
Security minister Sydney Mufamadi has announced the
abolition of military ranks and the decentralisation of
command personnel and structures within the force.

The 1994/95 budget foresees the spending of R9,43-billion
on the police services.

Attempting to adjust to the demands of a participatory
democracy, the South African Police has added the word
Service to its title. The suffix is an attempt to signal a move
away from the old style of paramilitary law enforcement on
behalf of a hated regime and towards a style of policing which
satisfies community requirements. But the addition is perhaps
more telling than the minister would like to believe, signalling
as it does that the old force remains intact, if amended.

As with South Africa's military and intelligence organisations, real change can be expected to come slowly to the

police, with the old guard still firmly in the saddle for some time to come and old military habits and thought patterns refusing to disappear.

Although he has said the reorganisation and integration of the old SAP and the homelands police forces would be centred around local community policing and a devolution of responsibilities, Mufamadi has made it clear that he and the national commissioner will remain firmly in charge country-wide. The police are due to be devolved into nine provincial forces, each with its own commissioner appointed by and responsible to the national commissioner, and reporting to a local Safety and Security minister.

Mufamadi has said even those powers which were to be ceded to the provinces remained 'shared powers and all policing functions remain under the supervision of the national police service and the national minister and commissioner'.

His insistence on retaining central control could be of particular significance in kwaZulu/Natal. The fear is that the provincial force will become an Inkatha private army much as the kwaZulu Police did.

But despite his strong words on central control, Mufamadi has made it clear that he intends managing change within the police force with the co-operation of regional police ministers and commanders. A Committee of Ministers from all nine regions is assisting in the implementation of reforms. A similar body comprising the commissioners of the former homelands police forces and the SAPS chief has been instituted. The 11 commissioners command about 115 000 former SAP and 26 000 former homelands police personnel.

Although Mufamadi has refused to be drawn on whether the numbers are adequate to achieve his goals of a force responsible to community needs and demands and a significant reduction in crime levels, he has indirectly confirmed the view of foreign policing experts who have said manning levels are too low by as much as 50 per cent, and that civilians should take over certain administrative functions so that more uniformed officers can be put back on the beat.

Mufamadi has agreed that many administrative tasks currently performed by uniformed police would in future go to civilians in an effort to 'improve productivity and motivation'. A number of Pretoria-based senior officers and experts are moving to the provinces so that their skills and abilities can be used where they are needed most.

While attempting to allay the fears of white police officers, Mufamadi has said affirmative action would play an increasing role in making the force 'visibly more representative of the population. It is vital for the legitimacy and credibility of the SAPS that more blacks be brought into the top structure.' He has added that a police force which more closely mirrors the population needs more women, and has promised a plan to combat gender discrimination.

Yet the police services have other problems to overcome. The Waddington report, written by an English policing expert following the 1992 Boipatong massacre, was particularly critical of the SAPS's professional shortcomings. Standards of detective work, scene-of-crime techniques and other specialist areas are said to lag years behind the current international norm.

Perhaps most important in the short term will be how the senior officer corps, with its roots in apartheid, responds to direction from the new government, and whether they can change enough to give the force legitimacy. A campaign in August 1994 to cut the toll of police deaths in action seemed to be gathering popular support, an indication that a change in the general perception of the force might be on the way.

Ministry of Safety and Security: (021) 45-7400/
(012) 323-8880/1/2/3

Truth Commission

The Truth Commission to probe apartheid-era crimes has
been variously labelled a witch-hunt, South Africa's own
Nuremberg Trials — and a toothless, useless, waste-of-time
investigation.

It will rely on the consciences of those involved in human
rights violations to prompt them to come forward and
'confess'. The carrot is likely to be amnesty. The stick is
prosecution if they do not volunteer information and their
misdeeds are subsequently discovered.

The names of the perpetrators and the crimes to which
they confess will be published in the Government Gazette.
Although the commission will make recommendations to the
president about who should be given amnesty, he will take
the final decision.

Despite the expectations of some of the victims, compensation has been ruled out because of the cost involved.
Relatives of some people killed by state agents to maintain
apartheid strongly object to the commission and to amnesty
being granted from criminal prosecution and civil action.
They feel their grievances are being ignored and that the state
is leaving them in the lurch by agreeing to a commission
without the power to prosecute.

Ministry of Justice: (021) 45-7506/(012) 323-8581

Water Affairs and Forestry

This ministry was long considered a dumping ground for
disgraced politicians awaiting their pensions, but the
appointment of African National Congress heavyweight

Kader Asmal to head it is a sign of its importance to the Reconstruction and Development Programme.

It is not hard to see why: the provision of safe water is fundamental to the success of any other reconstruction projects and basic to the restoration of human dignity in many rural and informal settlement areas. The new minister inherits a situation where more than a third of South Africans have no ready access to clean and safe water and half the population has no hygienic sanitation. So, while the department has notched up a number of notable engineering feats — the construction of huge dams, even the reversal of the flow of the Vaal River — it has paid little attention to the needs of the mass of the population.

Asmal has embarked on what he has called 'my department's revolutionary new mission'. This involves rewriting the law, redirecting the expertise and channelling the funds into water and sanitation provision for the most needy. Asmal plans a programme of Community Water Supply and Sanitation to co-ordinate these activities, reform of the Water Boards, and the reshaping of subsidies so that heavy household water users support those with least access to the service.

How difficult it will be to meet the needs of ordinary households became clear when Asmal announced within weeks of taking office that clean drinking water and sanitation would be provided to the entire population within three years. Afterwards, it was estimated that supplying water would cost between R200 and R250 per head, and sanitation between R300 and R350 — a total cost of between R10-billion and R13-billion.

Ministry of Water Affairs and Forestry: (021) 45-5541/
    (012) 299-2083

3

POLITICAL PARTIES

In this chapter, we profile the seven parties that won seats in
the National Assembly. They appear in order of size: the
African National Congress, the National Party, Inkatha
Freedom Party, Freedom Front, Democratic Party, Pan
Africanist Congress and African Christian Democratic Party.

African National Congress (ANC)

The African National Congress emerged from the April 1994
elections overwhelmingly dominant, winning three times as
many votes as its nearest rival. The ANC's 12,2-million votes,
or 62,65 per cent of the electorate, gave it 252 of the 400
National Assembly seats; and the party won control of seven
of the nine provincial governments. Its election victory was
the culmination of the extraordinary transformation the
ANC had undergone in the four years since its unbanning,
from the world's oldest liberation movement to the ruling
party in the one country that had engineered a relatively
peaceful transition from minority rule to democracy.

The ANC's most striking feature is just how broad a
church it is. While changing to a political party, it has
managed so far to keep the varied constituency more
characteristic of a liberation movement. Its support crosses
the barriers of ethnicity, language, religion, geography, age,
gender and ideology. In formal terms, it leads an alliance of
trade unionists, civic associations, communists, women's
organisations, youth organisations and former homeland
politicians, known as the 'Congress Alliance' or the

'Tripartite Alliance' (from the three major members: the ANC, Cosatu and the South African Communist Party).

It is a tribute to the standing, political skill and commitment to unity of President Nelson Mandela that this alliance not only held its ground in the 1994 elections, but emerged stronger than ever. From a rich mixture of liberal businessmen, radical socialists and conservatives, he has forged a party that is broadly social democratic in outlook and held together by his pragmatic vision of a multicultural, multireligious, multilingual society based on racial and gender equality.

The ANC was founded in 1912 as the South African Native National Congress. It was a gathering of intellectuals — led by legendary black leaders such as Pixley ka Izaka Seme, John Dube and Sol Plaatje — seeking to unite their people across tribal lines. But when their representations against, for example, what was to become the 1913 Land Act and the 1924 Hertzog racial Bills went unheard, it became little more than a talk shop.

This changed in the post-war ferment of the late 1940s, when a new generation of more radical and impatient leaders of the ANC Youth League — Mandela, Oliver Tambo, Walter Sisulu and Anton Lembede — galvanised the organisation into a more militant stance and pushed in into a Programme of Action involving the 'new weapons' of protest, boycott, strike and civil disobedience.

Their successful takeover of the ANC led to the passive resistance and stayaways of the 1950s. It was also during this period that the Congress Alliance was formed, bringing the ANC together with parallel coloured, Indian and white organisations. In 1956, a Congress of the People, an informal Parliament-like gathering, adopted the Freedom Charter, which was to define the ANC's credo for the next three decades: non-racialism, equality, democracy and a soft socialist demand for social reform through redistribution and nationalisation.

In 1959, ANC stalwart Robert Sobukwe led a breakaway of those disgruntled with non-racialism and the influence of white communists and Indians to form the Pan Africanist Congress. For decades thereafter, the ANC and PAC — both recognised by the Organisation of African Unity and the United Nations — competed for recognition as the primary liberation movement.

The 1950s also brought the first wave of serious government repression which was to last, and grow steadily more brutal, until 1990. The process began with the lengthy 1956 Treason Trial of 156 leaders and continued with the banning of the ANC and PAC in 1960 and the decision of both organisations to abandon peaceful resistance and take up armed struggle through a military wing, Umkhonto weSizwe. It also brought the 'dirty war' of the 1980s when hundreds of ANC members were detained, jailed or assassinated.

The first few, rather ineffectual, bomb blasts of the armed struggle led to the arrest in Rivonia, north of Johannesburg, of the ANC military leadership, including Sisulu, Govan Mbeki, Ahmed Kathrada and Dennis Goldberg. With Mandela, who was already serving a sentence for leaving the country illegally, they were tried and sentenced to life imprisonment.

Tambo led the organisation into exile to begin three decades of long, hard slog in London and Lusaka. His steady, unifying leadership saw the organisation through the relatively inactive and militarily unsuccessful 1960s and 1970s, but the organisation was rejuvenated by the new influx of young radicals after the 1976 uprising. The next few years saw some spectacular, if isolated and infrequent, displays of military action in line with a policy of 'armed propaganda' — the use of high-profile military activities to boost morale and resistance inside the country. These included the bombing of the Sasol refinery in 1980, the Koeberg plant in 1982 and a massive bomb outside Air Force headquarters in central Pretoria in 1983.

Tambo's greatest success, however, was in the field of diplomacy where, with current deputy president Thabo Mbeki at his side, he quietly worked to establish the ANC as the primary voice of the liberation struggle in the international community and to bring about the political, economic, sporting and cultural isolation of the Pretoria government.

Tambo led the ANC through its crisis conference in Mogorogoro in 1969 and its consolidation conference in Kabwe in 1985 — both landmarks in the development of the organisation. The Mogorogoro conference allowed whites to become members and some were elected to the national executive for the first time at Kabwe. Throughout this period, the ANC kept its close alliance with the Communist Party.

Snubbed by most Western leaders for many years, the ANC found its main support in the Soviet Union, Eastern Europe, Scandinavia and southern African governments under the banner of the Frontline States. As a rule, Scandinavia supplied money, the Soviet Union arms, and the Frontline States bases. Gradually, the ANC built up support in anti-apartheid movements in the West and in the mid-1980s Tambo's reception by the United States State Department signalled a breakthrough in Western acceptance. This was fuelled by the massive popular support garnered by the anti-apartheid movements in each of these countries, and the growing status of Mandela as the world's best-known prisoner.

The ANC's fortunes also grew with the shift inside the country away from the black consciousness organisations of the 1970s to bodies such as the United Democratic Front, essentially ANC-front organisations. Through them, the ANC led the move to boycott apartheid institutions, undermine partial reforms and resist the conditional release from prison of the Rivonia trialists, who had been offered their freedom if they would officially renounce violence.

While building a new, broad-based, internal alliance, the ANC also constructed a ramshackle government-in-exile, with representatives in dozens of countries, a large bureaucracy around its Lusaka headquarters, and armies based in African countries. South Africa's military dominance of its neighbours frustrated the ANC's attempts to infiltrate guerrillas but in the late 1980s the organisation adopted a new strategy: Operation Vula, devised to build a new underground network within South Africa, with the long-term intention of promoting insurrection.

By the time the government moved to reform and negotiation in the late 1980s, the ANC was established strongly enough, both internally and internationally, to make it impossible for changes to take place without the organisation. Talks with the still-imprisoned Mandela began in 1988 and public contact with the ANC in exile — such as by businessmen who visited Lusaka in 1985 and a group of prominent Afrikaners who met ANC leaders in Dakar in 1987 — broke the ice. The ANC, meanwhile, had succeeded in getting its blueprint for negotiations, known as the Harare Declaration, adopted by most international bodies.

The ANC's pre-eminent status was confirmed when it was unbanned in 1990. Its leaders returned to open headquarters in Johannesburg. The organisation led the next four years of negotiations with the government, proving to be a more formidable opponent than the government had anticipated.

Those four years culminated in the election victory and the ANC's ascendancy to government in 1994.

The ANC ran an election campaign based on 'peace, jobs and freedom' and 'a better life for all', built on Mandela's personal credibility and a candidates list that brought together every element of its broad-based constituency. The party swept the black vote, winning about 11,5-million of the 14,2-million ballots cast by black voters, but managed less than 30 per cent of the coloured and Indian votes and only a tiny fraction of the white vote. The extent to which it swept black votes was matched by its failure in the coloured and Indian communities.

As a political organisation, the ANC has now been depleted by the rush of its leading members to state and parliamentary jobs and it is burdened by a large election debt. Only a few leaders, notably secretary-general Cyril Ramaphosa and Cheryl Carolus, remained behind in the party structures to help prepare for the important local government elections due in 1995.

The challenge for the ANC will be to hold together its vast constituency, particularly when Mandela's powerful figure is no longer present to lead it. But there is no shortage of formidable leaders to replace Mandela, notably Ramaphosa, Mbeki and Gauteng premier Tokyo Sexwale, all of whom command sufficient respect to lead the ANC in future. Mbeki, however, had by the end of 1994 established himself as the heir apparent.

National Party (NP, members often called Nats)

The dominant party in white parliamentary politics since it came to power in 1948, the National Party has been cut down to its proper size by the first democratic elections of 27 April 1994 — what African National Congress (and former NP) member Jannie Momberg now dismisses as 'the 20 per cent party'. With 82 members in the 400-member National Assembly, the NP is the second biggest party after the ANC (252 members). However, the election results reflected the 'worst scenario' predictions of its strategists. Instead of the expected 30 per cent, the NP mustered 20,39 per cent of the vote countrywide, against the ANC's 62,65 per cent.

But the party is still relatively strong, representing mostly the interests of the previous — and still influential — establishment: civil servants, farmers, the security forces and big business. In terms of agreements reached during the negotiations in Kempton Park in 1993, the party's leader, FW de Klerk, was inaugurated as second deputy president in the government of national unity. Nats also share the senior posts in Parliament with ANC members and have — De Klerk excluded — five NP members in President Nelson Mandela's 27-member cabinet.

The NP's poor showing at the polls forced it to compromise on its pre-election insistence to be represented by either a minister or deputy minister in all the so-called security portfolios: Safety and Security, Defence, Correctional Services, and Justice. In the end it had to be satisfied with only one of these posts, that of deputy minister of Justice.

The present power-sharing relationship between the NP and the ANC is to last until the next general elections, due in April 1999.

In the April 1994 elections, the NP won control of only one of the nine provincial governments, that of the Western Cape. In the Northern Cape it was narrowly beaten by the ANC (12 seats against the ANC's 15).

The NP has come a long way since it was founded by General JBM Hertzog in 1914 in an effort to unify Afrikaners politically. The aim right from the start was to achieve a more prominent role for Afrikaners in society and in government, to resist British imperialism, to develop the country and to keep blacks, coloureds and Indians socially and politically apart from whites.

In 1924, with the assistance of the (white) Labour Party under Colonel FHP Creswell, the NP came to power for the first time, ousting Jan Smuts's South African Party (SAP). The NP had the active support, in that election, of the ANC, which in May 1924 had urged the few blacks who qualified to 'vote solidly for changes in government'.

Having secured equal language rights for Afrikaans and English, and sovereign independence for South Africa, the NP and SAP were fused into the United Party. Afrikaner ideals were now subject to broader national interests — which led in 1934 to a breakaway by Dr DF Malan and his followers, who formed the Purified National Party.

The present NP grew from the Purified NP, a very different party from Hertzog's NP; it was strongly republican and ethnically exclusive, and it openly set out to uplift Afrikaners materially and promote their group interests at the cost of other communities.

When Malan's NP came to power in a surprise victory in the all-white 1948 poll, it immediately set out to implement its policy of racial separation, or apartheid, aimed at entrenching white minority rule to the exclusion of all other population groups. A plethora of racist Acts followed. In 1949 the Prohibition of Mixed Marriages Act was accepted by Parliament, followed by the Population Registration Act (1950), the Group Areas Act (1950), the Separate Representation of Voters Act (1951) which stripped coloured voters of the franchise, the Bantu Authorities Act (1951), Bantu Education (1953), Natives' Resettlement Act (1954), Reservation of Separate Amenities Act (1953), the Preservation of

Coloured Areas Act (1961), and the Urban Bantu Councils Act (1961). There were other Acts, ranging from the barring of blacks from 'white' universities to legislation allowing for the independence of black homelands.

During the 1960s, under the premiership of Dr HF Verwoerd, the apartheid structures were further entrenched. In 1961, the great Afrikaner ideal of an independent republic was realised.

The racist policies of the NP led to increasing internal resistance and international isolation. When PW Botha came to power in 1978, the state was beginning to lose legitimacy. A 'total strategy' was developed against what was perceived as a 'total onslaught', with the security establishment playing an increasingly prominent role.

The 'total strategy' was supplemented by limited reforms to apartheid laws. Trade unions were legalised, the prohibition on mixed marriages was scrapped, limitations on the movement of blacks were lifted.

Botha's political reforms were supported by verligtes in the NP, including Afrikaner cultural leaders, academics, business people and senior civil servants. They were rejected, however, by the NP's right wing which felt Botha was moving too fast, and broke away in 1982 to form the Conservative Party (CP). The reforms were also rejected by those who were supposed to have benefited from them but felt they were insufficient: the majority of black people.

In 1983 a new constitution was forced through Parliament, allowing for an executive state president. Power-sharing with coloureds and Indians was introduced, allowing these groups a minority share of Parliament in two separate, racially based chambers. The exclusion of blacks led to a countrywide popular revolt, precipitating a State of Emergency in 1985.

Parliament became increasingly less important as power shifted to the National Security Management System and the security establishment in general. By May 1987, when Botha called a general election, it had become clear that the new state president had lost his will for further reform. However, Botha succeeded in broadening the NP's base beyond its ethnic origins: as right-wing Afrikaners flocked to the CP, the NP polled more English votes than ever before in its history.

In 1989, after suffering a stroke, Botha was succeeded by FW de Klerk, following an unsavoury behind-the-scenes power tussle. Previously known as a conservative member of the NP caucus, De Klerk promised a 'new South Africa' free from racism and domination. At its federal congress in Pretoria in June 1989, the NP accepted a 'five-year plan' towards democracy. However, groups still formed the basis of the new plan and no allowance was made for negotiations with banned organisations.

On 2 February 1990, De Klerk astounded friend and foe by announcing the unbanning of the African National Congress, the Pan Africanist Congress and the South African Communist Party, fundamentally changing the rules of the political game.

Negotiations with black-dominated organisations which had been excluded from power started later in 1990. Indications are that the NP thought it would be possible to co-opt the ANC. The negotiations at Kempton Park soon showed that it had seriously underestimated its erstwhile enemies.

The NP has now committed itself to democracy and is promising an image of itself as a party of reform for the whole country, claiming that its principles are based on capitalism and 'Western thinking'. But in defining its future role, it will have to take a close look at the make-up of its current support. The NP did better in the white community in the April 1994 elections than ever before, routing its right wing and its liberal rivals, and reversing the gradual decline it had experienced since the formation of the CP in the early 1980s. In his *Election '94 South Africa*, analyst Andrew Reynolds estimates that the NP won 65 per cent of white votes in April 1994, as opposed to 48 per cent in the 1989 general election, 53 per cent in the 1987 general election, and 58 per cent in the 1981 general election.

However, whites make up only 15 per cent of the electorate, and although the NP did better than expected in the coloured and Indian communities, winning 60-70 per cent of their votes, these three racial groups together constitute only 27 per cent of the voters. Thus, even in the unlikely event of the NP's winning every single white, coloured and Indian vote, it will still remain a small minority party. Its major problem is that it won only three to four per cent of the black vote — and it will never mount a significant challenge to the ANC unless it makes serious inroads among these voters.

The NP is now in an awkward situation as both a member of the government and the largest party in opposition. It has to assert itself as a party in its own right, while not being seen to undermine the government of national unity. It has to oppose the government while playing a part in it — not an easy position from which to build a party.

It will also have to prove itself in the one province it controls, the Western Cape. It will want to show that it can deliver on reconstruction and development as well as the ANC can, but will depend on central government's co-operation and assistance to do this.

The party's greatest asset is undoubtedly the leadership of De Klerk, whose personal image contributed enormously to the NP's ability to overcome its burdensome past. Its strength is also greater than its numbers, because it commands more support than the ANC in key areas, such as the civil service, the security forces and the business community.

Inkatha Freedom Party (IFP)

The April 1994 election proved Inkatha to be a formidable regional party in kwaZulu/Natal, but a negligible national force. It won kwaZulu/Natal with 50,3 per cent of the vote in this, the most populous province. But it won only 10,5 per cent nationally, giving it 43 National Assembly seats and three cabinet places. Votes for the IFP came almost entirely from Zulus and about 85 per cent were from kwaZulu/Natal. It was a dream result for those who placed peace highest on their agenda: not enough to give the bellicose IFP ambitions for central power, but just enough provincial clout to allow it to accept the outcome with dignity.

The IFP, for long the ruling party in the kwaZulu homeland, was founded in 1975 as Inkatha Yenkululeku Yesizwe, a Zulu cultural organisation named for the coil heirloom representing Zulu unity and used to soften the weight of goods carried by women on their heads. It was originally formed with the blessing of the then banned African National Congress, since its founder, Chief Mangosuthu Buthelezi, was an ANC member with a close relationship with Nelson Mandela. The two organisations, however, fell out in the late 1970s and a steady deterioration in their relationship led to bloody conflict in many parts of the country. Inkatha was renamed the Inkatha Freedom Party when it transformed itself into a political party in 1990 and made a bid for the national vote.

For many years, Buthelezi positioned Inkatha as the liberal, non-violent, pro-capitalist alternative to the ANC, and for this won much support from moderate South African whites and Western politicians. But there was little to back up this positioning; in reality, Inkatha was a top-heavy, not very democratic organisation that based its appeal on ethnic nationalism and homeland patronage.

The organisation took a series of knocks with the exposé in 1991 of the secret financial and logistical support it received from the Security Police and Military Intelligence and lost a good deal of support during the early 1990s because of its belligerent and ethnocentric attitude towards negotiations. Buthelezi and the IFP gradually shed their liberal, non-violent image and took on a much more warlike and intolerant one. This was reinforced when Buthelezi showed he was prepared to go to the brink of war to win concessions before he would enter the elections, agreeing to put his name on the ballot only at the last minute.

The IFP has also been tainted by the involvement in violence of the kwaZulu Police, which fell under the personal ministership of Buthelezi himself. A number of its leaders, including current provincial Justice minister JC Mthethwa, and Transvaal leaders Themba Khoza and Humphrey Ndlovu, have been implicated in gun smuggling and the trial of 'third force' leader Eugene de Kock.

The party's claim to kwaZulu/Natal is not unchallenged. Serious allegations of election fraud were pushed aside for the sake of peace, leaving disgruntled ANC members believing that their party had sold them out for the sake of national reconciliation. In truth, all that is in dispute is the exact number of votes making up the IFP's clear majority; there is little doubt that the party soundly beat the ANC in the province.

The provincial leadership got off to a stormy start, with disputes over cabinet positions and the location of the capital. The IFP faces a formidable challenge in the province, proving it can deliver reconstruction and development at least as well as the ANC can in other provinces, but relying on the central government for resources. The IFP is likely to provide the strongest provincial challenge to central government powers. Throughout negotiations, the IFP took a strong federalist line, arguing for much greater provincial powers and even indirectly threatening secession for kwaZulu/Natal.

Although Buthelezi was given the important national ministry of Home Affairs, he has shown much greater interest in the politics of his home province, looking over the shoulder of kwaZulu/Natal premier, Dr Frank Mdlalose. A shrewd politician, Buthelezi is certain to make sure, first and foremost, that his home base is secure.

He has suffered one major political blow: losing the support of Zulu King Goodwill Zwelithini. The national ascendancy of the ANC, and the quiet diplomatic work of ANC provincial leader Jacob Zuma, appears to have drawn the king away from Buthelezi's control.

The king is a key to the traditionalist, rural Zulu vote — and this is the IFP's heartland. In the elections, the ANC won most of the kwaZulu/Natal urban areas, and the IFP dominated the rest of the region. Now the test will be how the IFP fares without the kind of absolute control it held in the homeland — and the patronage it dispensed there — and without the support of the king.

In its annual conference after the election, the IFP moved to democratise itself, diluting Buthelezi's personal power and influence. A new constitution was adopted, similar to a 1990 constitution which had similar intentions but was never implemented. Now, however, Buthelezi faces a strong push from the more moderate and pragmatic members of his party who favoured negotiations and were uncomfortable with Buthelezi's brinkmanship, notably Ziba Jiyane, Joe Matthews,

Ben Ngubane and Mdlalose. The constitutional change, however, is not fundamental: Buthelezi still retains the power to choose the leaders of his party executive.

Freedom Front (FF)

The Freedom Front was ostensibly registered to serve as an election vehicle for a possible coalition party consisting of members of the now defunct Freedom Alliance. But the party was eventually used by General Constand Viljoen and his supporters to contest the election. Riding on the ticket of a volkstaat to be pursued after the election by the peaceful means of the Volkstaatraad (Volkstaat Council), Viljoen was hounded by hard-core right-wingers for his decision to participate in the election.

But Viljoen brushed aside radical right-wing war-talk, seeking — with the realism of a battle-weary soldier — the solution that would give Afrikaners the best of a losing situation, and leaving behind a rather rudderless Afrikaner Volksfront (AVF).

Although Viljoen announced his decision barely a month before elections, the FF's participation was not an absolute certainty until a few days before the poll. Using a combination of brinkmanship and promises, Viljoen eventually succeeded in getting the National Party and the African National Congress to sign a tripartite accord on 23 April, making provision for the creation of the Volkstaatraad and clearing the way for his participation in the ballot. Viljoen, ditching the hard-core right wing, went to vote in the Voortrekkerhoogte military base in the company of 35 former generals, including former police commissioner Mike Geldenhuys and former head of the Bureau for State Security (Boss), Hendrik van den Berg.

The FF polled a total of 424 555 votes on a national level and notably more, 639 643, on a provincial level, giving it nine National Assembly seats and a handful of seats in the three provinces in which it did best: Gauteng, the Orange Free State and the Northern Cape. This was notably less than the one million predicted by Viljoen beforehand and even less than the 670 000 votes won by the Conservative Party in 1989 and 547 000 in 1987.

But it did represent 14 per cent of the national white vote, and 20 per cent of the provincial white vote, and Viljoen viewed the latter as 'real and proven' support for the ideal of a volkstaat among Afrikaners. There were only pockets of the country, a few lone districts, in which he could claim majority support among whites. However, according to Viljoen, the FF's showing in the polls gave his Volkstaatraad the support of 35 to 40 per cent of the 1,8-million Afrikaners.

Democratic Party (DP, or Democrats)

Once the proud bearer of the liberal torch, the Democratic Party has been all but wiped out in the country's first democratic elections. It succeeded in winning only seven seats in the National Assembly, and did not fare much better in the provinces: in kwaZulu/Natal it won two seats, in the PWV (renamed Gauteng in December 1994) five, in the Western Cape three, in the Eastern Cape one, and in the Northern Cape one. The disappointing election results led to the resignation of party leader Dr Zach de Beer. Tony Leon, the dynamic but controversial young PWV leader of the party, was named leader.

The party was founded in Johannesburg in April 1989, when the Progressive Federal Party (PFP), the Independent Party (IP) and the National Democratic Movement (NDM) joined forces. Of these, only the PFP had a history of resisting apartheid, going back to the breakaway of a group of liberals from the United Party in 1959 to form the Progressive Party. The Progressive Party had been associated with the redoubtable Helen Suzman who for many years was its only representative in Parliament, maintaining a lone but influential liberal voice that earned her universal respect and international honour.

The IP and NDM were formed shortly before the 1987 general elections, and consisted mainly of a so-called 'fourth force' of Afrikaners disenchanted with the refusal of then prime minister PW Botha to implement inevitable political reforms.

Initially the Democratic Party, combining the full spectrum of left-wing forces in Parliament, was led by a triumvirate of leaders: the PFP's Zach de Beer, the IP's Denis Worrall, and the NDM's Wynand Malan. De Beer was later elected sole leader.

Espousing liberal values and predominantly representing English speakers, the DP played an important role in the previous white-controlled Parliament as a moral watchdog over the excesses of the National Party's policies. In addition, many of its members were involved in monitoring both the state's oppression and the popular groundswell against the NP's apartheid policies. The DP was represented at the multiparty negotiations by party stalwarts Colin Eglin and Ken Andrew, who both played an important role in the drafting of the transitional constitution.

But in the April 1994 elections, the DP failed to overcome its image as a party of comfortable white liberals, making few inroads into the coloured, Indian or black communities that make up 85 per cent of the voters. Between 80 and 90 per cent of its votes came from the 15 per cent of the community that is white. Yet even within that racial group, it did not fare well, polling only 10 per cent of the national votes of the white community, down considerably from the 20 per cent enjoyed by it, or its predecessor, the PFP, in 1989 and 1981.

Pan Africanist Congress of Azania (PAC)

The Pan Africanist Congress, formed from an Africanist breakaway from the African National Congress in 1959 under the charismatic and respected Robert Sobukwe, gave voice after February 1990 to those demanding a much more radical form of transformation than the ANC was delivering through negotiations. It was therefore expected to ride the rising tide of disillusionment of the most dispossessed and disempowered South Africans.

But it was not to happen. The PAC's radical — even racist — slogans cost it votes, seemingly fuelling the electorate's desperate desire for peace above all else. The PAC had misread the signs and paid dearly, being all but wiped out in the April 1994 elections. It won just 243 000 votes, or 1,25 per cent, and five seats in the National Assembly — not anywhere near enough to join the government of national unity. Even in its radical heartland, the Eastern Cape, the PAC came a pathetic fourth behind the Democratic Party.

The main reason for this seems to be poor leadership, which led to an abominable election campaign. President Clarence Makwetu made few public appearances, and failed to impress when he did. The PAC was a reluctant negotiator and peacemaker, continuing with war-talk even as the war ended after 1990. It was ridden with internal conflicts over negotiations and the laying down of arms and never succeeded in presenting an alternative vision to the ANC's policy of reconciliation and compromise.

Its election collapse is certain to lead to challenges to the leadership, but the critical question is whether the PAC — long expected to provide the most significant challenge to the

ANC at the next election — will survive its disastrous performance in the first.

African Christian Democratic Party (ACDP)

The African Christian Democratic Party failed to make any significant impression in the elections. It won a single seat in the National Assembly, one seat in the Eastern Cape legislature and one in kwaZulu/Natal.

The party was founded under controversial circumstances by Dr Johan van der Westhuizen, a former front man for Military Intelligence in the previous dispensation. For several years, beginning in 1986, Van der Westhuizen ran state-sponsored organisations, often behind Christian front groups, involved in anti-African National Congress activities.

The party's leader is Kenneth Meshoe. During the election campaign the ACDP underscored its capitalist approach with a clear Christian message, stating that all legislation 'must be ultimately measured against the Word of God'. The party's manifesto said there could be no human rights without 'all people committing themselves to fulfilling their responsibilities and duties to God'.

4

THE PROVINCES

One of the richest new elements of South African politics emerges from the creation of nine new provincial governments. Since their powers in relation to the central government are not yet clearly defined, there will be fascinating battles between the provinces and the central authority over the extent and the nature of their respective responsibilities. Two of the provinces — kwaZulu/Natal and the Western Cape — are not in African National Congress hands, and their relationship with the central government will be particularly important to long-term national politics and to the future of the second and third largest political parties. In this chapter, we outline the political dynamics of each of these provinces against the background of each province's socio-economic conditions.

Eastern Cape

Capital: Bisho/King William's Town
Premier: Raymond Mhlaba (ANC)
Regional executive:
Ezra Sigwela (ANC) — Land Reform, Administration and Departmental Planning
Smuts Ngonyama (ANC) — Economic Affairs
Sheperd Mayatula (ANC) — Finance

This chapter draws on the work of: The Bureau for Market Research of the University of South Africa, Report No 207, 'Socio-economic Profile of the Nine Provinces, 1994', by JH Martins, AA Ligthelm, M Loubser and H de J van Wyk; *Fast Facts*, Number 7, produced by the South African Institute of Race Relations; and *Elections '94*, edited by Andrew Reynolds (David Philip).

Trudie Thomas (ANC) — Health and Welfare
Nosimo Balindlela (ANC) — Education and Culture
Malizo Mpehle (ANC) — Safety and Security
Thobile Mhlahlo (ANC) — Public Works
Mandisa Marasha (ANC) — Transport
Max Mamase (ANC) — Housing and Local Government
Tertius Delport (NP) — Agriculture and Environmental
   Planning
Prince Msutu — Provincial government spokesperson

Telephone: (0401) 91415/92319
Fax: (0471) 95-1166

Population: 6 665 400 (16,4% of total)
Area: 170 616 square kilometres (13,9% of total)
Languages: Xhosa 85%; Afrikaans 9%; English 3%
Proportion of country's GDP: 7,4%
Proportion of country's direct tax: 5,4%

1994 Election		
Party	Votes	Seats
African National Congress	84,4%	48
National Party	9,8%	6
Democratic Party	2,1%	1
Pan Africanist Congress	2,0%	1
TOTAL	2 922 154	56
Spoilt ballots	0,45%	

This province, which incorporates parts of the former
Transkei and Ciskei, is marked by its poverty and
unemployment, and its history of radical politics. A focal
point of the struggles of the 1970s and 1980s, it is the region

that spawned Nelson Mandela, Oliver Tambo, Chris Hani, Thabo Mbeki and Steve Biko.

The main surprise, therefore, in the ANC's overwhelming election victory was that the PAC, which viewed this as its stronghold, did little better than in the rest of the country. It is also worth noting that the combined vote for the NP, DP and the Freedom Front (which failed to win a seat) was 12,6 per cent, a proportion higher than the eight per cent constituted by the province's white voters.

Motor manufacturing is the key industry, providing a base for powerful trade unions. But much of the male population migrates to work in other provinces, such as on the mines of the Witwatersrand.

Among the first items that the new provincial government will have to deal with are demands that the province be split into two parts: an eastern Cape region and a Border/Kei region. The ANC opposes this because it does not believe the latter region will be viable on its own. The other two parties in the provincial assembly support the split. The NP won many of the Border/Kei districts in the election, though it was overwhelmed in the vast bulk of the province.

There will also have to be a decision on a proposal to cede the Kokstad area to kwaZulu/Natal.

Tertius Delport sits as the sole NP member in the executive and the recipient of ANC goodwill, as his party did not get the 10 per cent of the vote that would have entitled it to an executive seat.

Eastern Transvaal

Capital: Nelspruit
Premier: Mathews Phosa (ANC)
Regional executive:
Jacob Mabena (ANC) — Economic Affairs

The Nine Provinces

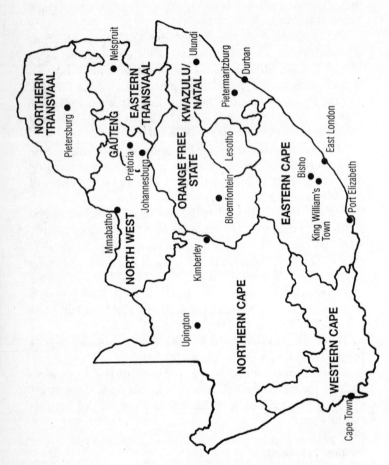

NORTHERN TRANSVAAL

Pietersburg

Nelspruit

GAUTENG

EASTERN TRANSVAAL

Pretoria

Johannesburg

KWAZULU/NATAL

Ulundi

Pietermaritzburg

Durban

Mmabatho

NORTH WEST

ORANGE FREE STATE

Lesotho

Bloemfontein

EASTERN CAPE

East London

Bisho

King William's Town

Port Elizabeth

Kimberley

NORTHERN CAPE

Upington

WESTERN CAPE

Cape Town

Jacques Modipane (ANC) — Finance
January Masilela (ANC) — Local Government
Craig Padayachee (ANC) — Housing
Jabulane Mabona (ANC) — Law and Order
David Mkwanazi (ANC) — Environmental Affairs
Ntimane Mathebula (ANC) — Public Works, Roads and Transport
Steven Mbuyisa (ANC) — Without portfolio
David Mabuza (ANC) — Education and Training
Lucas Nel (NP) — Agriculture

Telephone: (01311) 55-1476
Fax: (01311) 55-1172

Population: 2 838 500 (6,9% of total)
Area: 81 816 square kilometres (6,7% of total)
Languages: Siswati 40%; Zulu 28%; Afrikaans 9%
Proportion of country's GDP: 8,5%
Proportion of country's direct tax: 5,4%

1994 Election		
Party	Votes	Seats
African National Congress	80,7%	25
National Party	9,0%	3
Freedom Front	5,7%	2
TOTAL	1 338 699	30
Spoilt ballots	0,94%	

This farming area is solid ANC territory, with pockets in which the FF outnumbers the NP. It has the fourth strongest provincial economy in the country, largely because of its agriculture, though premier Mathews Phosa has indicated that he intends to develop tourism and build a university and a casino to attract revenue for his reconstruction and development work. Game reserves are already a significant part of the economy.

The NP did not get the 10 per cent of the vote that would have entitled it to an executive seat, but the premier not only gave the party one seat in the name of goodwill, but handed over the important agriculture portfolio.

Gauteng (formerly PWV)

Capital: Johannesburg
Premier: Tokyo Sexwale (ANC)
Regional executive:
Amos Masondo (ANC) — Health
Jessie Duarte (ANC) — Public Safety and Security
Sicelo Shiceka (ANC) — Development Planning, Environment and Works
Dan Mofokeng (ANC) — Housing and Local Government
Mary Metcalfe (ANC) — Education
Jabu Moleketi (ANC) — Economic Affairs and Finance
Peter Skosana (ANC) — Sports, Recreation, Arts and Culture
John Mavuso (NP) — Agriculture and Conservation
Olaus van Zyl (NP) — Public Transport and Roads
Johannes Blance (NP) — Social Welfare

Telephone: (011) 240-1500
Fax: (011) 836-7219/8558

Population: 6 850 000 (16,8% of total)
Area: 18 760 square kilometres (1,5% of total)
Languages: Afrikaans 20%; Zulu 18%; English 15%
Proportion of country's GDP: 37% (1988)
Proportion of country's direct tax: 49,3%

1994 Election		
Party	Votes	Seats
African National Congress	57,6%	50
National Party	23,9%	21
Freedom Front	6,2%	5
Democratic Party	5,3%	5
Inkatha Freedom Party	3,7%	3
Pan Africanist Congress	1,5%	1
African Christian Democratic Party	0,6%	1
TOTAL	4 223 633	86
Spoilt ballots	0,6%	

This province is effectively a single greater metropolitan area defined by the Pretoria-Witwatersrand-Vereeniging triangle. Formerly known as the PWV, it was renamed Gauteng in December 1994. Geographically, it is by far the country's smallest province, but as the country's mining, industrial and financial centre, it provides the economic hub for the whole subcontinent. It is easily the most densely populated province, and contributes a totally disproportionate amount of South Africa's wealth, tax and jobs.

As the most powerful province, it will be critical to the success of the country's democratic experiment. Its achievement in implementing the ANC's Reconstruction and Development Programme, for example, will play a large part in the success or failure of the national programme.

It has a powerful leader in premier Tokyo Sexwale, who combines a military background, moderate and pragmatic politics and populist rhetoric, and will probably play a major role in the push by regional leaders to enhance their powers in relation to the central government. Considering his high national profile, however, this post may be a stepping-stone to a national position.

Sexwale has made a strong impression, visiting troubled township areas regularly and making bold promises on housing and other redevelopment projects. He began his period in office by promising to build 150 000 low-cost housing units in a year and announcing plans for his own provincial community bank. The housing figure was met with widespread scepticism and his plans were called into question by the national minister of Housing. Delivering on these promises will now be the key test of his period of office.

It will not be an easy one. As the country's economic hub, this province attracts many people and the cities are increasingly being circled by informal settlements.

The East Rand townships have been areas of intense conflict and will need resources and constant attention to avoid a resurgence of the bloody violence of 1985-1990. Conflict between hostel-based IFP supporters and the ANC supporters who live around these areas will need to be defused and self-defence units on both sides will need to be disbanded or incorporated into formal security forces.

Another personality worth noting in this high-crime, high-violence area is the executive member for Safety and Security, the spunky Jessie Duarte, a former detainee now facing the test of winning over a new police force.

Seven parties are represented in the provincial assembly, more than in any other province. The NP's votes entitled the party to two executive seats which were filled by the national campaign manager Olaus van Zyl, and a man who had served them well in regional government when most other black leaders were boycotting, John Mavuso.

Nevertheless, the province is firmly in the hands of the ANC, which lost only one district in the elections. In Germiston, the ANC managed only 28 per cent and 29 per cent in the regional and national votes respectively; and the NP scored 43 per cent and 50,4 per cent. There were three other areas in which the ANC did not get a majority, but was still well ahead of its rivals: Pretoria, Randburg and Roodepoort.

The IFP polled 153 000 votes in this province, just 3,6 per cent of the votes and about 20 per cent of the Zulu voters. The FF polled 258 935 or 6,3 per cent of the overall vote, but did notably better in Pretoria where it took 14 per cent of the overall votes. Since the FF polled only 640 000 nationally, this makes Gauteng its strongest base.

kwaZulu/Natal

Capital: Under dispute — between Ulundi and Pietermaritz-
    burg
Premier: Dr Frank Mdlalose (IFP)
Regional executive:
Celani Mthethwa (IFP) — Police Services
Peter Miller (IFP) — Housing and Local Government
Nyanga J Ngubane (IFP) — Nature Conservation and
    Traditional Authorities
Vincent Zulu (IFP) — Education and Culture
Senzele Mhlungu (IFP) — Finance
Gideon Zulu (IFP) — Social Welfare
George Bartlett (NP) — Agriculture
Sibusiso Ndebele (ANC) — Roads, Transport and Traffic
    Control
Zweli Mkhize (ANC) — Health
Jacob Zuma (ANC) — Economic Affairs and Tourism

Telephone: (0331) 95-2001 / (0358) 20-2432
Fax: (0331) 42-7368 / (0358) 20-2470

Population: 8 540 000 (21% of total)
Area: 91 481 square kilometres (7,5% of total)
Languages: Zulu 80%; English 15%; Afrikaans 2%
Proportion of country's GDP: 14,5%
Proportion of country's direct tax: 12,9%

1994 Election		
Party	Votes	Seats
Inkatha Freedom Party	50,324%	41
African National Congress	32,2%	26
National Party	11,2%	9
Democratic Party	2,2%	2
Minority Front	1,3%	1
Pan Africanist Congress	0,7%	1
African Christian Democratic Party	0,7%	1
TOTAL	3 703 693	81
Spoilt ballots	1,06%	

The magnificent rolling hills of kwaZulu/Natal, its green
sugar cane fields and its rich subtropical vegetation disguise
an ugly political situation. As the province that has seen the
most violence in the last five years, kwaZulu/Natal contains
an explosive political mixture. It is one of only two provinces
not controlled by the ANC and is the power base of the
country's only significant regional party, the IFP. It enters
the new era with a powerful legacy of bitterness and
animosity between the ANC and the IFP and will be the

most difficult testing ground for the policy of national and regional reconciliation.

This policy passed its first test with the announcement of the province's election results: the ANC chose not to contest allegations of fraud in kwaZulu, and the IFP in turn did not challenge national or other regional results. In effect, the ANC ceded control over the province for the sake of national reconciliation. kwaZulu/Natal saw more electoral fraud than any other area, but secret negotiations allowed the ballots to be counted without reference to fraud, which is believed to be what gave the IFP its slim majority.

The result provided the IFP with its regional base, but caused a degree of disenchantment among many ANC radicals who felt they had been sacrificed for the sake of national reconciliation.

In fact, the IFP won 30 of the province's 43 electoral districts, many of them overwhelmingly. The ANC, however, won the urban areas of greater Durban and Pietermaritzburg. The split was therefore neat: most of the province is IFP territory, with relatively small but highly populated urban enclaves dominated by the ANC.

An interesting exception was the traditionally Indian area of Chatsworth, where the NP thrashed everyone else and Amichand Rajbansi's Minority Front scored 19,5 per cent.

The premier, the IFP's Dr Frank Mdlalose, is a moderate, but it is expected that the IFP president, minister of Home Affairs Mangosuthu Buthelezi, will give his home base much personal attention.

This province, with an assertive and pro-federalist IFP leadership, is certain to provide the major focus of a push to grant maximum power to the provinces. At the same time, the IFP regionally will face the same test that the ANC faces nationally: to deliver on socio-economic reform and development. This means it will have to slot into the ANC's Reconstruction and Development Programme, and it will need the central ANC government to allocate it sufficient resources to do so.

kwaZulu/Natal has a particularly harsh set of socio-economic problems to deal with — a major reason for the high level of violence. Health, education and welfare systems are notoriously rickety.

Tension became evident in the very first days of the new kwaZulu/Natal administration, when the ANC refused to take up its cabinet posts because it was dissatisfied with the allocation of key portfolios, in particular the sensitive safety and security office. The appointee is Celani Mthethwa, former homeland minister of Justice, whose dubious reputation is due to his involvement in the violence of the early 1990s. His job is particularly important because the former kwaZulu Police, an important IFP power base with a reputation for taking sides in the conflict, has to be incorporated into the new national police service. It will require delicate handling to end the partisanship of the KZP, successfully incorporate it and prevent the spread of violence.

Another early point of conflict was the choice of capital. The IFP favoured its traditional homeland base, Ulundi, while the other parties argued that one of the major cities, Pietermaritzburg or Durban, would be more practical. It was agreed to put the question to a ballot when voting lists are drawn up and to appoint an independent commission to decide on an interim capital.

Another point of conflict was the revelation, by the *Weekly Mail & Guardian*, that all Zulu tribal land (about 1,2-million hectares) had been secretly transferred on the eve of the election to the Ingonyama Trust, of which King Goodwill Zwelithini is the sole trustee. Under the new constitution, this land was due to become the property of the central state. A four-person cabinet committee was set up to look into and make recommendations on the issue.

The ANC is led by the moderate Jacob Zuma, who has the ultra-radical Midlands leader Harry Gwala constantly snapping at his heels. Zuma has gone far to win the all-important support of Zwelithini away from the IFP. The king's allegiances remain a major factor in the politics of this province. So do those of the powerful sugar barons, who dominate the economy of the province. Also notable are its two busy and strategically important ports, Durban and Richards Bay.

North West

Capital: Mmabatho
Premier: Popo Molefe (ANC)
Regional executive:
Mamokoena Gaoretelelwe (ANC) — Education
Molefi Sefularo (ANC) — Health and Social Welfare
Darkey Africa (ANC) — Local Government and Housing
Martin Kuscus (ANC) — Finance
Zacharia Tolo (ANC) — Public Works
Satish Roopa (ANC) — Justice and Police
Frans Vilakazi (ANC) — Transport and Aviation
Johannes Tselapedi (ANC) — Agriculture
Riani de Wet (ANC) — Media
Abraham Venter (NP) — Economic Affairs

Telephone: (0140) 84-3690
Fax (Premier's office): (0140) 84-3695

Population: 3 506 800 (8,6% of total)
Area: 118 710 square kilometres (9,7% of total)
Languages: Setswana 63%; Xhosa 14%; Sesotho 8%

Proportion of country's GDP: 7,12%
Proportion of country's direct tax: 3,5%

1994 Election		
Party	Votes	Seats
African National Congress	83,3%	26
National Party	8,8%	3
Freedom Front	4,6%	1
TOTAL	1 591 116	30
Spoilt ballots	1,2%	

This province combines much of the former Bophuthatswana and a strong far-right wing element. But with Africans making up 86 per cent of the population, the ANC victory was overwhelming. It was some surprise, however, that the FF did not do better in the voting.

This is a province with large racial discrepancies in living conditions, and the new government has a tough administrative task in uniting the old homeland structures and finances with those of the former Transvaal Provincial Administration.

Premier Popo Molefe announced early on his plans to build 25 000 houses in the first year of office, a target he claimed to be realistic. The focus of this activity is the giant squatter area of Winterveld, north of Pretoria.

Once again, an NP representative was drawn into the executive as an act of goodwill, since the party did not win sufficient votes to entitle it to an executive role.

Towards the end of 1994, Molefe was involved in an ugly power struggle with his first choice as MEC for Agriculture, Rockey Malabane-Metsing, resulting in the latter's dismissal.

Northern Cape

Capital: Kimberley
Premier: Manne Dipico (ANC)
Regional executive:
Goolam Akharwaray (ANC) — Economic Affairs,
    Trade and Industry
Tina Joemat (ANC) — Education and Culture
Modise Matlaopane (ANC) — Health and Welfare
Ouneas Dikgetsi (ANC) — Local Government,
    Housing and Land Reform
Eunice Komane (ANC) — Police Services,
    Safety and Security
Jacobus Marais (NP) — Agriculture
Jan Brazelle (NP) — Finance
Peggy Hollander (NP) — Public Works
Charl van Wyk (NP) — Transport
Jozef Henning (FF) — Without portfolio (Youth Affairs)

Telephone: (0531) 81-4760
Fax: (0531) 81-4776

Population: 763 900 (1,9% of total)
Area: 363 389 square kilometres (29,7% of total)
Languages: Afrikaans 65%; Setswana 22%; Xhosa 4%
Proportion of country's GDP: 2,3%
Proportion of country's direct tax: 1,5%

1994 Election		
Party	Votes	Seats
African National Congress	49,7%	15
National Party	40,5%	12
Freedom Front	6,0%	2
Democratic Party	1,9%	1
TOTAL	407 306	30
Spoilt ballots	0,86%	

This is far and away the largest province, with by far the lowest population density (2,1 persons per square kilometre, compared with the national ratio of 33,3 and Gauteng's ratio of 365). It is also highly urbanised, with the bulk of the population clustered around Kimberley.

The NP won 16 of the province's 26 voting districts, meaning that it controls most of the province. But the ANC swept Kimberley with 60 per cent of its 101 000 voters, and 78 per cent of Barkly West with its 22 000 voters, giving it the edge but no clear majority.

The strong NP showing mirrors that in the Western Cape: these are the only two provinces with a majority of coloured voters. In this case, 51 per cent of the voters are coloured, 31 per cent black and 18 per cent white.

The election results created a hung provincial assembly, evenly balanced at 15 ANC seats against 15 for the rest, but the ANC managed to hold power, with the support of the DP and the decision by the FF to abstain rather than support the NP. The ANC responded to the DP's show of support by making its sole representative, Ethne Papenfus, speaker of the house, and to the FF's neutral stance by inviting the party to take an executive seat, even though it was not automatically entitled to one.

The FF's six per cent of the poll represents about one-third of the 18 per cent of voters who were white, a strong showing and well above its two per cent national figure.

Although current living standards in this province are, in some respects at least, better than those in most of the country, there are questions being raised about the Northern Cape's viability as an entity without a strong economic base.

Northern Transvaal

Capital: Pietersburg
Premier: Ngoako Ramathlodi (ANC)
Regional executive:
Thaba Mafumadi (ANC) — Economic Affairs, Commerce and Industry
Aaron Motsoaledi (ANC) — Education and Culture
John Dombo (ANC) — Local Government, Housing and Land Affairs
Tinie Burgers (ANC) — Agriculture
Marie-Stella Mabitje (ANC) — Environmental Affairs and Tourism
Dikeledi Magadzi (ANC) — Public Works
Seth Nthai (ANC) — Police and Protection Services
Edgar Mushwane (ANC) — Finance
Johan Kriek (FF) — Public Transport

Telephone: (0152) 291-4870
Fax: (0152) 295-2197

Population: 5 120 600 (12,6% of total)
Area: 119 606 square kilometres (8,9% of total)
Languages: Sepedi 56%; Shangaan 22%; Venda 12%

Proportion of country's GDP: 3,1%
Proportion of country's direct tax: 2%

1994 Election		
Party	Votes	Seats
African National Congress	91,6%	38
National Party	3,3%	1
Freedom Front	2,2%	1
TOTAL	1 933 962	40
Spoilt Ballots	0,7%	

This area, which is 96 per cent black, is poor and rural, with the lowest urbanisation rate in the country. It provided the ANC's most overwhelming victory, entitling it to command all the seats on the provincial executive and ensuring that this would be one area with a low level of political conflict. Interestingly, when the premier wanted to show goodwill, he offered an executive seat to the FF rather than the NP, even though the latter had polled marginally more votes.

Orange Free State

Capital: Bloemfontein (proposed new name Mangaung)
Premier: Patrick 'Terror' Lekota (ANC)
Regional executive:
Tate Makgoe (ANC) – Finance and Expenditure
Saki Belot (ANC) – Education and Culture
Lizzie Kubushe (ANC) – Police Services
Gregory Nthatisi (ANC) – Public Works and Roads
Senorita Ntlabathi (ANC) – Health and Welfare

Cas Human (ANC) — Agriculture and Environmental Affairs
Ace Magashule (ANC) — Economic Affairs
Ouma Motsumi (ANC) — Local Government Management
Vax Mayekiso (ANC) — Housing
Louis van der Watt (NP) — Public Transport

Telephone: (051) 405-5804
Fax: (051) 405-4803

Population: 2 804 600 (6,9% of total)
Area: 129 437 square kilometres (10,6% of total)
Languages: Sesotho 56%; Afrikaans 14%; Xhosa 9%
Proportion of country's GDP: 7,2%
Proportion of country's direct tax: 5,3%

1994 Election		
Party	Votes	Seats
African National Congress	76,6%	24
National Party	12,6%	4
Freedom Front	6,0%	2
TOTAL	1 364 552	30
Spoilt ballots	0,75%	

The traditional heartland of the NP and of conservative Afrikanerdom was won overwhelmingly by the ANC under former United Democratic Front activist, the popular 'Terror' Lekota — who has already made a point of winning white support for his reconstruction and development plans.

The FF did less well than expected.

Western Cape

Capital: Cape Town
Premier: Hernus Kriel (NP)
Regional executive:
Gerard Morkel (NP) — Housing
Kobus Meiring (NP) — Finance, Expenditure and Service Commission
Lampie Fick (NP) — Agricultural Development and Sport
Patrick MacKenzie (NP) — Police Services
Peter Marais (NP) — Local Government and Development Planning
Martha Olckers (NP) — Education, Training and Cultural Affairs
Chris Nissen (ANC) — Economic Affairs
Ebrahim Rasool (ANC) — Health and Social Services
Lerumo Kalako (ANC) — Environmental Affairs, Nature Conservation and Tourism
Leonard Ramatlakane (ANC) — Roads, Transport and Public Works

Telephone: (021) 483-4705/6
Fax (Premier's office) : (021) 24-5650

Population: 3 620 200 (8,9% of total)
Area: 129 386 square kilometres (10,6% of total)
Languages: Afrikaans 63%; English 20%; Xhosa 16%
Proportion of country's GDP: 13%
Proportion of country's direct tax: 15,7%

1994 Election		
Party	Votes	Seats
National Party	53,3%	23
African National Congress	33,0%	14
Democratic Party	6,6%	3
Freedom Front	2,1%	1
African Christian Democratic Party	1,2%	1
TOTAL	3 703 693	42
Spoilt ballots	1,06%	

This is another province of particular political interest because it is the only one that remains in the hands of the NP, which won a surprisingly comfortable victory in the election. Its showing was based on its success in winning the coloured vote, using quite crude tactics of racial division. The Western Cape is one of only two provinces which does not have an African majority; it is 55 per cent coloured, 25 per cent white, 19 per cent African, and one per cent Indian.

It is clear from the voting results that the ANC swept up to 90 per cent of the African vote, but less than 30 per cent of the coloured vote. But it is noteworthy for future election-watching that there are sharp changes in the demographics of the region, with a strong influx of Africans from other regions.

This makes the Western Cape an important political base for the NP, which will use it to assert its position in relation to the government of national unity. But that will take a delicate balancing act, because to show that it can deliver on socio-economic reform it will have to embrace the ANC's Reconstruction and Development Programme and win resources from the central government. Its success will depend on its relationship with the ANC leadership in the province. Premier Hernus Kriel has said he will undertake reconstruction and development based on both ANC and NP plans.

The ANC was led by the charismatic but controversial Allan Boesak. Shortly after the election, however, he was offered a diplomatic post and Chris Nissen replaced him as regional party leader and MEC for Economic Affairs.

The NP, on the other hand, is burdened by leadership that is not particularly strong, considering the importance of this province to the party's future. Kriel is not a popular figure — indeed, he kept a low profile during the election; likewise Meiring, now the provincial Housing minister. Neither of them comes with a strong reputation after their performances in apartheid structures.

This province is facing a tough battle to keep Parliament, in the face of a push to save money by moving it from Cape Town to Pretoria or Johannesburg. Losing Parliament would deliver a blow to Cape Town, already suffering from the gradual disappearance of import protections for its largest employers, the textile industry. However, it is likely to be sustained by its tourist potential, with its growing reputation as a holiday playground for the rich and famous.

With its breathtaking coastlines, magnificent wine farm areas and famous Table Mountain, the greater Cape Town area is better off than most of the country. It has the highest recent growth rates, the highest human development index in the country in 1991, the highest literacy rate, lowest pupil:teacher ratio, and the lowest infant mortality rate. But these figures mask huge inequalities, heightened by massive influx from rural areas, that provide a strong challenge to the NP leadership, whose long-term national prospects will depend to a large extent on its performance here.

While the DP did notably better here (6,6 per cent) than nationally (four per cent), it did not do as well as expected in what is one of its traditionally strong areas.

5

ELECTION RESULTS — APRIL 1994

South Africa went to vote on April 26, 27 and 28 (and, when it was realised that mistakes threatened to deprive some of the vote, on April 29 in certain homeland areas).

It was the country's first-ever democratic election, which accounts for its failures and successes. Too little time, too little preparation and bureaucratic incompetence on the part of the Independent Electoral Commission (IEC) contributed to organisational chaos that threatened the process. But this was overcome by the high level of hope invested in the election, the patience and determination of voters and the collective will to make the process succeed. In the end, these factors overrode the problems and the elections were marked by only limited violence (a series of right-wing bombs on the eve of polling), heartfelt celebrations and general acceptance of the outcome.

But the election was not without its idiosyncrasies. When breakdowns and fraud in the counting system led to lengthy delays, the IEC had to negotiate its way through to a conclusion. Allegations of cheating in some areas (notably kwaZulu/Natal, the Eastern Cape and the Northern Transvaal), combined with bureaucratic incompetence in almost all areas, meant that objections and disputes threatened the timely announcement of a credible result. IEC chairman Judge Johann Kriegler called representatives of all the parties together and gave them an ultimatum: he could investigate

This chapter draws on the book *Elections '94*, edited by Andrew Reynolds (David Philip).

all these disputes, thus running the risk of bogging the process down in conflict, or all the parties could reconsider their objections. The parties bit the bullet and withdrew almost all their objections, allowing the IEC to proceed.

Was the election free and fair? There seems little doubt — despite the extraordinary business of negotiating the outcome — that it was a reasonable reflection of the national will. The negotiated parts of the outcome would be unlikely to change the national picture and the only region where the outcome was seriously threatened by dispute was kwaZulu/Natal. But since there was no question that the Inkatha Freedom Party had won the region, and the matter in dispute was whether the IFP had an absolute majority, the result was accepted in the interests of national peace.

The most extraordinary aspect of the outcome was how clearly the African National Congress had won countrywide. Its 62 per cent was nothing short of overwhelming. However, it fell short of the 66 per cent that would give it a free hand in drawing up a new constitution, and this averted much of the potential tension. The second notable aspect was that the party with the most racially tainted past, the National Party, was the only one drawing anything like cross-racial support. Almost all of the smaller parties did worse than anticipated, with the IFP the major exception. Its respectable 10 per cent nationally and its regional victory in kwaZulu/Natal were more than most pundits had predicted and enough for its satisfaction.

The overall result left the country with two major parties — the ANC and the NP — and one significant regional party — the IFP.

Two other notable factors were the high voter turnout, estimated at 86 per cent, and the low spoilt ballot count, just over one per cent. The latter in particular contradicted all the research which had indicated that the country's low levels of literacy would yield an exceptional rate of spoilt ballots, prejudicing the ANC. The final figure indicates either that these predictions were wrong, or that the extensive voter education programme worked.

1. The electorate and the turnout

Without a voters' roll and with only an unreliable 1992 census to go on, the 1994 election figures were based on rough estimates. How rough these were was borne out by the IEC's vastly misplaced estimates of the number of voting papers needed in each region, which led to massive shortages in some areas. Nevertheless, it was all they had — and all we have — to go on.

Estimated electorate		
Total	National votes cast	Provincial votes cast
22 754 152	19 726 578 (86,7%)	19 633 751 (86,3%)

Racial breakdown of voters (estimated)				
	Black	White	Coloured	Indian
Voters	14,2-m	2,9-m	1,8-m	0,6-m
% of total	73	15	9	3

Voter turnout 1994 (National ballot — IEC estimates)				
Area	Electorate	Votes cast	% Poll	Spoilt (%)
South Africa	22,75-m	19,50-m	86,7	1,0
Eastern Cape	3,17-m	2,87-m	90,5	0,5
Eastern Tvl	1,55-m	1,32-m	85,4	0,9
kwaZulu/Natal	4,58-m	3,79-m	82,8	1,0
Northern Cape	0,43-m	0,41-m	93,3	0,8
Northern Tvl	2,28-m	1,94-m	84,7	0,7
North West	1,76-m	1,61-m	91,2	1,2
OFS	1,63-m	1,38-m	84,5	0,8
PWV*	4,86-m	4,23-m	87,2	0,6
Western Cape	2,40-m	2,15-m	87,8	0,5

* Renamed Gauteng in December 1994.

2. National results

Party	Votes	%	Nat Assembly seats
African National Congress	12 237 655	62,65	252
National Party	3 983 690	20,39	82
Inkatha Freedom Party	2 058 294	10,54	43
Freedom Front	424 555	2,17	9
Democratic Party	338 426	1,73	7
Pan Africanist Congress	243 478	1,25	5
African Christian Dem Party	88 104	0,45	2
African Moderate Party	34 466	0,18	0
AMCP	27 690	0,14	0
Dikwankwetla Party	19 451	0,10	0
Federal Party	17 663	0,09	0
Minority Front	13 433	0,07	0
Soccer Party	10 575	0,05	0
African Democratic Movement	9 886	0,05	0
Women's Rights for Peace Party	6 434	0,03	0
Ximoko Progressive Party	6 320	0,03	0
Kiss Party	5 916	0,03	0
Workers List Party	4 169	0,02	0
Luso-SA	3 293	0,02	0

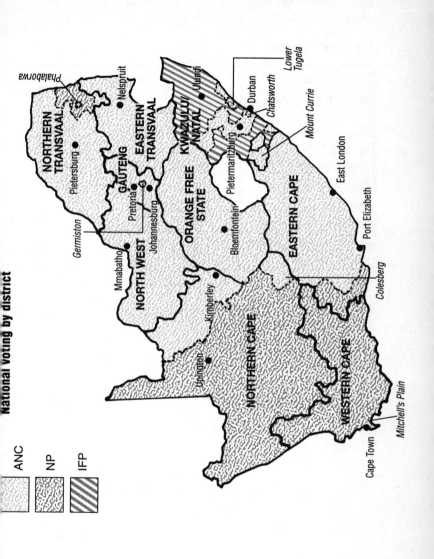

ANC

NP

IFP

Phalaborwa

NORTHERN TRANSVAAL

Pietersburg

Nelspruit

GAUTENG

EASTERN TRANSVAAL

Germiston

Pretoria

Johannesburg

Mmabatho

NORTH WEST

ORANGE FREE STATE

KWAZULU/ NATAL

Ulundi

Pietermaritzburg

Durban

Chatsworth

Lower Tugela

Mount Currie

Bloemfontein

Kimberley

NORTHERN CAPE

Upington

EASTERN CAPE

East London

Port Elizabeth

Colesberg

WESTERN CAPE

Mitchell's Plain

Cape Town

3. Provincial results

Party	Seats	Legislatures controlled
African National Congress	266	6 (PWV, E.Cape, North West, OFS, N.Tvl, E.Tvl)
National Party	82	1 (Western Cape)
Inkatha Freedom Party	44	1 (kwaZulu/Natal)
Freedom Front	14	0
Democratic Party	12	0
Pan Africanist Congress	3	0
African Christian Dem Party	3	0
Minority Front	1	0

The remaining province, Northern Cape, had no majority party.

For the breakdown of votes in each province, see Chapter 4, The Provinces.

Provincial voting by district

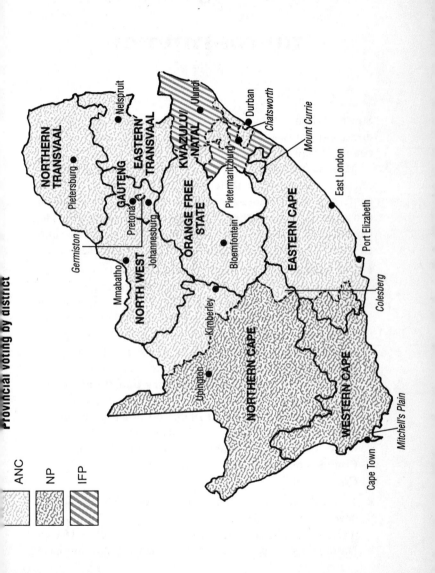

ANC

NP

IFP

NORTHERN TRANSVAAL

Pietersburg

GAUTENG

EASTERN TRANSVAAL

Nelspruit

Germiston

Pretoria

Johannesburg

NORTH WEST

Mmabatho

KWAZULU/ NATAL

Ulundi

Pietermaritzburg

Durban

Chatsworth

Mount Currie

ORANGE FREE STATE

Bloemfontein

Kimberley

NORTHERN CAPE

Upington

EASTERN CAPE

East London

Port Elizabeth

Colesberg

WESTERN CAPE

Cape Town

Mitchell's Plain

6

THE CONSTITUTION

South Africa's interim constitution is a most unusual document, drawn up to meet the specific needs of the country's delicately negotiated transition.

Most constitutions are written with the straightforward purpose of defining state and government structures, conferring and limiting powers. The South African interim constitution performs these functions, and others as well. The Constitution of South Africa Act, 200 of 1993, that came into effect on 27 April 1994, has four additional purposes:

- To replace the apartheid government with a five-year government of national unity. As the preamble states, '(Whereas) there is a need to create a new order in which all South Africans will be entitled to a common South African citizenship in a sovereign and democratic constitutional state in which there is equality between men and women and people of all races so that all citizens shall be able to enjoy and exercise their fundamental rights and freedoms.'

   To do this, a large part of the document sets out the structures of democracy and a government of national unity, and creates a number of new institutions, such as a Commission on Gender Equality and a Human Rights Commission.

- To create an elected Constitutional Assembly to adopt a new constitution. This is why the current constitution is an interim constitution. In order to balance the African National Congress's demand that a new constitution have the stamp of an elected assembly with the National Party's refusal to cede power without the protection of a new constitution, negotiators compromised by agreeing to a set of 34 principles to guide a Constitutional Assembly; the agreement dealt with NP concerns and the new constitution will have to conform to them.

- To provide for governance while the Constitutional Assembly works on the new constitution. To do this, the interim document sets out the structures and rules of procedure of a new government. This means that the new Parliament is both a conventional law-making Parliament and a Constitutional Assembly. Much of this part of the constitution is of a routine nature, the sort that defines powers and responsibilities for standard government bodies and which would be found in any constitution.

- To protect citizens. The constitution establishes the equality of all citizens, and, in addition, a number of protections are built into it. These include: a chapter on fundamental rights, a rule that all legislation has to conform to the agreed 34 constitutional principles, and the creation of a Constitutional Court and a Human Rights Commission.

This constitution, unlike its predecessor, is supreme. Until now, Parliament has been supreme in South African law. This no longer applies. In future, Parliament and all other governing bodies will be subordinate to the constitution. No other law can contradict any provision of the constitution, including the chapter on fundamental rights.

The constitution is made up of 15 chapters and seven schedules, including the Bill of Fundamental Rights (Chapter III) and the constitutional principles that will define the next constitution (Schedule 4).

Chapter I: Flags, Anthems, Languages

This chapter stipulates that the Republic shall be one sovereign state, establishes the constitution as the supreme law of the Republic, and deals with national symbols and languages.

The constitution leaves the choice of flag and national anthem to the president. This was done to avoid conflict over emotional symbolic matters during the negotiations. In fact, negotiators agreed that the Transitional Executive Council would recommend a decision to the president, and the TEC designed a new flag and chose two anthems: Die Stem and Nkosi Sikelel' iAfrika. A lesser-known fact is that the old coat of arms and the seal of the Republic under the previous constitution were kept in place.

Eleven languages are named as 'the official South African languages at a national level'. Once again, this was conflict avoidance: rather than alienate any group, the negotiators gave recognition to all the significant language groups. But with the words 'at a national level', they left the way open for different languages to be recognised at a regional level. And when they granted any person the right to be dealt with in the official language of his or her choice, they left themselves an escape hatch by adding 'wherever practicable'. (The constitution itself has only been made available in English and Afrikaans.)

The official languages are: Afrikaans, English, isiNdebele, Sesotho sa Leboa, Sesotho, siSwati, Xitsonga, Setswana, Tshivenda, isiXhosa and isiZulu.

Regional legislatures may, with a two-thirds majority, choose their own official languages from any of the above, but may not diminish the status of any official language in place at the time this constitution comes into effect. This is clearly intended to deal with the fear that Afrikaans may be de-recognised.

This section instructs Parliament to create a Pan South African Language Board to promote the development of the 11 official languages and the principle of multilingualism. In case anybody feels left out, this body is also instructed to promote German, Greek, Gujerati, Hindi, Portuguese, Tamil, Telegu, Urdu and 'other languages used by communities in South Africa'.

Chapter II: Citizenship and the Franchise

This is the basic clause of democracy that gives equality to all citizens, including universal franchise for any citizen over the age of 18, thereby wiping out the structure of minority rule.

Chapter III: Fundamental Rights

This is known as the Bill of Rights and is dealt with separately in Chapter 7.

Chapter IV: Parliament

Parliament consists of the National Assembly and the Senate, which have the power to make laws, providing they do not conflict with the constitution. Parliament will sit for a fixed term of five years and may only be dissolved under specific circumstances: to call another election under the same constitution if there is a failure of all the deadlock-breaking mechanisms for the passing of a new constitution; or if there is a vote of no confidence in the president or cabinet and he/ they decline to resign.

There is a ban on being a member of more than one of: the National Assembly, the Senate, a regional assembly or a local government.

MPs have indemnity for anything said in Parliament.

There is allowance for joint sittings of the two houses, though not to vote on Bills that affect the powers of provinces. The constitution can only be amended by a two-thirds majority of a joint sitting of both houses.

Bills appropriating revenues may only be introduced in the National Assembly, not the Senate.

National Assembly   The National Assembly consists of 400 members, elected by proportional representation. Two hundred are elected on a national ballot, and the other 200 on a regional basis. These latter 200 seats are divided as follows: Western Cape 21; Eastern Cape 26; Northern Cape 4; kwaZulu/Natal 40; Orange Free State 15; North West 17; Northern Transvaal 20; Eastern Transvaal 14; Gauteng 43.

A limited number of regional MPs may live outside their region; only 10 per cent of a party's representatives may live outside the region they represent.

An MP must be a South African citizen of sound mind and financial solvency, and must not be employed by the state, but there are fewer restrictions than usual on people with criminal histories. The constitution says only that an MP loses the seat if he or she is serving a sentence of more than 12 months when elected, or is sentenced any time in the future to more than 12 months.

Section 43(b) of this chapter is one of the most controversial in the constitution. It states that a person who ceases to be a member of the party which nominated him or her loses the National Assembly seat. This is designed to stop the floor-crossing that became rampant in the previous Parliament, when MPs seeking position and reward sometimes switched parties more than once a day. However, there is a fear that this section will prevent the emergence of dissenting voices in the caucus. The possibility that any MP who votes against the party line can be expelled and automatically lose his or her seat hardly makes for backbench dissent.

There is provision for a speaker and a deputy speaker. A quorum is one-third of MPs, or one-half for a vote on a Bill.

A vacancy in the National Assembly is filled by a person nominated by the political party which initially nominated the member who has vacated his or her seat. This party has to nominate the person whose name appears at the top of the party's last list of election candidates.

Senate   The Senate has 90 members − 10 from each region, appointed by the parties in each regional assembly on the basis of proportional representation. It will sit during the five years of this Parliament and then, once the national and regional assemblies are elected, a new Senate will be appointed.

The same rules of membership apply as those applicable to the National Assembly. There will be a president and a deputy president of the Senate. The quorum rule is also the same as that for the National Assembly.

If a Senate seat becomes vacant, the party that nominated the person who vacated the seat may nominate a new senator. If a regional assembly dissolves, then its 10 senators immediately vacate their seats.

Chapter V: Adoption of the New Constitution

This is an unusual clause, which turns Parliament into the Constitutional Assembly when the National Assembly and the Senate sit together for the purpose of adopting a new constitution.

There is a chairperson and a deputy chairperson of the Constitutional Assembly, distinct from the speaker of the National Assembly or the president of the Senate.

The new constitution has to conform with the 34 constitutional principles (and the Constitutional Court has to certify this) and be passed by a two-thirds majority of the Constitutional Assembly. Any provisions relating to the powers of regions also need the assent of two-thirds of the Senate.

The new constitution has to be passed within two years. If it fails to gain the necessary 67 per cent support, but is supported by a majority of the Constitutional Assembly, it will be referred to a panel of constitutional experts to make recommendations which may secure its approval. If this fails, the president may put the draft to a national referendum; this must be passed by 60 per cent of the electorate. If it fails to achieve this 60 per cent support, then the president is obliged to dissolve Parliament and call a new election.

The new Constitutional Assembly that emerges from this election needs only a 60 per cent majority to pass a new constitution and must do it within a year. Any powers relating to regions must also get the support of 60 per cent of the Senate.

The constitutional principles are firmly entrenched. They, or the provisions which ensure that the new constitution must comply with them, may not be amended or repealed.

Chapter VI: The National Executive

This is the section which entrenches the government of national unity, by giving minority parties representation on the cabinet and in the vice-presidency.

The President The role of president combines head of government with head of state. There are some critics who argue that this is a messy mixture, not allowing the head of state to rise above party politics.

The National Assembly elects the president from its members, though he immediately vacates his parliamentary seat. He serves for five years.

There is no provision, as there was previously, for the president to be exempt from tax. There is, however, a ban on freelancing: the president cannot 'perform remunerative work outside the duties of his or her office'.

His powers include: signing Bills passed by Parliament; convening cabinet meetings; referring constitutional disputes to the Constitutional Court; conferring honours; appointing and receiving ambassadors; appointing commissions of inquiry; signing international agreements; pardoning or reprieving offenders; commanding the national defence force.

An interesting addition, entrenching the concept of national unity, obliges the president to consult his executive deputy presidents in the development and execution of policies; in all matters relating to cabinet management and performance; on ambassadorial appointments; and commissions of inquiry.

Executive Deputy Presidents Every party with more than 80 seats in the National Assembly (or 20 per cent of the total) can choose from its number an executive deputy president. Should no party or only one party achieve this, then the two biggest parties in the National Assembly can each choose one executive deputy president.

An executive deputy president serves for five years and may choose to give up or keep his or her National Assembly seat. Powers and duties are assigned by the president in consultation with the executive deputy president in question.

The constitution contains no hierarchy of deputy presidents. Although it has become common to refer to a senior or first deputy president, there is no such title granted by the constitution.

Impeachment   The president or the executive deputy presidents can be impeached by a two-thirds majority of both houses of Parliament on the grounds of a serious violation of the constitution or other laws, misconduct or inability rendering him or her unfit to perform his or her functions.

The Cabinet   Once again, the government of national unity is firmly entrenched.

The cabinet consists of the president, executive deputy presidents and not more than 27 ministers. Any party holding at least 20 seats in the National Assembly (five per cent of the total) is entitled to cabinet seats and deputy minister positions in proportion to its number of National Assembly seats.

The president must consult with his executive deputy presidents when appointing or dismissing ministers and deputy ministers and when designating portfolios. He must do this in the spirit of a government of national unity, though his decisions shall prevail.

'The Cabinet shall function,' according to the very important but not easily understood Section 89(2) of the constitution, 'in a manner which gives consideration to the consensus-seeking spirit underlying the concept of a government of national unity as well as the need for effective government.'

Chapter VII: The Judiciary

The judiciary provides one of the all-important checks and balances of government power – if, that is, it is independent. However, a new set of provisions govern the hiring and firing of judges, taking the power away from the government and vesting it in the combination of the government, a new Judicial Service Commission (JSC) and Parliament.

The JSC consists of the chief justice, president of the Constitutional Court, one judge president designated by all the judge presidents, the minister responsible for Justice, two practising advocates chosen by their peers, two practising attorneys chosen by their peers, one professor of law chosen by the deans of all the law schools, four senators approved by two-thirds of the Senate, four persons (including at least two practising lawyers) chosen by the president in consultation with the cabinet, and, on any matter affecting a provincial decision of the supreme court, that region's judge president and premier.

Supreme court judges and most of the Constitutional Court judges can only be appointed by the president when nominated by the JSC. A judge can be removed only on the recommendation of the JSC and only on specific, circumscribed grounds.

The chief justice and Constitutional Court president are chosen by the president in consultation with the cabinet and after consultation with the JSC.

The Constitutional Court, which will be based in Johannesburg, will be the most powerful court in the country with jurisdiction 'of final instance over all matters relating to the interpretation, protection and enforcement' of the constitution. It is particularly interesting that its members have to be chosen with 'regard to the need to constitute a court which is independent and competent and representative in respect of race and gender'. The Constitutional Court thus may include not just judges but people 'who, by nature of their training and experience, (have) expertise in the field of constitutional law'. This means the court is this country's first not to consist entirely of white males.

The constitution specifies that this court shall consist of a Constitutional Court president and 10 others. Four are supreme court judges chosen by the president in consultation with the cabinet and the chief justice; the other six are chosen by the president in consultation with the cabinet and after consulting with the Constitutional Court president, from a list of nine nominations from the JSC. If they reject these nominations, they require further ones from the JSC. They must all be citizens, ruling out the practice of other African countries of seeking to bolster their courts by importing judges.

There will also be a Magistrates' Commission to oversee the appointment of those who sit on the Benches of the lower courts.

Chapter VIII: Establishing a Number of New Offices to Restore and Protect Human Rights

The Public Protector   Despite the Orwellian title, this person will be a powerful, official ombudsman. There cannot be many constitutions in the world that protect the citizen against discourteous officials. This one, however, gives the public protector powers to investigate maladministration at any level of government; abuse or unjustifiable use of power; unfair, capricious or discourteous conduct by a person performing a public function; any improper or dishonest act, or omission, or corruption involving public money; improper or unlawful enrichment of officials; or any act or omission by a public servant which results in improper prejudice to any person.

This person will be nominated by a joint committee of both houses of Parliament and approved by 75 per cent of each house. He or she is obliged to be impartial and independent, and all organs of state are instructed to give reasonable assistance to the public protector.

Provincial legislatures may also appoint their own public protectors.

Human Rights Commission This body, consisting of a chairperson and 10 members, is obliged to promote the observance of, respect for and protection of fundamental rights, and to develop a public awareness of these rights. It is nominated by a joint committee of both houses of Parliament and must be approved by 75 per cent of each house. The commission is given a staff and a budget, and must present an annual report to the president.

Commission on Gender Equality This clause instructs Parliament to pass a law creating a commission to promote gender equality and to make recommendations to Parliament.

Restitution of Land Rights Parliament is obliged to pass a law providing for the restitution of land rights to any person or community dispossessed of their land at any time after a date still to be fixed, if that land was taken away under a racially discriminatory law. Parliament is instructed to create a Commission on Restitution of Land Rights to investigate, mediate and settle such claims.

This Act, and any activity of this commission, will of course have to comply with the relevant land rights section of the Bill of Rights.

Chapter IX: Provincial Government

This chapter establishes nine provinces: Eastern Cape, Eastern Transvaal, Natal, Northern Cape, Northern Transvaal, North West, OFS, PWV (renamed Gauteng in December 1994), and Western Cape. These names may be changed if requested by the provincial legislatures (to allow the name kwaZulu to come into play).

Because some of the borders are not yet clear, the constitution allows for referendums to allow residents in these border areas to choose their province.

Each province will have its own legislature of between 30 and 100 members, a speaker and a deputy speaker, and rules similar to those of Parliament. Each provincial legislature will elect a premier from among its members who has the power to sign provincial Bills, refer them back to the legislature, convene the executive council, appoint commissions of inquiry and proclaim referendums.

The executive council consists of the premier and not more than 10 others, elected in proportion to party representation in the legislature. As with the cabinet, the premier allocates portfolios to these executive council members after consultation with the participating parties. Once again, the premier has to act 'in accordance with the spirit underlying the concept of a government of national unity'.

A province is entitled to an equitable share of revenue collected by the national government and may levy taxes only if authorised by the central Parliament. Each province has to pass its own constitution by a two-thirds majority, providing its provisions are not inconsistent with the national constitution. A late amendment to the constitution recognised the position of the Zulu king as a regional constitutional monarch.

A national Commission on Provincial Government, consisting of 10 to 15 people, is to facilitate the development of a system of provincial government.

Chapter X: Local Government

This uncontroversial section empowers the government to pass a law creating and regulating local authorities.

Chapter XI: Traditional Authorities

Traditional authorities are given recognition in the constitution. This chapter preserves their existing legal powers and authority and allows any traditional leader to be a member, *ex officio*, of a local authority.

Provinces which have traditional authorities are obliged to form a House of Traditional Leaders to be consulted on draft legislation in a manner left to each province to establish.

This chapter also establishes a national Council of Traditional Leaders, consisting of a chairman and 19 members elected by traditional authorities. It will advise the president and government on any matter affecting indigenous law and shall be consulted on legislation affecting tradition or customs.

Volkstaat Council   Another late addition to the constitution is the provision for a Volkstaat Council, consisting of 20 members elected by members of Parliament who support the notion of an Afrikaner homeland. The council is defined as a mechanism to pursue the concept of a volkstaat by constitutional means. The council may study the possible boundaries, powers, functions, and the legislative and executive structures of a volkstaat, the constitutional relationship between it and the national and provincial governments, and the feasibility of the concept. It may then make submissions and recommendations to the Constitutional Assembly. Thereafter, the procedures to be followed must be determined by an Act of Parliament.

Chapter XII: Financial Affairs

This is a straightforward technical chapter dealing with matters such as the annual budget, the Reserve Bank and the Financial and Fiscal Commission. It creates, for the first time, a Commission on Remuneration of Representatives, which will make recommendations to Parliament on the remuneration of all elected officials at all levels, including traditional leaders.

Chapter XIII: Public Service Commission

This keeps in place the Public Service Commission, sets out the rules for public service (it shall be non-partisan, it shall loyally execute the policies of the government of the day, etc), and allows for provincial service commissions. It also allows for the office of the auditor general to audit and report on the financial statements of all levels of government.

Chapter XIV: Police and Defence

South African Police Service   This chapter changes the name of the police, adding the word Service to its title, and gives it a structure appropriate to the provincial system. This was the subject of tough negotiations, with the ANC and the police themselves favouring a single national police force, and the NP seeking to enhance provincial powers. In the end, there will be one police force, but provincial authorities will hold certain, quite limited powers.

A national commissioner has executive command of the force and control of such elements as training, international liaison and forensic laboratories. He bears responsibility for the recruitment, appointment, promotion and transfer of all policemen.

But provincial commissioners control transfers in their regions and promotions up to the rank of lieutenant-colonel.

Interestingly, there is no restriction on a policeman acting outside the province in which he or she is stationed.

The constitution specifically instructs Parliament to legislate for community policing forums and to promote accountability to local communities.

National Defence Force   This is a straightforward section that allows for the continued operation of the South African Defence Force, renamed the South African National Defence Force.

Chapter XV: General and Transitional Provisions

This chapter keeps in place existing laws, unless repealed or amended, and international treaties. Notably, for a country just being reintroduced to the world community, it makes customary international law part of the country's law, except where it may contradict this constitution.

It also allows for transitional arrangements for a whole range of state offices and for the rationalisation of civil services and security forces, to bring them in line with the new provincial structures. It gives some protection to civil servants, in that it ensures that their employment continues subject to the same terms and conditions as before, unless the law governing that employment is amended. This is clearly intended to placate anxious civil servants.

However, the president may appoint a judicial commission to review any contract, appointment or promotion since April 1993. This provision was intended to prevent the wholesale signing of contracts or granting of appointments or promotions by the outgoing government.

National Unity and Reconciliation   The constitution ends strangely with a section on the need for reconciliation 'to transcend the divisions and strife of the past, which generated gross violations of human rights, the transgression of humanitarian principles in violent conflicts and a legacy of hatred, fear, guilt and revenge.

'These can now be addressed on the basis that there is a need for understanding but not for vengeance, a need for reparation but not for retaliation, a need for ubuntu (humanity) but not for victimisation.'

It then instructs Parliament to pass an amnesty law for political crimes with a firm cut-off date of between October 1990 and December 1993. Having begun with 'humble submission to Almighty God', the constitution ends with the words 'Nkosi sikelel' iAfrika', repeated in six of the 11 official languages.

The Thirty-four Principles

The negotiators of the interim constitution agreed on 34 principles which must be adhered to in the drafting of a final constitution. These principles cannot be changed. Any new law must comply with these principles. The Constitutional Court has final adjudication on whether new laws do comply with the 34 principles, as it does in certifying that the new constitution does not contradict them.

The principles are:

1. The Constitution of South Africa shall provide for the establishment of one sovereign state, a common South African citizenship and a democratic system of government committed to achieving equality between men and women and people of all races.

2. Everyone shall enjoy all universally accepted fundamental rights, freedoms and civil liberties, which shall be provided for and protected by entrenched and justiciable provisions in the Constitution, which shall be drafted after having given due consideration to inter alia

the fundamental rights contained in Chapter III of this Constitution.

3. The Constitution shall prohibit racial, gender and all other forms of discrimination and shall promote racial and gender equality and national unity.

4. The Constitution shall be the supreme law of the land. It shall be binding on all organs of state at all levels of government.

5. The legal system shall ensure the equality of all before the law and an equitable legal process. Equality before the law includes laws, programmes or activities that have as their object the amelioration of the conditions of the disadvantaged, including those disadvantaged on the grounds of race, colour or gender.

6. There shall be a separation of powers between the legislature, executive and judiciary, with appropriate checks and balances to ensure accountability, responsiveness and openness.

7. The judiciary shall be appropriately qualified, independent and impartial and shall have the power and jurisdiction to safeguard and enforce the Constitution and all fundamental rights.

8. There shall be representative government embracing multiparty democracy, regular elections, universal adult suffrage, a common voters' roll, and, in general, proportional representation.

9. Provision shall be made for freedom of information so that there can be open and accountable administration at all levels of government.

10. Formal legislative procedures shall be adhered to by legislative organs at all levels of government.

11. The diversity of language and culture shall be acknowledged and protected, and conditions for their promotion shall be encouraged.

12. Collective rights of self-determination in forming, joining and maintaining organs of civil society, including linguistic, cultural and religious associations, shall, on the basis of non-discrimination and free association, be recognised and protected.

13. The institution, status and role of traditional leadership, according to indigenous law, shall be recognised and protected in the Constitution. Indigenous law, like common law, shall be recognised and applied by the courts, subject to the fundamental rights contained in the Constitution and to legislation dealing specifically therewith.

14. Provision shall be made for participation of minority political parties in the legislative process in a manner consistent with democracy.

15. Amendments to the Constitution shall require special procedures involving special majorities.

16. Government shall be structured at national, provincial and local levels.

17. At each level of government there shall be democratic representation. This principle shall not derogate from the provisions of Principle 13.

18. The powers, boundaries and functions of the national government and provincial governments shall be defined in the Constitution. Amendments to the Constitution which alter the powers, boundaries, functions or institutions of provinces shall in addition to any other procedures specified in the Constitution for constitutional amendments, require the approval of a special

majority of the legislatures of the provinces; alternatively, if there is such a chamber, a two-thirds majority of a chamber of Parliament composed of provincial representatives, and if the amendment concerns specific provinces only, the approval of the legislatures of such provinces will also be needed. Provision shall be made for obtaining the views of a provincial legislature concerning all constitutional amendments regarding its powers, boundaries and functions.

19. The powers and functions at national and provincial levels of government shall include exclusive and concurrent powers as well as the power to perform functions for other levels of government on an agency or delegation basis.

20. Each level of government shall have appropriate and adequate legislative and executive powers and functions that will enable each level to function effectively. The allocation of powers between different levels of government shall be made on a basis which is conducive to financial viability at each level of government and to effective public administration, and which recognises the need for and promotes national unity and legitimate provincial autonomy and acknowledges cultural diversity.

21. The following criteria shall be applied in the allocation of powers to the national government and the provincial governments:

(1) The level at which decisions can be taken most effectively in respect of the quality and rendering of services, shall be the level responsible and accountable for the quality and the rendering of the services, and such level shall accordingly be empowered by the Constitution to do so.

(2) Where it is necessary for the maintenance of essential national standards, for the establishment of minimum standards required for the rendering of services, the maintenance of economic unity, the maintenance of national security or the prevention of unreasonable action taken by one province which is prejudicial to the interests of another province or the country as a whole, the Constitution shall empower the national government to intervene through legislation or such other steps as may be defined in the Constitution.

(3) Where there is necessity for South Africa to speak with one voice, or to act as a single entity — in particular in relation to other states — powers should be allocated to the national government.

(4) Where uniformity across the nation is required for a particular function, the legislative power over that function should be allocated predominantly, if not wholly, to the national government.

(5) The determination of national economic policies, and the power to promote interprovincial commerce and to protect the common market in respect of the mobility of goods, services, capital and labour, should be allocated to the national government.

(6) Provincial governments shall have powers, either exclusively or concurrently with the national government, inter alia —

(a) for the purposes of provincial planning and development and the rendering of services; and

(b) in respect of aspects of government dealing with specific socio-economic and cultural needs and the general well-being of the inhabitants of the province.

(7) Where mutual co-operation is essential or desirable or where it is required to guarantee equality of opportunity or access to a government service, the powers should be allocated concurrently to the national government and the provincial governments.

(8) The Constitution shall specify how powers which are not specifically allocated in the Constitution to the national government or to a provincial government, shall be dealt with as necessary ancillary powers pertaining to the powers and functions allocated either to the national government or provincial governments.

22. The national government shall not exercise its powers (exclusive or concurrent) so as to encroach upon the geographical, functional or institutional integrity of the provinces.

23. In the event of a dispute concerning the legislative powers allocated by the Constitution concurrently to the national government and provincial governments which cannot be resolved by a court on a construction of the Constitution, precedence shall be given to the legislative powers of the national government.

24. A framework for local government powers, functions and structures shall be set out in the Constitution. The comprehensive powers, functions and other features of local government shall be set out in parliamentary statutes or in provincial legislation or in both.

25. The national government and provincial governments shall have fiscal powers and functions which will be defined in the Constitution. The framework for local government referred to in Principle 24 shall make provision for appropriate fiscal powers and functions for different categories of local government.

26. Each level of government shall have a constitutional right to an equitable share of revenue collected nationally so as to ensure that provinces and local governments are able to provide basic services and execute the functions allocated to them.

27. A Financial and Fiscal Commission, in which each province shall be represented, shall recommend equitable fiscal and financial allocations to the provincial and local governments from revenue collected nationally, after taking into account the national interest, economic disparities between the provinces as well as the population and developmental needs, administrative responsibilities and other legitimate interests of each of the provinces.

28. Notwithstanding the provisions of Principle 12, the right of employers and employees to join and form employer organisations and trade unions and to engage in collective bargaining shall be recognised and protected. Provision shall be made that every person shall have the right to fair labour practices.

29. The independence and impartiality of a Public Service Commission, a Reserve Bank, an Auditor-General and a Public Protector shall be provided for and safeguarded by the Constitution in the interests of the maintenance of effective public finance and administration and a high standard of professional ethics in the public service.

30. (1) There shall be an efficient, non-partisan, career-orientated public service broadly representative of the South African community, functioning on a basis of fairness and which shall serve all members of the public in an unbiased and impartial manner, and shall, in the exercise of its powers and in compliance with its duties, loyally execute the lawful policies of the government of

the day in the performance of its administrative functions. The structures and functioning of the public service, as well as the terms and conditions of service of its members, shall be regulated by law.

(2) Every member of the public service shall be entitled to a fair pension.

31. Every member of the security forces (police, military and intelligence), and the security forces as a whole, shall be required to perform their functions and exercise their powers in the national interest and shall be prohibited from furthering or prejudicing party political interest.

32. The Constitution shall provide that until 30 April 1999 the national executive shall be composed and shall function substantially in the manner provided for in Chapter VI of this Constitution.

33. The Constitution shall provide that, unless Parliament is dissolved on account of its passing a vote of no-confidence in the Cabinet, no national election shall be held before 30 April 1999.

34. (1) This Schedule and the recognition therein of the right of the South African people as a whole to self-determination, shall not be construed as precluding, within the framework of the said right, constitutional provision for a notion of the right to self-determination by any community sharing a common cultural and language heritage, whether in a territorial entity within the Republic or in any other recognised way.

(2) The Constitution may give expression to any form of self-determination provided there is substantial proven support within the community concerned for such a form of self-determination.

(3) If a territorial entity referred to in paragraph 1 is established in terms of this Constitution before the new constitutional text is adopted, the new Constitution shall entrench the continuation of such territorial entity, including its structures, powers and functions.

7

THE BILL OF RIGHTS

The key document for the protection of citizens from human rights abuses is contained in the constitution — Chapter III, headed Fundamental Rights. This Bill of Rights is the document that rids South Africa of apartheid — defining all citizens as equal and guaranteeing basic freedoms and rights — and empowers citizens to defend themselves against government abuses.

It is a crucial document, allowing individuals and groups to demand a range of rights previously denied them. For minority groups, it is their protection against rampant majoritarianism.

The Constitutional Court will have to set policy on all sorts of controversial issues — such as abortion, the death penalty, environmental rights and affirmative action — on the basis of this document, balancing the rights set out in Chapter III against each other. Does the right to life overrule a right to human dignity, for example; or does a right to dignity limit the right to freedom of speech?

Because it is part of the interim constitution, the Bill of Rights is subject to further negotiation over the next two years. At the moment, it consists of Sections 7-35 in Chapter III of the constitution.

This chapter has drawn extensively on analysis of the Bill of Rights by the staff and associates of the Centre for Applied Legal Studies at the University of the Witwatersrand, Johannesburg.

Section 7: Application

7. (1) This Chapter shall bind all legislative and executive organs of state at all levels of government.

    (2) This Chapter shall apply to all law in force and all administrative decisions taken and acts performed during the period of operation of this Constitution.

    (3) Juristic persons shall be entitled to the rights contained in this Chapter where, and to the extent that, the nature of the rights permits.

    (4) (a) When an infringement of or threat to any right entrenched in this Chapter is alleged, any person referred to in paragraph (b) shall be entitled to apply to a competent court of law for appropriate relief, which may include a declaration of rights.

    (b) The relief referred to in paragraph (a) may be sought by:

     (i) a person acting in his or her own interest;

    (ii) an association acting in the interest of its members;

    (iii) a person acting on behalf of another person who is not in a position to seek such relief in his or her own name;

    (iv) a person acting as a member of or in the interest of a group or class of persons; or

    (v) a person acting in the public interest.

This opening clause sets out which laws and which people are covered by the Bill of Rights. It raises the crucial — and so far unresolved — question of whether the Bill applies to the relationship between individuals and non-state organisations (does it protect, for example, an individual against discrimination by a private company or club?), or just between individuals/organisations and the state.

The Bill of Rights applies to all laws in force on 27 April 1994, the day the constitution came into effect, and all laws which come into force during the life of the constitution. The only exception is current labour law, which is valid until it has been repealed or amended by Parliament.

All other legislation is subject to this chapter, which sets up many existing laws for challenge, ranging from the Internal Security Act, which allows for detention without trial, to the Income Tax Act because it discriminates in favour of men. It will also apply to common and customary law.

The more controversial issue relates to the scope of the Bill for individuals. It is stated in this section that the Bill binds the legislative and executive organs of state at all levels of government. Some experts argue that because the judiciary is not mentioned, it does not have the power to enforce the Bill in terms of relationships between citizens − a 'horizontal' application. If the Bill does apply to relationships between citizens, it would mean that an ordinary person who faced discrimination at the hands of another, such as a hotelier, restaurateur or employer who excluded someone on the basis of race or gender, could rely on the court to enforce the fundamental right of equality.

But it is the opinion of a number of eminent legal commentators that the omission of the word 'judiciary' is not fatal to the horizontal application of the Bill. This view is supported by the way many of the rights have been phrased, indicating that they apply beyond the relationship of an individual to the state.

This clause also opens the way, for the first time in South Africa, to class actions − allowing one person to take action on behalf of a group or class of persons.

Section 8: Equality

8. (1) Every person shall have the right to equality before the law and to equal protection of the law.

   (2) No person shall be unfairly discriminated against, directly or indirectly, and, without derogating from the generality of this provision, on one or more of the following grounds in particular: race, gender, sex, ethnic or social origin, colour, sexual orientation, age, disability, religion, conscience, belief, culture or language.

   (3) (a) This section shall not preclude measures designed to achieve the adequate protection and advancement of persons or groups or categories of persons disadvantaged by unfair discrimination, in order to enable their full and equal enjoyment of all rights and freedoms.

   (b) Every person or community dispossessed of rights in land before the commencement of this Constitution under any law which would have been inconsistent with subsection (2) had that subsection been in operation at the time of the dispossession, shall be entitled to claim restitution of such rights subject to and in accordance with sections 121, 122 and 123.

   (4) Prima facie proof of discrimination on any of the grounds specified in subsection (2) shall be presumed to be sufficient proof of unfair discrimination as contemplated in that subsection, until the contrary is established.

It is no surprise, in a society trying to right the wrongs of apartheid, that the first right mentioned in the Bill is the right to equality. It would not be possible to treat all people identically. So the court will have to decide when distinctions can be made between individuals and when not.

The starting point for this debate is usually that equals should be treated equally and those who are not alike can be treated unequally. This applies most obviously to questions of gender and disability.

But the Canadian courts (of great influence, because much of the wording of our Bill is derived from theirs) have developed the notion of a 'similarly situated' test: those who are similarly situated should be similarly treated and, of course, the converse. This means a law giving privileges to a woman who is pregnant would not get knocked down because it discriminates against men.

Slipped in, virtually unnoticed, is more constitutional protection against discrimination on the basis of sexual orientation than in most countries. Gay rights are, therefore, strongly protected.

The section also intends to exempt affirmative action programmes from challenges on the basis of unequal treatment. It exempts laws 'designed to achieve the adequate protection and advancement' of certain specified groups. But what does 'designed to achieve' mean? It seems to rule out challenges to, for example, a racial quota system in the civil service designed to advance categories of disadvantaged persons. But could a court argue that such a quota system was not likely to undo disadvantage and set it aside on this basis? Such an interpretation would give the court a very wide power to scrutinise affirmative action programmes.

Section 9: Life

Every person shall have the right to life.

This will be the source of much crucial debate over three issues: abortion, euthanasia and the death penalty.

The death penalty is likely to be decided in Parliament, rather than the courts, since the government has indicated that it will legislate against it; moreover, it is difficult to see how anyone could go to court to claim the right to execute someone.

The decision concerning abortion will hinge on the question that has bedevilled constitutional courts around the world: at what point does a foetus have a right to life? In some countries, like the United States and Canada, the issue has also been decided on the woman's right to security and/or privacy. In a recent German case, abortion legislation was set aside on the basis that the state had a primary duty to protect human life even before birth.

On the question of euthanasia, the court will have to balance the right to life against, inter alia, the right to dignity.

This clause has, in some countries, also been very widely interpreted to give 'secondary rights'. The Indian Supreme Court has ruled that the right to life includes the right to certain social and economic rights: it also relates to the quality of life. In one memorable case, this included the rights of residents of a rural village to a road, the absence of which affected the inhabitants' livelihood and development.

Section 10: Human Dignity

Every person shall have the right to respect for and protection of his or her dignity.

The rights protected by this section include the right of persons to have their dignity respected by the state in its dealing with or treatment of them. It may also include an obligation on the part of the state to protect their dignity against attack by others.

Section 11: Freedom and Security of the Person

11. (1) Every person shall have the right to freedom and security of the person, which shall include the right not to be detained without trial.

    (2) No person shall be subject to torture of any kind, whether physical, mental or emotional, nor shall any person be subject to cruel, inhuman or degrading treatment or punishment.

Many of the basic freedoms are dealt with elsewhere in the Bill of Rights, but the court is likely to take the view — upheld by courts in other countries — that this section encompasses those rights and privileges recognised as being essential for 'the orderly pursuit of happiness by a free people'.

The prohibition against detention raises important issues. Detention without trial is rendered unconstitutional in this section but is recognised in Section 25 under the provision for a state of emergency. Moreover, there is even some difficulty in relation to non-emergency detention because Section 25, dealing with 'detained, arrested and accused persons', lists the rights of detainees separately from the others. And Section 30 on the rights of children requires that a child in detention must be treated in a manner that takes account of his or her age.

Although one may hope that the Constitutional Court will conclude that non-emergency detention has been outlawed, it is possible that an executive-minded approach could read other sections to allow for non-emergency political detention.

The concept of 'cruel and unusual punishment' has been at the heart of many of the legal challenges to the death penalty. American courts have held that a punishment is cruel if it makes no measurable contribution to legitimate goals and thus is nothing more than a purposeless and gratuitous imposition of pain and suffering. The prohibition in this section now invites the Constitutional Court to examine the legitimate and permissible aims of punishment. The Namibian Bench used this section to outlaw corporal punishment.

The inclusion of the word 'emotional' in this section makes our provision broader than elsewhere in the world.

The European Court of Human Rights has held that the notion of inhuman treatment covers treatment that deliberately causes severe suffering, mental or physical, which in the particular situation is unjustifiable.

The combined application of various forms of interrogation techniques such as the occasional slap, the deprivation of sleep and restrictions of diet, which separately might not constitute inhuman treatment, have been cumulatively considered to fall within this category. The same conclusion would apply to the solitary confinement of a person under interrogation or awaiting trial.

Section 12: Servitude and Forced Labour

No person shall be subject to servitude or forced labour.

This covers any law, or state practice or policy which promotes, legitimates or sustains servitude or forced labour. Servitude would include debt bondage, such as the pledging of personal services as security for a debt, serfdom or the delivery of women or children against their will to another with the view to the exploitation of their labour.

The International Labour Organisation defines forced labour as 'all work or service which is exacted from any person under the menace of any penalty and for which the said person has not offered himself voluntarily'. But most courts have gone narrower than this, insisting that the work must not just be involuntary, it must also be unjust, oppressive or involve unavoidable hardship. This means that this clause does not cover military service, prison labour or civil service in an emergency situation.

There are other limitations. The European Commission on Human Rights rejected a claim of 'servitude or forced labour' by volunteers who had joined the armed services as minors and, having reached majority, were unable to leave because of threats of penal sanction.

The same commission was divided on whether this clause prevented the Norwegian authorities obliging doctors to do compulsory medical service in remote areas on the grounds that it was 'forced labour'. But it did reject a claim by lawyers that they could not be forced to represent clients on legal aid. The court argued that the lawyer had freely chosen his profession, knowing the legal obligation to represent poor clients if appointed by the court.

Section 13: Privacy

Every person shall have the right to his or her personal privacy, which shall include the right not to be subject to searches of his or her person, home or property, the seizure of private possessions or the violation of private communications.

This clause will create a hotly contested area.

For a start there are a number of existing laws which fall foul of this protection. The Criminal Procedure Act gives extensive powers of search and seizure, and other Acts grant similar powers. For example, the Drugs and Drug Trafficking Act confers powers upon a police officer to seize anything which in his opinion is connected with or may provide proof of a contravention of a provision of the Act. This would not stand up to the test of this clause.

A crucial question flowing out of this is whether the courts will accept evidence that has been obtained improperly or in violation of the constitution. If they don't, this could be a strong deterrent to police misconduct.

The ambit of this clause is certain to be tested. Does a right to privacy apply, for example, to a corporation facing a demand to disclose correspondence to a trade union? In the European Convention, the right extends to the protection of a person's private and family life and his or her home, and respect for his or her correspondence.

The general protection of privacy has also been used to uphold the right of a woman to an abortion: that it is a private, personal decision. In the famous case of Roe vs Wade, the United States Supreme Court found that the right of privacy was broad enough to encompass a woman's decision whether or not to terminate her pregnancy.

Section 14: Religion, Belief and Opinion

14. (1) Every person shall have the right to freedom of conscience, religion, thought, belief and opinion, which shall include academic freedom in institutions of higher learning.

(2) Without derogating from the generality of subsection (1), religious observances may be conducted at state or state-aided institutions under rules established by an appropriate authority for that purpose, provided that such religious observances are conducted on an equitable basis and attendance at them is free and voluntary.

(3) Nothing in this Chapter shall preclude legislation recognising:

(a) a system of personal and family law adhered to by persons professing a particular religion; and

    (b) the validity of marriages concluded under a system of religious law subject to specified procedures.

This section guarantees the right to freedom of religion. On a first reading, this might be thought to guarantee freedom from government action which favours one religion over another with, for example, compulsory school prayer, religious education in state schools, state support for private religious education and the observance of religious rituals in state institutions. This is how the United States Supreme Court has read the right to freedom of religion.

But the second section of this clause goes on to provide that religious observances may be conducted at state or state-aided institutions providing that it is done on an equitable basis and attendance is free and voluntary.

Section 15: Freedom of Expression

15. (1) Every person shall have the right to freedom of speech and expression, which shall include freedom of artistic creativity and scientific research.

    (2) All media financed by or under the control of the state shall be regulated in a manner which ensures impartiality and the expression of a diversity of opinion.

This should bring an end to South Africa's long tradition of suppression of speech which has seen the banning of thousands of books and films and the silencing of individuals, organisations and media. Current censorship legislation and the mechanism for censorship will, in all probability, fall foul of this clause. To defend any form of censorship, the state will have to justify it on the grounds of the limitations clause (Section 33).

This does not mean that 'anything goes'. The right to freedom of expression will have to be balanced against other rights, such as the rights to privacy, equality or dignity. Anti-pornographers, for example, will argue that the right to dignity limits offensive sexual material. Others will argue that restrictions on race hate speech are justified in terms of Section 9, which guarantees equality.

This section will also force a change in defamation law. In future, a person alleging defamation will have to prove that the press intended to defame or, at least was negligent. This does not rule out defamation actions, but it does give the media better defences against them.

Section 16: Assembly, Demonstration and Petition

Every person shall have the right to assemble and demonstrate with others peacefully and unarmed, and to present petitions.

This could be characterised as the right to South Africa's traditional form of political expression: mass action.

South Africa is a country that has seen more petitions than most, and this clause is designed to keep up the flow. There is no suggestion, however, that it confers immunity regarding the contents of a petition; these would still be subject to defamation law, for example.

The inclusion of the right to demonstrate is unusual; it is normally considered to fall under assembly and its specific mention here is probably to emphasise its importance in the light of South Africa's history of breaking up meetings and suppressing demonstrations of opposition to the government.

Some limitations are written in: the demonstration must be peaceful. Others have been established in international jurisprudence, such as restrictions that are necessary for public safety, the protection of public health or morals, or the protection of the rights and freedoms of others. However, the United States Supreme Court has emphasised that any restriction of the right to assembly 'carries a heavy burden of justification'.

Some courts see the right to peaceful assembly as an overriding right, like freedom of expression. However, trade unions have not always enjoyed it. In Canada, for example, the courts upheld a ban on secondary picketing, saying that freedom of assembly was not infringed because primary picketing was still allowed.

Section 17: Freedom of Association

Every person shall have the right to freedom of association.

This is usually seen as a core right, but can be expected to give rise to controversy. Does it give the right to associate on the basis of race or gender? Can this be a shield behind which privatised racism can take place?

The United States Supreme Court has said no, this right does not provide a defence against otherwise valid anti-discrimination laws.

This clause also has implications for trade unions. Does it exclude a closed shop? Does it prevent legal restrictions on striking? Does it imply a freedom to disassociate? This is one of the reasons why labour legislation has been excluded from testing in terms of the Bill of Rights.

Section 18: Freedom of Movement

Every person shall have the right to freedom of movement anywhere within the national territory.

Our Bill of Rights is unusual in that it separates the right to freedom of internal movement, and the right to leave or re-enter the country.

This is an important right, given South Africa's history of forced removal and forced segregation. It would, naturally, have to be weighed against the rights to property in, for example, cases of trespass.

Section 19: Residence

Every person shall have the right freely to choose his or her place of residence anywhere in the national territory.

Once again, this is a clause that arises from our history of influx control and forced removal. Whom does it apply to? The use of 'persons' rather than citizens implies that non-citizens could fall within it. International precedent has established its application to permanent residents. It excludes 'juristic' persons (such as companies or organisations).

Section 20: Citizens' Rights

Every person shall have the right to enter, remain in and leave the Republic, and no citizen shall without justification be deprived of his or her citizenship.

This provision stops the long-standing practice of with-holding passports from dissidents. The right to leave must include the right to a passport, making this document a right, not a privilege, as has been the case in the past.

This section must also give scope for a challenge by anyone who is extradited from the country.

Section 21: Political Rights

21. (1) Every citizen shall have the right:

    (a) to form, to participate in the activities of and to recruit members for a political party;

    (b) to campaign for a political party or cause; and

    (c) freely to make political choices.

   (2) Every citizen shall have the right to vote, to do so in secret and to stand for election to public office.

The topical aspect here is whether this rules unconstitutional that part of the Electoral Act that prevented certain classes of prisoners from voting. It also raises the question of whether a prisoner could stand for office.

This clause also establishes the right to form, join and recruit members of a political party. It is unlikely, however, to be seen as an absolute right, as the courts are likely to accept restrictions on parties that advocate civil war, for example, or race hatred or violence. This right could also be suspended in an emergency.

Section 22: Access to Court

Every person shall have the right to have justifiable disputes settled by a court of law or, where appropriate, another independent and impartial forum.

This is an unusual clause, in that it is usually held to be included under the right to equal protection of the law. It ensures that there cannot be attempts to exclude the jurisdiction of the courts, which happened under previous states of emergency.

Does it, however, obligate the state to give meaningful access to the courts, for example through legal aid? If people cannot afford properly to defend themselves, has their right to have their disputes settled in a court been violated?

Section 23: Access to Information

Every person shall have the right to access to all information held by the state or any of its organs at any level of government in so far as such information is required for the exercise or protection of any of his or her rights.

This interesting clause sets in stone the principle of transparent government. However, it does not by any means give an absolute right to information.

Firstly, it only applies vertically — that is between the state and the individual requesting such information held by the state. Secondly, the right is qualified in that the information requested must be required for the exercise of one's rights. The limitations clause — allowing the right to be limited if such limitation is reasonable and justifiable in an open and democratic society — would apply. So, for example, the courts might deny access to a police docket during an investigation. Or it could deny access to information that would threaten state security. Or it could balance the right to information against another person's right to privacy.

But it seems that this clause puts a heavy onus on the state to prove that any denial of information is not just reasonable but also necessary.

There are some who argue that the strength of this clause renders unnecessary a Freedom of Information Act that would regulate access to state information. This clause may give more access and greater flexibility than a specific Act would allow for. But such an Act would set up mechanisms for the preservation and dissemination of such information.

Section 24: Administrative Justice

Every person shall have the right to:

(a) lawful administrative action where any of his or her rights or interests is affected or threatened;

(b) procedurally fair administrative action where any of his or her rights or legitimate expectations is affected or threatened;

(c) be furnished with reasons in writing for administrative action which affects any of his or her rights or interests unless the reasons for such action have been made public; and

(d) administrative action which is justifiable in relation to the reasons given for it where any of his or her rights is affected or threatened.

Lurking within this seemingly innocuous technical jargon are rights which go a long way to empowering ordinary citizens and protecting them from the kind of administrative abuses which characterised apartheid. One of the worst features of Nationalist rule was the way in which state officials wielded awesome and largely unchecked discretionary powers. For the majority of South Africans, virtually every aspect of their daily lives was controlled by the often arbitrary whim of a petty bureaucrat.

This clause seeks to make state officials accountable for their actions. Official discretion must not be exercised unfairly and, most importantly, officials will be required to furnish written reasons for their decisions. This will constitute a significant safeguard against the abuse of power.

Section 25: Detained, Arrested and Accused Persons

25. (1) Every person who is detained, including every sentenced prisoner, shall have the right:

(a) to be informed promptly in a language which he or she understands of the reason for his or her detention;

(b) to be detained under conditions consonant with human dignity, which shall include at least the provision of adequate nutrition, reading material and medical treatment at state expense;

(c) to consult with a legal practitioner of his or her choice, to be informed of this right promptly and, where substantial injustice would otherwise result, to be provided with the services of a legal practitioner by the state;

(d) to be given the opportunity to communicate with and to be visited by his or her spouse or partner, next of kin, religious counsellor and a medical practitioner of his or her choice; and

(e) to challenge the lawfulness of his or her detention in person before a court of law and to be released if such detention is unlawful.

(2) Every person arrested for the alleged commission of an offence shall, in addition to the rights which he or she has as a detained person, have the right:

(a) promptly to be informed, in a language which he or she understands, that he or she has the right to remain silent and to be warned of the consequences of making any statement;

(b) as soon as it is reasonably possible, but not later than 48 hours, or on a day which is not a court day, on the first court day after such expiry, to be brought before an ordinary court of law and to be charged or to be informed of the reason for his or her further detention, failing which he or she shall be entitled to be released;

(c) not to be compelled to make a confession or admission which could be used in evidence against him or her; and

(d) to be released from detention with or without bail, unless the interests of justice require otherwise.

(3) Every accused person shall have the right to a fair trial, which shall include the right:

(a) to a public trial before an ordinary court of law within a reasonable time after having been charged;

(b) to be informed with sufficient particularity of the charge;

(c) to be presumed innocent and to remain silent during plea proceedings or trial and not to testify during trial;

(d) to adduce and challenge evidence, and not to be a compellable witness against himself or herself;

(e) to be represented by a legal practitioner of his or her choice or, where substantial injustice would otherwise result, to be provided with legal representation at state expense, and to be informed of these rights;

(f) not to be convicted of an offence in respect of any act or omission which was not an offence at the time it was committed, and not to be sentenced to a more severe punishment than that which was applicable when the offence was committed;

(g) not to be tried again for any offence of which he or she has previously been convicted or acquitted;

(h) to have recourse by way of appeal or review to a higher court than the court of first instance;

(i) to be tried in a language which he or she understands or, failing this, to have the proceedings interpreted to him or her; and

(j) to be sentenced within a reasonable time after conviction.

This provision will revolutionise criminal law and procedure in South Africa, affecting virtually all police and court activity.

Among the far-reaching provisions in this section, it introduces the prospect of a 'Miranda rule' — the court ruling that forces American policemen to read a formal and detailed warning to suspects as they are arrested. The rule is that an incriminating statement made in police custody is not admissible in evidence unless the suspect has been clearly informed of his or her rights. It will be interesting to see if the South African courts use this section to oblige police to give similar warnings and whether they exclude evidence obtained in violation of a suspect's rights.

Section 26: Economic Activity

26. (1) Every person shall have the right freely to engage in economic activity and to pursue a livelihood any-where in the national territory.

(2) Subsection (1) shall not preclude measures designed to promote the protection or the improvement of the quality of life, economic growth, human develop-ment, social justice, basic conditions of employment, fair labour practices or equal opportunity for all, provided such measures are justifiable in an open and democratic society based on freedom and equality.

The first part of this clause is *laissez-faire* in the extreme and would, alone, rule out any regulation or control.

The second section recognises this and sets out the basis for such regulation. To what extent this clause applies to the work of the Competition Board, the common law rules on restraint of trade or to the regulation by professional bodies on entry into certain professions (such as law) could all be the subject of constitutional challenges.

Section 27: Labour Relations

27. (1) Every person shall have the right to fair labour practices.
    (2) Workers shall have the right to form and join trade unions, and employers shall have the right to form and join employers' organisations.
    (3) Workers and employers shall have the right to organise and bargain collectively.
    (4) Workers shall have the right to strike for the purpose of collective bargaining.
    (5) Employers' recourse to the lockout for the purpose of collective bargaining shall not be impaired, subject to section 33(1).

This section is the result of a peculiar compromise, hammered out in last-minute negotiations involving World Trade Centre negotiators and representatives of organised labour and business. It has a limited impact because all existing labour legislation is exempted from this Bill of Rights (by Section 33). But it will affect employees not covered by existing legislation, such as domestic workers and certain civil servants, giving them protection against 'unfair labour practices'. This section will also protect the rights of unions against potential challenges under the freedom of association clause.

Section 28: Property

28. (1) Every person shall have the right to acquire and hold rights in property and, to the extent that the nature of the rights permits, to dispose of such rights.

(2) No deprivation of any rights in property shall be permitted otherwise than in accordance with a law.

(3) Where any rights in property are expropriated pursuant to a law referred to in subsection (2), such expropriation shall be permissible for public purposes only and shall be subject to the payment of agreed compensation or, failing agreement, to the payment of such compensation and within such period as may be determined by a court of law as just and equitable, taking into account all relevant factors, including, in the case of determination of compensation, the use to which the property is being put, the history of its acquisition, its market value, the value of the investments in it by those affected and the interests of those affected.

Such tortuous wording is a sure sign that this was another hotly argued clause that emerged as a messy compromise. Controversy will focus on what is meant by expropriation for 'public purposes'. If this means expropriation for the purpose of building a road or a public building, but not for the purpose of land redistribution from one person or group of persons to another, the clause will severely jeopardise a future government's ability to engage in all-important land reform. Thus the court will have to make the crucial decision of what the phrase 'public purpose' means.

The clause is widely couched, in that it protects rights *in* property. It would seem to include a right to a pension and to immaterial property such as patent trademarks and copyrights.

The provision related to compensation was also a compromise. Concern was expressed that if the only criterion was fair market value, then no land transformation could take place.

Section 29: Environment

Every person shall have the right to an environment which is not detrimental to his or her health or well-being.

The critical issue here will be whether the courts allow this clause to be applied horizontally (between individuals and groups other than the state) or only vertically (between individuals/groups and the state).

It is couched as an individual right to a healthy environment and would clearly empower an individual to prevent the state from any activity which is harmful to the health of that person.

It would also allow a court to set aside any law which private agencies such as corporations might use to defend their rights to emit harmful effluent. The question is whether these rights can be enforced against private concerns such as factories which might emit a harmful effluent. That, the Constitutional Court will have to decide.

Section 30: Children

30. (1) Every child shall have the right:

(a) to a name and nationality from birth;

(b) to parental care;

(c) to security, basic nutrition and basic health and social services;

(d) not to be subject to neglect or abuse;

(e) not to be subject to exploitative labour practices; and

(f) not to be required or permitted to perform that which is hazardous or harmful to his or her education, health or well-being.

(2) Every child who is in detention shall, in addition to the rights which he or she has in terms of Section 25, have the right to be detained under conditions and to be treated in a manner that takes account of his or her age.

(3) For the purposes of this section, a child shall mean a person under the age of 18 years and in all matters concerning such child his or her best interests shall be paramount.

This special protection for children follows international precedent. The International Covenant of Political and Civil Rights and the European Social Charter include specific provisions for children.

This is one of the very few provisions in the Bill of Rights which gives 'second generation rights': it not only protects rights, but places an obligation on the state to provide certain goods or objects for citizens. In this case, the state is obliged to provide security, basic nutrition, health and social services for children.

One of the first acts of President Nelson Mandela, after coming to power, was to order the enforcement of some of these rules by requiring hospitals to supply free medical attention to children under the age of six.

There is also special provision in this section for the detention of children, a sore point under apartheid. The Bill of Rights recognises the right of children not to be incarcerated with adults, as well as their right to have access to educational material and appropriate access to parents and relatives.

Section 31: Language and Culture

Every person shall have the right to use the language and to participate in the cultural life of his or her choice.

This is an attempt to ensure the equal protection of all cultures — a major departure from the Christian nationalism of the past. It provides the constitutional basis for Mandela's celebration of the 'rainbow nation'. The upshot of this clause was the totally impracticable recognition of 11 official languages.

Section 32: Education

Every person shall have the right:
(a) to basic education and to equal access to educational institutions;
(b) to instruction in the language of his or her choice where this is reasonably practicable;
(c) to establish, where practicable, educational institutions based on a common culture, language or religion, provided that there shall be no discrimination on the ground of race.

This is another example of an unusual 'second generation' right, which obliges the state to provide citizens with services.
    Of most interest will be the parameters for exclusive private schools. On the face of it, one could, on the basis of this clause, start a school for any social group, provided it did not discriminate on grounds of race. Does a Jewish school fit this Bill? Or an Afrikaans nationalist school?

Section 33: Limitation

33. (1) The rights entrenched in this Chapter may be limited by law of general application, provided that such limitation:

(a) shall be permissible only to the extent that it is:

 (i) reasonable; and

(ii) justifiable in an open and democratic society based on freedom and equality; and

(b) shall not negate the essential content of the right in question, and provided further that any limitation to:

(aa) a right entrenched in section 10, 11, 12, 14(1), 21, 25 or 30(1)(d) or (e) or (2); or

(bb) a right entrenched in section 15, 16, 17, 18, 23 or 24, in so far as such right relates to free and fair political activity, shall, in addition to being reasonable as required in paragraph (a)(i), also be necessary.

(2) Save as provided for in subsection (1) or any other provision of this Constitution, no law, whether a rule of the common law, customary law or legislation, shall limit any right entrenched in this Chapter.

(3) The entrenchment of the rights in terms of this Chapter shall not be construed as denying the existence of any other rights or freedoms recognised or conferred by common law, customary law or legislation to the extent that they are not inconsistent with this Chapter.

(4) This Chapter shall not preclude measures designed to prohibit unfair discrimination by bodies and persons other than those bound in terms of section 7(1).

(5) (a) The provisions of a law in force at the commencement of this Constitution promoting fair

employment practices, orderly and equitable collective bargaining and the regulation of industrial action shall remain of full force and effect until repealed or amended by the legislature.

(b) If a proposed enactment amending or repealing a law referred to in paragraph (a) deals with a matter in respect of which the National Manpower Commission, referred to in section 2A of the Labour Relations Act, 1956 (Act No 28 of 1956), or any similar body which may replace the Commission, is competent in terms of a law then in force to consider and make recommendations, such proposed enactment shall not be introduced in Parliament unless the said Commission or other such body has been given an opportunity to consider the proposed enactment and to make recommendations with regard thereto.

This is the most important clause in the Bill of Rights, and the one which will be the basis of almost every Constitutional Court debate. It allows for the limitations of all the other rights, ensuring that there is no absolute right in the Bill, but setting the parameters for when these rights can be denied or restricted. 'Your right to swing your fist ends where someone else's nose begins' was how one United States Supreme Court justice expressed the balancing of individual rights, and it is this clause that instructs the courts in how to do it.

An astonishing part is that every single right can be limited in terms of this section. Not even the restrictions on torture, servitude or slavery is immune from limitation. The drafters have followed the examples of the Canadian Charter of Rights and Freedoms and the European Convention of Human Rights. While the US Bill of Rights has no such limitations clause, its courts have still found — with some creative jurisprudence — that a right is not absolute and can be limited by legislation. For example, the US Bill of Rights says that no law can limit freedom of expression, but it has never been suggested that it cannot be limited by the law of defamation. The US model, however, ensures that such limitations can only be introduced in very restricted circumstances.

Our clause, based on the German model, says that any of our rights can be limited by a law that is reasonable, justifiable in an open and democratic society and does not negate the essential content of the right in question. But certain rights get greater protection than this. These include the provisions on human dignity, freedom, security, servitude, forced labour, religion, belief and opinion, political rights, the protection of detained or arrested persons, children's rights and a number relating to free and fair political activity. Before it can limit these rights, the state has to convince the court that, in addition to meeting all the above requirements, this limitation is also necessary.

Section 34: State of Emergency

34. (1) A state of emergency shall be proclaimed prospectively under an Act of Parliament, and shall be declared only where the security of the Republic is threatened by war, invasion, general insurrection or disorder or at a time of national disaster, and if the declaration of a state of emergency is necessary to restore peace or order.

(2) The declaration of a state of emergency and any action taken, including any regulation enacted, in consequence thereof, shall be of force for a period of not more than 21 days, unless it is extended for a period of not longer than three months, or consecutive periods of not longer than three months at a time,

by resolution of the National Assembly adopted by a majority of at least two-thirds of all its members.

(3) Any superior court shall be competent to enquire into the validity of a declaration of a state of emergency, any extension thereof, and any action taken, including any regulation enacted, under such declaration.

(4) The rights entrenched in this Chapter may be suspended only in consequence of the declaration of a state of emergency, and only to the extent necessary to restore peace or order.

(5) Neither any law which provides for the declaration of a state of emergency nor any action taken, including any regulation enacted in consequence thereof, shall permit or authorise:

(a) the creation of retrospective crimes;

(b) the indemnification by the state of persons acting under its authority for unlawful actions during the state of emergency; or

(c) the suspension of this section, and sections 7, 8(2), 9, 10, 11(2), 12, 14, 27(1) and (2), 30(1)(d) and (e) and (2) and 33(1) and (2).

(6) Where a person is detained under a state of emergency the detention shall be subject to the following conditions:

(a) An adult family member or friend of the detainee shall be notified of the detention as soon as is reasonably possible;

(b) The names of all detainees and a reference to the measures in terms of which they are being detained shall be published in the Gazette within five days of their detention;

(c) When rights entrenched in section 11 or 25 have been suspended:

(i) The detention of a detainee shall, as soon as it is reasonably possible but not later than 10 days after his or her detention, be reviewed by a court of law, and the court shall order the release of the detainee if it is satisfied that the detention is not necessary to restore peace or order;

(ii) A detainee shall at any stage after the expiry of a period of 10 days after a review in terms of subparagraph (i) be entitled to apply to a court of law for a further review of his or her detention, and the court shall order the release of the detainee if it is satisfied that the detention is no longer necessary to restore peace or order;

(d) The detainee shall be entitled to appear before the court in person, to be represented by legal counsel, and to make representations against his or her continued detention;

(e) The detainee shall be entitled at all reasonable times to have access to a legal representative of his or her choice;

(f) The detainee shall be entitled at all times to have access to a medical practitioner of his or her choice; and

(g) The state shall for the purpose of a review referred to in paragraph (c)(i) or (ii) submit written reasons to justify the detention or further detention of the detainee to the court, and shall furnish the detainee with such reasons not later than two days before the review.

(7) If a court of law, having found the grounds for a detainee's detention unjustified, orders his or her release, such a person shall not be detained again on the same grounds unless the state shows good cause to a court of law prior to such re-detention.

This is another section that, in its attention to detail, reflects the concerns inherited from a past in which emergencies were used and abused with abandon. This section limits the exercise of emergency powers. It makes it much harder than before to declare an emergency, forcing the state to fill a number of mandatory requirements first.

Particularly important are those rights that cannot be suspended, even under a state of emergency. These include the right not to be discriminated against, the right to life, the right to dignity, freedom from torture, prohibition against servitude, freedom of religion, labour rights and children's rights.

There was some controversy in that the Bill of Rights allows for detention without trial in an emergency. There are, however, safeguards: review by a court within 10 days of detention, the right to defence, the right to appeal in person, and the right of access to a medical practitioner of one's choice. And, for the first time, the jurisdiction of the court cannot be ousted by emergency law.

Section 35: Interpretation

35. (1) In interpreting the provisions of this Chapter a court of law shall promote the values which underlie an open and democratic society based on freedom and equality and shall, where applicable, have regard to public international law applicable to the protection of the rights entrenched in this Chapter, and may have regard to comparable foreign case law.

(2) No law which limits any of the rights entrenched in this Chapter shall be constitutionally invalid solely by reason of the fact that the wording used prima facie exceeds the limits imposed in this Chapter, provided such a law is reasonably capable of a more restricted interpretation which does not exceed such limits, in which event such law shall be construed as having a meaning in accordance with the said more restricted interpretation.

(3) In the interpretation of any law and the application and development of the common law and customary law, a court shall have due regard to the spirit, purport and objects of this Chapter.

This important section provides guidance to the Constitutional Court in the interpretation of the rest of Chapter III. The court's touchstone will be to develop the Bill in accordance with the principles which underlie an open and democratic society based on freedom and equality.

Of particular significance is that, despite the debate over whether the Bill of Rights applies horizontally, this clause enjoins our courts to develop all our law, including private law, in the spirit and purpose of the chapter. This will give wide scope for lawyers to argue for substantial changes to many areas of private law.

For the first time, South African lawyers will not rely on that archaic body of law known as the Roman-Dutch authorities. These will only apply in the − most unlikely − event that these authorities promote the values enshrined in the Bill of Rights. Otherwise, a wide body of international precedent can be called on by the Constitutional Court and the most likely sources will be those countries with a strong Bill of Rights tradition, such as the United States, Canada and Germany.

8

A STATISTICAL PROFILE OF
THE NINE PROVINCES

The five-year interim constitution which came into effect after the April 1994 election restructures government on national, regional and local levels.

The national government will rule a unitary state with boundaries as they were in the 1910 Union of South Africa. This comprises the land which was previously administered by the four provinces of 'white' South Africa, the six self-governing homelands and the four nominally independent homelands.

This territory will be administered in nine new provinces: Northern Transvaal, Eastern Transvaal, Gauteng, North West, kwaZulu/Natal, Orange Free State, Eastern Cape, Northern Cape, and Western Cape. New local government structures are due to be elected in April 1995.

Surface areas and population densities

South Africa's 1994 population is estimated to be 40 346 000 (40,7-million according to DBSA, 1994:17), with an overall population density of 33,1 people per square kilometre.

The population is very unevenly spread. The Northern Cape is the largest province (almost 30 per cent of the country) and the most sparsely populated (2,1 people per square kilometre). Gauteng has the highest population density (364,9 per square kilometre) and the smallest surface area (1,54 per cent). KwaZulu/Natal is by far the most populous province, accounting for 21,2 per cent of the population with a very dense 92,8 people per square kilometre. The high population density of Gauteng should be seen in the context that this tiny province is extremely urbanised and that most of the country's economic activity is concentrated there.

	Area (km^2)	% Area of SA	Population 1994	Population density per km^2
W Cape	129 370	10,61	3 635 000	28,1
N Cape	361 800	29,68	749 000	2,1
E Cape	169 600	13,91	6 504 000	38,3
OFS	129 480	10,61	2 767 000	21,4
kwaZulu/Natal	92 180	7,56	8 553 000	92,8
E Transvaal	78 370	6,43	2 911 000	37,1
N Transvaal	123 280	10,11	5 013 000	40,7
Gauteng	18 810	1,54	6 864 000	364,9
North West	116 190	9,53	3 349 000	28,8
TOTAL	1 219 080	100,00	40 346 000	33,1

Source: BMR, 1994:7

Distribution of population by province and race

Of the total estimated population in 1994, 76,1 per cent is black, 12,8 per cent white, 8,5 per cent coloured and 2,6 per cent Asian. Africans are in the majority in seven of the nine provinces. Coloureds are in the majority in the remaining two — the Northern Cape and the Western Cape.

	Asian '000	African '000	Coloured '000	White '000	TOTAL '000	% of total
W Cape	30	632	2 101	872	3 635	9,01
N Cape	2	237	389	121	749	1,86
E Cape	15	5 678	433	377	6 503	16,11
OFS	1	2 325	73	368	2 767	6,86
kwaZulu/Natal	809	7 024	107	612	8 552	21,19
E Transvaal	11	2 589	16	296	2 912	7,21
N Transvaal	4	4 863	6	140	5 013	12,42
Gauteng	15	4 302	279	2 132	6 864	17,01
North West	8	3 039	38	264	3 349	8,3
TOTAL	1 031	30 689	3 442	5 182	40 344	100,00

Source: BMR, 1994:23-9

Population: urban:non-urban, male:female

Gauteng and Western Cape have very high levels of urbanisation (99,6 per cent and 95,1 per cent respectively) and relatively low rates of population growth. The most rural provinces (Northern Transvaal, Eastern Transvaal, North West and kwaZulu/Natal) have very high rates of population growth. Northern Transvaal is the most extreme example of this — only 12,1 per cent of its population is urbanised and its population growth rate is a massive 3,95 per cent per year.

Women outnumber men in predominantly rural areas with poor economic prospects, the homeland migrant labour system being the historical reason for this. Men are also more mobile than women and are more likely to migrate to look for work, explaining why men outnumber women in

provinces which offer employment in mining, agriculture or
industry (Orange Free State and Gauteng).

	Functional urbanisation %	Male:Female %	Population growth 1985-93 %
W Cape	95,1	50,18:49,81	1,70
N Cape	78,2	50,50:49,49	0,79
E Cape	55,4	44,67:55,32	2,60
OFS	73,7	52,35:47,64	1,50
kwaZulu/Natal	77,9	47,44:52,55	2,79
E Transvaal	43,2	50,70:49,29	3,03
N Transvaal	12,1	45,44:54,55	3,95
Gauteng	99,6	53,27:46,72	1,29
North West	43,9	49,80:50,19	3,10
TOTAL	65,5	48,79:51,20	2,44

Source: DBSA, 1994:18,81. Gender percentages are rounded off.

Language

In South Africa as a whole, more people — 9,1-million —
speak Zulu as a home language than any other, followed by
Xhosa (7,4-million) and Afrikaans (5,9-million), North Sotho
(3,7-million), English (3,4-million) and Setswana (3,1-
million). In the Western and Northern Cape, the most
widely understood language is Afrikaans; in the Orange Free
State, Sesotho; in kwaZulu/Natal and Eastern Transvaal,
Zulu. The pattern is not so clear-cut in the other provinces —
the most widely understood language by a small majority in

Northern Transvaal is North Sotho, and in Gauteng, Zulu. (*Source: DBSA, 1994:21,86-7.*)

Potential voters

There are about 23-million potential voters in South Africa. Gauteng and kwaZulu/Natal are the biggest voting blocks, both with about 20 per cent of the total. The Eastern Cape has about 13 per cent of the total; the Western Cape, Northern Transvaal and North West all have about 10 per cent; Orange Free State and Eastern Transvaal about seven per cent; and Northern Cape about two per cent. (*Source: DBSA, 1994:22.*)

Employment

Labour absorption capacity (the percentage of the labour force employed in the formal sector of the economy) gives an indication of the extent of unemployment in South Africa. The national average of 50 per cent indicates that half the labour force is unemployed. The Western Cape is the province with the highest labour absorption capacity but even there less than 57 per cent of the labour force is employed in the formal sector.

The unemployment rate refers only to that part of the labour force which is neither active in subsistence agriculture nor involved in non-market activities. KwaZulu/Natal has the highest unemployment rate (25,2 per cent), followed closely by the Northern Transvaal, Eastern Cape and North West provinces. Dependency ratio statistics show the number of people supported by a single member of the labour force (employed or unemployed), excluding the person himself or herself.

The poverty of the Northern Transvaal and the Eastern Cape has come to the fore here again with very high dependency ratios of 4,8 and 3,7 respectively. The provinces with the strongest economies have the lowest dependency ratios — Gauteng (0,9) and Western Cape (1,2).

	Unemployment rate (%)	Dependency ratio	Labour absorption capacity (%)
W Cape	13,3	1,2	56,9
N Cape	16,7	1,6	52,9
E Cape	23,6	3,7	44,8
OFS	15,3	1,4	55,8
kwaZulu/Natal	25,2	2,3	44,8
E Transvaal	16,3	2,1	51,8
N Transvaal	24,8	4,8	40,3
Gauteng	16,6	0,9	54,4
North West	22,3	1,6	48,0
TOTAL	19,4	1,9	50,0

Source: DBSA, 1994:18

Economic growth districts of the provinces

A Bureau for Market Research study (Van Wyk, 1994) measured economic activity in major centres and likely growth until 1995. The study's 'growth index' is a composite indicator in which 100 represents the national average.

Gauteng has by far the most important concentration of economic activity in South Africa. By 1995 it is expected to account for 29,9 per cent of all employment and 42,2 per cent of all employees' remuneration, and will maintain its relative prominence by growing at the national average. The Cape Peninsula (Western Cape) is the second most important economic region with 7,3 per cent of total employment and 10,1 per cent of remuneration. Durban (kwaZulu/Natal) employs 6,5 per cent of the country's workforce. The Eastern Transvaal is the fastest growing region in the country — its proportion of total economic activity grew at seven per cent per year between 1970 and 1990 and all of its economic centres will grow faster than the national average.

	Employment % of SA total	Growth index by 1995 (National average: 100)
W Cape		
Cape Town	7,3	100,1
Southern Cape	0,6	102,6
N Cape		
Kimberley	0,5	94,3
E Cape		
Port Elizabeth-Uitenhage	2,7	98,5
East London-Ciskei area	1,6	101,5
OFS		
Bloemfontein	1,8	104,3
OFS Goldfields	2,4	98,0
kwaZulu/Natal		
Pietermaritzburg	1,4	100,9
Durban	6,5	97,6
Pinetown-Chatsworth	1,1	98,3
Lower Umfolozi	0,6	113,3
Klip River-Emnambithi	0,5	106,1
Newcastle-Madadeni	0,7	104,4

	Employment % of SA total	Growth index by 1995 (National average: 100)
E Transvaal		
Middelburg-Witbank	1,3	105,2
Nelspruit	1,0	105,9
Highveld Ridge	0,8	102,5
N Transvaal		
Pietersburg-Seshego	0,6	100,0
Gauteng		
Johannesburg-Randburg	9,1	96,8
Pretoria	8,7	103,4
East Rand	7,1	99,9
West Rand	3,1	97,5
North West		
Klerksdorp	1,4	98,7
Potchefstroom	0,8	101,4
Rustenburg-Bafokeng	1,4	102,4

Source: BMR, 1994:7-21

Personal income

Personal income in South Africa in 1994 is estimated at about R340-billion, including informal sector income and income in the form of goods and services. About R44,3-billion will be paid in income tax, leaving R295-billion in disposable personal income. Gauteng accounts for a massive 39 per cent of the total, with the Western Cape second (15,3 per cent) and kwaZulu/Natal a whisker behind (15,2 per cent). Between them, these three provinces account for 69,6 per cent of all personal disposable income in South Africa.

When income is divided by population to arrive at per capita disposable income (to give an average income), the stark differences between the provinces can be seen. Using an index of 100 to indicate the national average, Gauteng at 226 and the Western Cape at 169 are far better off than any of the other provinces. Northern Transvaal is the poorest province with a mere 29 on the scale. The Eastern Cape, the second poorest province in terms of income, is substantially better off at 49, even though this is less than half of the national income.

	Personal disposable income	% of total	Per capita disposable income, 1994	Per capita disposable income index
W Cape	R 45,0-bn	15,3	R12 387	169
N Cape	R 5,5-bn	1,9	R 7 403	101
E Cape	R 23,5-bn	8,0	R 3 616	49
OFS	R 28,7-bn	6,3	R 6 992	96
kwaZulu/Natal	R 44,9-bn	15,2	R 5 225	72
E Transvaal	R 16,6-bn	5,6	R 5 689	78
N Transvaal	R 10,6-bn	3,6	R 2 112	29
Gauteng	R115,2-bn	5,1	R16 570	226
North West	R 15,2-bn	39,0	R 4 533	62
TOTAL	R 295,2-bn	100,0	R 7 320	100

There are stark racial disparities in income across South Africa. Whites, who represent 12,8 per cent of the population, earn 48,9 per cent of all the income as opposed to Africans who, although they are 76,1 per cent of the population, earn only 38,3 per cent of the income.

	Proportion of population (%)	Proportion of total income (%)	Disposable income per capita	Relative to white income
White	12,8	48,9	R27 084	100
African	76,1	38,3	R 3 686	13
Coloured	8,5	8,9	R 7 650	27
Asian	2,6	3,9	R11 212	40

The average African person in Gauteng earns 30 per cent of the income of the average white person. The most extreme income gap is found in the Northern Transvaal where the average African person earns only seven per cent of the average white person's income. (*Source: BMR, 1994:31-9.*)

Human development

The human development index (HDI) is an international United Nations Development Programme indicator in which 1,0 represents the ideal. The 1990 HDI used three things: life expectancy and adult literacy as a measure of people's capacities, and income as a measure of their opportunities.

South Africa's 1990 HDI was 0,73, ranking it sixty-eighth out of 130 countries and putting it with medium human development countries.

A 1993 calculation using the same measures indicated South Africa had an average HDI of 0,69. The Western Cape was rated highest (0,76), followed by the Northern Cape and Gauteng (both above 0,70). The lowest level of human development is found in the Northern Transvaal (slightly more than 0,4) with the Eastern Cape (slightly less than 0,5).

	Literacy rate* (1991)(%)	Life expectancy (1991)(years)	HDI
W Cape	71,9	64,8	0,76
N Cape	67,6	64,0	0,73
E Cape	59,0	59,6	0,48
OFS	60,0	63,6	0,66
kwaZulu/Natal	58,7	62,6	0,58
E Transvaal	54,6	63,5	0,61
N Transvaal	52,7	62,7	0,40
Gauteng	69,0	65,6	0,71
North West	55,8	64,1	0,57
TOTAL	61,4	63,4	0,69

*People 13 years and older with at least a Standard Five education.
Source: DBSA, 1994: 18

The most recent HDI (1992), which incorporated numerous indicators not in the 1990 HDI, gave South Africa a rating of 0,65 and a ranking of 93 out of 173 countries. White South Africans on their own would rank twenty-fourth, and Africans if ranked alone, 123rd (*UNDP, 1994:130* and *Sapa-Reuter, 3 June 1994*).

Direct taxes

The relatively wealthy provinces generate more tax than the relatively poor provinces. Also, there are progressive increases in the proportion of tax payable on income: a married person with a taxable income of R80 000 per year pays 28 per cent to income tax as compared to a person who earns R15 000, who pays only 3,2 per cent. Gauteng pays almost half of all direct income tax in South Africa compared to the 1,5 per cent of the Northern Cape. Whites, being 12,8 per cent of the population and earning 48,9 per cent of all income, pay 83 per cent of all direct taxes.

	Proportion of total direct tax	Asian % of total	Black % of total	Coloured % of total	White % of total
W Cape	15,7%	0,8	2,1	17,0	80,2
N Cape	1,5%	0,6	7,0	13,8	78,5
E Cape	5,4%	1,8	19,4	8,0	70,8
OFS	5,3%	0,3	15,0	1,1	83,6
kwaZulu/Natal	12,9%	15,6	12,0	2,6	69,8
E Transvaal	5,4%	1,7	17,1	0,7	80,5
N Transvaal	2,0%	1,2	37,1	0,9	60,8
Gauteng	49,3%	1,8	6,1	1,8	90,3
North West	3,5%	1,2	20,4	1,4	76,9
TOTAL	100,0%	3,3	9,0	4,7	83,0

Source: BMR, 1994:39-40

Health

The Western Cape and Gauteng are the best resourced provinces in terms of health facilities and staff, but the Western Cape has the highest incidence of tuberculosis of any province (about 25 000 cases in 1992). Typhoid fever, associated with inadequate water supply and sanitation facilities, occurs mainly in the under-resourced provinces of Northern Transvaal, Eastern Transvaal and kwaZulu/Natal. In 1991, chronic malnutrition in the first two years of life caused stunting in more than a quarter of South Africa's children. This was particularly marked in the Northern Transvaal.

	Hospital beds per 1 000 population	Infant mortality rate*	Medical officials per 1 000 population	Nurses per 1 000 population
W Cape	5,6	26,8	1,5	7,0
N Cape	5,5	31,5	0,4	4,4
E Cape	4,6	58,2	0,3	3,3
OFS	4,1	45,4	0,5	3,9
kwaZulu/Natal	5,8	44,7	0,5	4,4
E Transvaal	2,4	41,2	0,3	2,8
N Transvaal	4,7	57,0	0,2	3,0
Gauteng	6,5	35,2	1,3	6,4
North West	4,5	43,3	0,2	2,7
TOTAL	5,1	41,8	0,6	4,3

*Infant mortality per 1 000 live births.

Education

The pattern of provincial inequality is repeated in education. Statistics in the following table are crude because they do not say much about the quality of education, but they do serve as a rough guide to the level of opportunity available to people to change their circumstances. The Western Cape and Gauteng are relatively well resourced and educated, along with the sparsely populated Northern Cape. KwaZulu/Natal, Eastern Cape, Northern Transvaal and North West have low levels of literacy, high pupil:teacher ratios, and large numbers of children not attending school at all.

	% 6-14 years not attending school	Pupil:teacher ratio	Schools	Literacy rate (%)*
W Cape	6,4	23	1 948	71,9
N Cape	7,3	25	565	67,6
E Cape	9,4	39	3 279	59,0
OFS	9,7	34	1 658	60,0
kwaZulu/Natal	11,3	37	5 079	58,7
E Transvaal	8,5	36	1 719	54,6
N Transvaal	8,6	35	3 466	52,7
Gauteng	8,7	27	2 295	69,0
North West	13,7	24	912	55,8
TOTAL	9,6	32	20 921	61,4

*People 13 years and older with at least a Standard Five education.
Source: DBSA, 1994:22,90,92

Conclusion

Gauteng and the Western Cape are the best resourced provinces in South Africa, and the Northern Transvaal and the Eastern Cape are the worst off. The Northern Transvaal in particular is extremely undeveloped, highly populated, very poor, and has very high unemployment.

In general, good infrastructures, urbanisation, high employment, strong economic activity and a high level of taxation go with the well-resourced provinces, and high population, poverty, unemployment, low development and low taxation are associated with the Northern Transvaal, Eastern Cape, kwaZulu/Natal and Eastern Transvaal.

It should be borne in mind that statistics on a provincial basis are inclined to provide a generalised picture which masks disparities within each region. For example, the Western Cape has the highest human development index in South Africa, with whites ranking among the world's top five developed countries. Coloured people in rural areas in the Western Cape would reflect an HDI comparable to the lowest in the world. A hint of this can be seen in health statistics — the Western Cape has the best health facilities in the country but also an incidence of tuberculosis which is more than double that of any other province. (*Source: DBSA, 1994:47.*)

References

BMR (Bureau for Market Research), 1994. Research Report no.207, 'Socio-economic profile of the nine provinces', by JH Martins, AA Ligthelm, M Loubser and H de J van Wyk. Pretoria: University of South Africa.

DBSA (Development Bank of Southern Africa), 1994. 'South Africa's nine provinces: a human development profile'. Midrand: DBSA.

UNDP (United Nations Development Programme), 1994. Human development report, 1994. New York: Oxford University Press.

LIST OF CONTRIBUTORS

Julia Beffon is a sports sub-editor at *Business Day*.

Farouk Chothia writes on politics for the *Weekly Mail & Guardian*, for whom he is Durban correspondent.

Jacklyn Cock, a founding member and trustee of the Group for Environmental Monitoring, is a professor of sociology at the University of the Witwatersrand, co-chairperson of the Military Research Group and author of, among others, *Maids and Madams* and *Colonels and Cadres*, and co-editor of *Going Green*.

Carole Cooper is senior research officer at the Centre for Applied Legal Studies, University of the Witwatersrand.

Lesley Cowling is the chief training officer of the South African Newspaper Education Trust.

Gaye Davis is parliamentary correspondent for the *Weekly Mail & Guardian*.

Shaun de Waal is *Weekly Mail & Guardian* literary editor.

David Fig is research director for the Group for Environmental Monitoring.

Philippa Garson is a free-lance journalist who writes on a range of subjects, including education.

Mark Gevisser is a free-lance journalist who writes regularly for the *Weekly Mail & Guardian*. He is co-editor of *Defiant Desire: Gay and Lesbian Lives in South Africa*.

Ferial Haffajee is an SABC radio reporter and a free-lance writer specialising in labour issues.

Anton Harber is co-editor of the *Weekly Mail & Guardian*.

Mduduzi ka Harvey is crime reporter for the *Weekly Mail & Guardian*.

Stephen Heyns is resource developer for the Community Development Resource Association in Cape Town.

Bafana Khumalo is a columnist and arts writer for the *Weekly Mail & Guardian*.

Eddie Koch, a founding member and trustee of the Group for Environmental Monitoring, writes on environmental matters for the *Weekly Mail & Guardian*. He is co-editor of *Going Green*.

Stephen Laufer, formerly a *Weekly Mail & Guardian* journalist specialising in politics and defence, is press secretary for the ministry of Housing.

Chris Louw is a free-lance journalist specialising in political affairs.

Barbara Ludman is assistant editor of the *Weekly Mail & Guardian*.

Jacques Magliolo, a financial journalist for the *Weekly Mail & Guardian*, is an industrial analyst for stockbrokers EW Balderson and author of *Share Analysis and Accurate Forecasting*.

Nombuyiselo Maloyi is a *Weekly Mail & Guardian* journalist.

Vuyo Mvoko, a former *Weekly Mail & Guardian* journalist specialising in labour issues, is a Master's student at the University of Wollongong, Australia.

Sibusiso Nxumalo is a *Weekly Mail & Guardian* journalist.

Justin Pearce is Cape Town bureau chief for the *Weekly Mail & Guardian*.

Ivor Powell is the editor of *Ventilator*, an arts magazine, and writes on art and culture for the *Weekly Mail & Guardian*.

Estelle Randall is media and communications co-ordinator for the Association for Rural Advancement and a free-lance journalist.

Carmel Rickard, a former Nieman fellow, writes on legal and religious subjects for the *Sunday Times*.

Reg Rumney is a published poet and business editor of the *Weekly Mail & Guardian*.

Pat Sidley is a *Weekly Mail & Guardian* journalist and correspondent for the Dutch news agency ANP.

Paul Stober is a free-lance journalist.

Jan Taljaard, a consultant and *Weekly Mail & Guardian* specialist writer on the right wing, runs Digi News, a bulletin board service.

Steuart Wright is a journalist for the East Cape News Agency, based in East London.

ACKNOWLEDGEMENTS

Thanks to: John Allen, Alison Lowry, Pam Thornley, Drew Forrest, Sophie Perryer, Palesa Motanyane, Annie Mapoma, Ann Stewart, East Cape News Agency and the librarians at Times Media Limited.

The maps on pages 276, 301 and 303, redrawn by Hadaway Illustration & Design, are based on the graphics by Fiona Krisch which appeared in the *Sunday Times* on 3 July 1994.

SELECTED INDEX